Lower-Middle-Class Nation

Lower-Middle-Class Nation

The White-Collar Worker in British Popular Culture

Nicola Bishop

BLOOMSBURY ACADEMIC
LONDON • NEW YORK • OXFORD • NEW DELHI • SYDNEY

BLOOMSBURY ACADEMIC
Bloomsbury Publishing Plc
50 Bedford Square, London, WC1B 3DP, UK
1385 Broadway, New York, NY 10018, USA

BLOOMSBURY, BLOOMSBURY ACADEMIC and the Diana logo are trademarks of
Bloomsbury Publishing Plc

First published in Great Britain 2021
Paperback edition published 2022

Copyright © Nicola Bishop, 2021

Nicola Bishop has asserted her right under the Copyright, Designs and Patents Act, 1988, to be
identified as Author of this work.

For legal purposes the Acknowledgements on p. ix constitute an extension
of this copyright page.

Cover image: Watching TV television while eating dinner at dining room table, interior of flat north
London, UK, 1970s. (© Homer Sykes / Alamy Stock Photo)
Cover designer: Terry Woodley

All rights reserved. No part of this publication may be reproduced
or transmitted in any form or by any means, electronic or mechanical,
including photocopying, recording, or any information storage or retrieval
system, without prior permission in writing from the publishers.

Bloomsbury Publishing Plc does not have any control over, or responsibility for, any
third-party websites referred to or in this book. All internet addresses given in this book were correct at
the time of going to press. The author and publisher regret any inconvenience caused if addresses have
changed or sites have ceased to exist, but can accept no responsibility for any such changes.

Every effort has been made to trace copyright holders and to obtain their permissions for the use of
copyright material. The publisher apologizes for any errors or omissions and would be grateful if notified
of any corrections that should be incorporated in future reprints or editions of this book.

A catalogue record for this book is available from the British Library.

Library of Congress Cataloging-in-Publication Data
Names: Bishop, Nicola, author.
Title: Lower-middle-class nation : the white-collar worker in British
popular culture / Nicola Bishop.
Description: New York, NY : Bloomsbury Academic, 2021. |
Includes bibliographical references and index.
Identifiers: LCCN 2020035913 (print) | LCCN 2020035914 (ebook) |
ISBN 9781350064355 (hardback) | ISBN 9781350064362 (ePDF) |
ISBN 9781350064379 (eBook)
Subjects: LCSH: Middle-class–Great Britain–History. |
Great Britain–Social conditions. | Popular culture–Great Britain–History.
Classification: LCC HT690.G7 B57 2021 (print) | LCC HT690.G7 (ebook) |
DDC 305.5/50941–dc23
LC record available at https://lccn.loc.gov/2020035913
LC ebook record available at https://lccn.loc.gov/2020035914

ISBN: HB: 978-1-3500-6435-5
PB: 978-1-3502-2804-7
ePDF: 978-1-3500-6436-2
eBook: 978-1-3500-6437-9

Typeset by Newgen KnowledgeWorks Pvt. Ltd., Chennai, India

To find out more about our authors and books visit www.bloomsbury.com
and sign up for our newsletters.

To mum, who began a new life away from the office

Contents

Lists of Figures	viii
Acknowledgements	ix
Introduction	1
1 The office	29
2 The desk	55
3 The commute	103
4 The suburbs	127
5 The home	153
Conclusion	185
Notes	191
Filmography	219
Bibliography	223
Index	237

Figures

1.1	'Half an office' in *Ever Decreasing Circles* (1987)	39
1.2	Desk duties in *The Rebel* (1961)	53
2.1	Introducing a new colleague in *The Squirrels* (1976)	84
2.2	Tim (Martin Freeman) back at his desk in *The Office* (2001)	89
3.1	Fighting for a seat on *The 7.39* (2014)	112
3.2	Enduring the silence in *Reggie Perrin* (2010)	115
4.1	Suburban Billericay in *Gavin and Stacey* (2007)	139
5.1	Margot Leadbetter (Penelope Keith) anxiously watches her neighbours in *The Good Life* (1975)	154
5.2	Richard (Clive Swift) attempts to tend the garden in *Keeping Up Appearances* (1995)	159
5.3	On the slim-line phone in *Keeping Up Appearances* (1995)	170

Acknowledgements

This book began one summer, sat at my parent's kitchen table, keeping one eye on my laptop and another on an eight-week old Labradoodle puppy. The puppy, now an old girl, has stuck with it and me, sleeping on my feet in the office or curled up on the wooden floor of our favourite coffee shop. She was joined, after a few years, by my daughter, Megan, whose education in the sitcom form has been unorthodox but, by hell, we've enjoyed it (and what seven-year old doesn't benefit from having Dame Judi Dench and Victoria Wood as personal heroes?).

Thanks are due to a whole host of people who have supported and mentored me over the last ten years. This includes James Taylor and John Schad for their sound advice and patience; my research mentor, fellow commuter and friend, David Cooper, who always lets me rant when I need to; and Tereza Valny, the original B-Wid and first-rate mad aunt. Life wouldn't run as smoothly without Sarah, John and Ezra Ilott, neighbours who couldn't be less like Hilda and Howard, even if they do sometimes wear matching clothes. My lifelong thanks as always to my parents for everything, including introducing me to the best that television has to offer (Dad, don't ever stop watching BBC3) – and for last-minute proof-reading and car-battery advice. I'm grateful to wider family and friends who have patiently listened to me talking about the lower middle class for the past ten years (Rob, Liz, Mairi, Kirsty and Sarah all deserve a mention). Tom and Gareth have always been ready to talk middlebrow culture (and Agatha Christie, in particular) at the pub or over Friday night bolognese, and Ruth and Robbie get a special shout out for being brave enough to read this before anyone else did.

Finally, to Sam. You are my metaphorical walking stick on life's path up the Fairfield Horseshoe. And you always pack me a spare hat for the top.

Introduction

At the end of the nineteenth century, the clerical white-collar worker captured the popular *zeitgeist*. With the new age of banking, the administration of London's vast commercial enterprises and the need to administer Britain's Empire, a growing tide of clerks crossed London Bridge from their suburban dwellings, destined for the rows of impressive new office buildings. Charles Dickens, George and Weedon Grossmith, George Gissing, Arnold Bennett and many others captured this phenomenon in fiction, while commentators in the press drew attention to the growing ubiquity of the clerical crowd. After a half century of bureaucratic expansion, the city was swollen with this new class of workers who increasingly could afford to live in the burgeoning suburban developments on the capital's outskirts and began to shape a culture of their own. They read the new *Daily Mail* (founded in 1896), browsed in the cheaper of the new department stores, and attempted to keep up with bourgeois fashions. This 'tribe of clerks', as Edgar Allan Poe called them, was the foundation of a newly aspirant lower middle class, a petite bourgeoisie that, at times, would provide a radical force for change in Europe, but which more often became emblematic of a quiet conservatism in Britain.

The first recorded usage of the label 'lower middle class' appeared in 1852, in a letter from early social theorist Harriet Martineau to G. J. Holyoake. The year before, as Gregory Anderson suggests, there were ninety-one thousand clerks recorded in the UK.[1] By 1891, as F. M. L. Thompson calculates, the number of male clerks working in the capital alone had already increased by 279,000, and by 1911, one recent estimate suggests that as many as 10 per cent of all male workers in London were clerks.[2] These numbers represent a bureaucratic revolution which dramatically altered the social landscape of London, in particular. Of these white-collar workers, at least 250,000 lived in the capital with a further 129,430 clerks – those whom novelist Norman Collins called the 'half-urban hordes' – commuting in each day from Middlesex, Essex, Surrey and Kent to office buildings across the city.³ This new lower middle class was increasingly visible to commentators, but they were also a class within which there were many differences. As a diverse and, at times, disparate sector in terms of pay, role and financial position – incorporating, as Geoffrey Crossick points out, shopkeepers, teachers, skilled artisans and clerks⁴ – the lower middle class was nonetheless characterized, in popular culture and the press, as possessing a series of notable traits. Most of these were based on widespread opinions about one prominent subsection of the lower middle class: the clerk. And, as Arlene Young suggests, this clerk 'bore the brunt of contemporary ill-will' towards the drastic growth of a new subsection of the middle classes who were, from the outset, seen as challenging existing social structures.⁵

T. W. H. Crosland used the term as an insult: in his witty study *The Suburbans* (1905), he denounced 'the clerks' who had, as John Carey later paraphrases it, 'virtually come to constitute society'.⁶ He referred to the sizeable growth in the number of suburban clerks as an invasion, an observation that lent credibility to a discourse of suburban colonization.⁷ In the 1970s, historian Richard Price continued this conflation when he remarked: 'I shall make no apology in what follows for concentrating on the clerk as a representative example of the lower middle classes.'⁸ Price's position was distant from Crosland's – his chapter was part of a revisionary collection that attempted to sketch out the widespread variations within the lower middle class*es*. While acknowledging this, Price makes it clear that clerks were 'universally recognized to be archetypal lower-middle-class workers'.⁹ Likewise, in 1998, Mark Clapson made a case for continuing to view the clerk as a symbolic and 'pejorative catch-all' for the lower middle class.¹⁰ It is important to recognize the wide range of socio-economic and cultural diversity within the class, but for the purpose of this study, which takes as its focus representations within popular culture, the clerk remains a meaningful figurehead.

By 1951, there were 2.4 million of these 'petty clerks and salesmen, insurance agents and shop assistants' across England.¹¹ Today, according to the most recent occupational surveys, there are currently 3.2 million administrative and secretarial workers (not including sales and customer services – which stand at 2.3 million) across the UK – of which 417, 200 work in London alone.¹² White-collar work has become ubiquitous, yet the implications of this on the class structure of British society remains largely understudied. What scholars such as F. D. Klingender, David Lockwood, Gregory Anderson and Michael Heller have considered, at various points across the twentieth and twenty-first centuries, were the effects of a bureaucratic 'revolution' on the identity of those who first made up a significant proportion of this new white-collar class in the mid-to-late nineteenth century. While several of these historians have explored the hostility with which the lower middle class has been treated, very little work has been done that examines where this emergent social group has ended up in the later twentieth, or even the twenty-first, century.

Existing scholarship on the lower middle class has often been characterized by what Arno Mayer has called a redrawing of class boundaries; he argues that this is an attempt to avoid a lower middle class 'in which so many [academics] originate and from which they seek to escape'.[13] More critical than even this, American scholar Stephen Mihm went as far as to suggest that many of these 'deskbound academics' actually have the same insecurities as the lower-middle-class clerks themselves, particularly when it came to discussing the implications of non-manual labour.[14] In the 1970s and 1980s, a generation of Marxist historians turned their attention to economic histories of the Victorian clerk, attempting to consider the implications of a 'proletarianization' thesis.[15] This is the ideological cul-de-sac that has attracted the attention of the few scholars who work on office life and at its core is a debate over the status of the white-collar worker. In two camps are historians who see the clerk as part of either the bourgeoisie or the proletariat – as alternatively skilled, salaried and with hope of career progression or deskilled, mechanized and thus precariously positioned. They have looked at career prospects, pay structures, labour division and clerical turnover in order to substantiate their positioning. While their conclusions are useful in understanding the economic position of the lower-middle-class office worker, preoccupation with the proleterianization thesis is problematic.[16] As Graham Lowe pointed out, in his 1980s exploration of women in the administrative revolution, gender is just one blind spot; he argues that many studies ignore the difference in wages amongst incoming women and existing male clerks as well as the restructuring that came as a consequence of the new technologies employed in the clerical workplace. As Lowe puts it, many roles such as stenographer and typist could not have been proletarianized because they were 'mechanized, routinized, and generally unrewarding almost from their inception'.[17] Meta Zimmeck picked up on this absence too, pointing out the obvious omission of women from several of the core studies, which is a particular misnomer, she argues, because by the time each of them was written, women already constituted 46 per cent of clerical workers (Klingender in 1931), rising to 60 per cent when Lockwood wrote his study (in the 1951 census) and 72 per cent by 1971 census data (the year of Anderson's work).[18]

Even recent studies of white-collar work continue to respond to much earlier histories, many of which are preoccupied with establishing the clerk-type office worker as either working or middle class. Very few scholarly studies take time to recognize the distinction that became coded in the 1911 census and which identified that the middle class was a plural set of classes; too wide and varied to be considered homogenous in any sense. As Simon Gunn argues, the terms 'upper', 'middle' and 'lower' came into middle-class discourse between 1880 and 1914 and, more crucially, as part of 'everyday' language, but academics tend to continue to talk about a single middle class as a social, cultural and economic entity.[19] The latest monograph on the clerk simply reiterates a debate that began in the 1930s: did the white-collar worker rise to join the middle classes 'proper' or become subsumed by the working class? Rather than asking if the Victorian clerk was skilled or unskilled, bourgeois or proletarian, this study establishes the office worker as the figurehead of a distinctive lower-middle-class culture, arguing that the clerk needs to be understood as distinctly and visibly lower middle class rather than as somebody who moves between the working and middle classes according to fortune.

To 'rescue' the clerk from the lower middle class through promotion or re-evaluation is to deny the existence of the class itself – that which has simultaneously been held responsible for so much and yet recognized for so little. Identified by many as a key swing electorate across Europe from the 1930s onwards, very few wanted to be associated with those seen as instrumental in the rise of Nazism in Germany[20] or as one of the neo-suburbanites who voted for Margaret Thatcher in Britain in the 1980s. As Rita Felski put it, no one wants to associate themselves with a class that has 'typically been an object of scorn amongst intellectuals, blamed for everything from exceedingly bad taste to the rise of Hitler'.[21] One of the first critics to write openly about being interested in the lower middle class *because* it is her own social origin, Felski also recognizes the inherent contradictions in a lower-middle-class identity:

> Being lower-middle-class is a singularly boring identity ... a non-identity ... yet as older forms of class polarization and class identification begin to dissolve, the lives of ever more individuals in the industrialized West are defined by occupations, lifestyles, and attitudes traditionally associated with the lower middle class.[22]

Given the obvious significance of the commonalities between contemporary lifestyles (suburbs, commuting, office work) and the historic lower middle class,[23] it is no wonder that Felski was critical of the limits of Geoffrey Crossick's edited collection. At the same time, in all fairness, *The Lower Middle Class in Britain* (1977) remains to date the only study that has ever attempted an evaluation of the broad sweep of lower-middle-class identities, however underwhelming its outcome in promoting further research. Instead, with the growth of labour history and the focus in the 1980s on the working classes (following E. P. Thompson's influential *The Making of the English Working Class* (1963)), the emphasis was placed on realigning the 'clerkly' class with '[Thompson's] rugged darlings', rather than challenging what Peter Bailey referred to as the 'condescension of posterity' that the lower middle class seemed to deserve.[24] Much of this condescension is a result of what Crossick admitted in the 1970s, that the lower middle class demonstrated what many saw as a 'sheer lack of heroism … fail[ing] to do anything very striking'.[25] The limited interest in trade unionism of the white-collar worker, in particular, rendered the petite bourgeoisie unremarkable in the eyes of Marxist historians, who saw in the working classes a definite call for action.

With the exception of Jonathan Wild's *The Rise of the Office Clerk in Literary Culture* (2006), broader historical studies likewise continue to fall foul of Michael Crozier's criticism that the clerk – and by extension the lower middle class – is viewed only through an economic lens in British history. And while Wild's study gives a comprehensive account of the Victorian and Edwardian office worker, just as several economic histories consider the same period, there is little scholarship that has considered the contemporary equivalent, despite the centrality of modern office work in twenty-first-century lives.

Almost no attention has been paid to the office worker after the Second World War. Wild talks about the lower middle class finding their voice in the early twentieth century, and this study attempts to trace that voice until the present day.[26] It also goes much further in positing that many fundamental tenets of early lower-middle-class culture are now deeply ingrained in stereotypes surrounding British identity. By the 1930s, this lower middle class made up the newly suburban masses, those who had followed a vision of ideal modern living out to suburbia, only to be who sneered at by writers, the press and the establishment (seen in George Orwell's fantasies of a bombed-out West Bletchley in *Coming Up for Air* (1939)). They had championed the supposed shift to 'privatised family and home-centred lives' that the 'suburban dream' had encouraged and were quietly enjoying their mock Tudorbethan semis, in what critics saw as a 'repressed and banal existence behind the net curtains and the front gardens of the suburban home'.[27] In the 1940s and 1950s, they were the new car owners who were exploring country roads and quiet seaside resorts in an attempt to evade the noisy working-class trippers, reinforcing the visibility of social hierarchies wherever they went. In the world of theatre, certain members of the class went on to become the Angry Young Men who railed against bed-sit living and the frustration of being the first generation of their class to go to university and the limited opportunities for social mobility once they graduated.

In the 1970s, the children of the lower middle class benefitted from the new grammar schools – just as the Victorian office class had risen through their Board School educations following Forster's Act – and their champion, Margaret Thatcher, was vociferously citing her credentials as a shopkeeper's daughter. The 1980s saw a new generation of suburbanites who longed to revolt against their parents and return to the city – see, for instance Julian Barnes's *Metroland* (1980) and Hanif Kureishi's *Buddha of Suburbia* (1990) – which was countered in the following decade by a reinforcement of the suburban utopia as the epitome of lower-middle-class everyday life in the television sitcom. In the noughties, and with the beginning of the email age, the office became an in-vogue location, the setting for a range of experimental new comedic media forms exploring the pathos of modern life. By 2013, when the BBC (alongside leading sociologists) offered a reworking of class structures for the Great British Class Calculator, their research suggested there were now seven different class groups and yet the wider conclusions drawn from the survey also spoke much about peoples' preference for considering themselves 'somewhere "in the middle"', preferring to label themselves with 'a less noticeable identity'.[28] This new model implied that the lower middle class no longer existed, and yet, the possible responses that were offered to the survey taker still focused on those attributes considered so defining for this culturally aspirational class – trips to the theatre, classical music and social activities are part of the survey, whereas levels of education are not.

This study examines the lower-middle-class office worker in popular culture and in doing so posits that the influence of this section of society is far more extensive than is usually recognized. By doing so, it also reiterates the significance of class more widely as a key part of our cultural, social, political and economic lives. As Brigitte Le Roux et al. have shown – as recently as 2008 – the language of class 'remains profoundly important in affecting cultural life'.[29] Taking this further, and using their analysis of respondents' attitudes to class – as well as the work of Mike Savage in looking at Mass Observation across the twentieth century – I argue that the class category that has been known at various points as the lower middle class, the petite bourgeoisie or the slightly less poetic CII (in the census from 1911) has become a 'default' status for many who view their position from a longitudinal perspective.

In popular cultural representations, however, lower middle class-ness has a much stronger identity; while in economic terms, historians and other scholars have struggled to find a position from which to examine the class, in fiction and on screen there have been an abundance of lower-middle-class settings and characters, all of which collectively reinforce an unanimously identifiable lower-middle-class discourse, even if it does, at times, fall into stereotyping. This study, like the work of Scott Banville, looks at the cultural longevity of certain tropes of the lower middle class as part of a 'remediation' that

> helps us see the extent to which previous cultural forms are taken up and reworked by later generations in ways that do not hinge on the idea of origin, but rather that hinge on the idea that all cultural forms and the media through which they are transmitted appropriate and supplement a vast range of other cultural forms.[30]

In this sense, the commonalities that are in evidence between representations of characters as wide ranging as Victorian literary figure Charles Pooter, John Cleese's iconic hotelier Basil Fawlty and *The Office*'s David Brent are drawn from a complex web of impressions and stereotypes formed through a multilayered history that includes ideological, political, social and economic influences. As Banville asserts, this is at times a transatlantic remediation, but it can also be attuned to particular understandings of national cultural significance, which forms the premise of this study.

In fact, as the title suggests, I suggest that lower-middle-class cultural values have become central to our national vision more widely, arguing that while there are economic, social and political aspects of the petite bourgeoisie that are not, perhaps, ubiquitous amongst British society, there are a series of cultural frameworks for self-identification that align with British, and indeed Western, contemporary life more widely. In this, the study follows Weberian views on status as defined by cultural taste rather than merely economic class.[31] The lower middle class, which has historically been poorly defined in economic terms – spanning the lowest paid clerks and shop-workers, through to middle management and white-collar workers in more elitist institutions, such as banking – are problematic in terms of wage differentiation. Instead of offering a reading that is situated economically, this study takes the 'matters of cultural identity [that] are [usually] of strictly limited relevance' and places these at the fore.[32] By reading popular cultural sources as a method of interpreting both historic and contemporary markers of class, I address the criticisms of scholarly analysis of class made by Gunn, who queried the assumption that 'social formation could or should exist separately from its representation'.[33]

In doing so, this study uses popular cultural texts to look for signs of the 'narratives of class' that Savage discusses, on the grounds that these self-articulations, so often defined by what one is not (or what one's grandparents were versus where one fits now), are critical to the ways that class is represented in our daily lives.[34] It is this same 'not-ness' which foregrounds the focus on self-deprecating or inferiority models that form the basis of much of British comedy, and in terms of class structures, becomes evident in the ways that people define themselves as 'not middle class' but 'not working class' either. Equally, this is what Felski identified as being crucial to the issues surrounding vocal belonging of the lower middle class; that people would rather define themselves not as lower middle class but through the terminology of the more venerable classes – even if in opposition: put simply, 'not working class' is preferable to a positive self-identification of lower middle class-ness.

Alongside this lies a less articulated thread of 'ordinariness' that once more fits the national narrative of self-deprecation. Identifying as part of the 'working class' continues to carry certain romantic and eulogized emotional connotations; we know, for instance, that despite 'dramatic shifts in the occupational structure', 'two thirds of Britons indicate they are working class in response to survey researchers, a proportion which has changed hardly at all over a fifty year period'.[35] This is, in part, connected to the ways that working-class identities are glorified, in a manner not replicated for the disparate middle classes. At the same time, being middle class carries certain widely understood cultural connotations; in Savage's surveys, for instance, respondents who have moved up into the middle class are keen to distance themselves often from ideas about snobbery or superiority, while those with professional careers are more willing to accept their position within the established middle class.[36] Often, though, there is an attempt to negotiate these through the language of 'ordinariness' or 'normality', and those who use these terms fall under the umbrella of the lower middle class – as one respondent put it rather more clearly: 'I would describe myself as a very normal, lower middle class person.'[37]

This book looks across the historical shifts and changes and identifies the threads of representational continuity that remain wedded to our imagined construction of the lower middle class. It spans early Victorian literary representations through popular fiction of the twentieth and twenty-first centuries and television from the 1960s onwards. It argues that the Victorian office clerk, hunched at a high stool over his hand-copied papers, may seem a distant forebear to the modern call-centre worker, reading from a script to placate irate customers, but that the two figures still have much in common. There are, of course, material differences between the two (which I will come on to in the later chapters), but if we step back to examine, for instance, the popular stereotypes that surround both, we can trace the continuities: the tedious and overcrowded commute into work from the bed-sit flat or, more optimistically, perhaps, the small suburban terrace; the stifling and regimented office environment; the endless performance-based assessment from the middle-manager; the condescension directed at the suburban family, enjoying their cloistered lives in a semi-detached home. Attitudes towards these crucial sites – the office, the commute, the suburbs – have changed very little since their development in the nineteenth century.

Comedy and class

The starting point for this study is a trivialization of the lower middle class that has lasted for over one hundred and fifty years. Even those who ostensibly understand or empathize with the white-collar worker recognize their intrinsically comedic value, particularly within a British context where humour is so often derived from differences between social strata.[38] As Carl Rhodes and Robert Westwood make clear, this is an explicitly British trait wherein class becomes a 'distinctly and relatively unique subtext' that is not necessarily translated into other popular cultures.[39] As a result, and perhaps without intention, the lower middle class have become significant in the construction of British comedy itself because they are used to help distinguish the comedy found in instances where 'those marked by difference are deemed inferior'.[40]

This principle forms the basis of early depictions of the lower middle class in literature. Arlene Young's detailed study of the impact of Charles Dickens on the construction of lower-middle-class stereotypes makes clear that the writer has dominated popular impressions of both the clerk and the wider class. There is an assumption that the clerk originates with Dickens, but Young draws attention to existing comic forms of the 1830s and 1840s that were significant when he was constructing his now-well-known clerical characters.[41] She challenges preconceptions about Dickens's lower-middle-class figures by seeing the author as both 'representing' and 'reinterpreting' the class.[42] In this sense, Dickens was potentially using comedy as a method to mock existing stereotypes, by their 'being re-invoked' in particularly exaggerated and parodied ways.[43] This might help to account for the fact that while Dickens was familiar with the plight of the white-collar worker, having experienced it first-hand, his portrayals are not straightforwardly sympathetic. In many ways, he simultaneously 'challenges middle-class assumptions', drawing attention to the methods through which the bourgeoisie were 'projecting its own faults onto those below them', while confirming a 'characteristic diminutiveness' that repressed or suppressed the lower middle class at all costs.[44] His characters, like so many that follow in their lower-middle-class footsteps, while not treated badly, or with total condescension, retain a marginal position in Dickens's own novels. Two important issues arise from this: it complicates assumptions that writers from within the lower middle class might naturally be more sympathetic, and it demonstrates the establishment of an important relationship between the bourgeoisie and the petite bourgeoisie in cultural portrayals.

Dickens casts a long shadow over the cultural construction of the lower middle class in his evocative male clerks. Read, for instance, this description given in *Sketches by Boz* (1837):

> He was a tall, thin, pale person, in a black coat, scanty grey trousers, little pinched-up gaiters, and brown beaver gloves. He had an umbrella in his hand – not for use, for the day was fine – but, evidently, because he always carried one to the office in the morning ... There was something in the man's manner and appearance which told us, we fancied, his whole life, or rather his whole day, for a man of this sort has no variety of days. We thought we almost saw the dingy little back office into which he walks every morning, hanging his hat on the same peg, and placing his legs beneath the same desk.[45]

This clerk captures so many of the traits that continue to shape depictions of the white-collar worker in popular culture. There are striking similarities between, for instance, the description of the clerk walking into his office at the beginning of the day and the episode of 1980s sitcom *Ever Decreasing Circles*, in which Martin Bryce climbs the steps of Mole Valley Valves, walks into his office and hangs his coat on the broken peg on the back of the door. Both examples make clear the fine line between poignancy and comedy that is so often invoked in the portrayals of the lower middle class from the Victorian period onwards and which has become a staple in their repertoire.

While fiction has long played an important role in the construction of lower-middle-class figures in popular culture, as the example above shows, this remit was taken on wholeheartedly by the rise of television, and from the 1960s, particularly the situational comedy. In fiction, there is more often pathos, sadness and a gritty realism to the narratives derived from lower-middle-class life – in, for instance, the work of Shan Bullock and Arnold Bennett – but on screen, petit-bourgeois characters are overwhelming comedic in form, borrowing more from the stage portrayals of the lower middle class that began in the Victorian music hall and the comedic writing that authors such as Jerome K. Jerome and Charles and Weedon Grossmith made famous. Indeed, the Grossmiths' *Diary of a Nobody* (1892) is deeply influential; in 2007, and as a new television adaptation of the text headlined the BBC's Edwardian season, columnist Jon Wilde wrote a feature on *Diary*, calling it 'among the very finest of English comic novels', inspiring both a 'curious devotion' and a 'fierce discriminatory zeal'.[46] The novel has constantly been in press since it first appeared in *Punch* in 1888, it has been adapted for radio and television multiple times across the twentieth and twenty-first centuries, has inspired responses like John Betjeman's 'Thoughts on "The Diary of a Nobody"' (1958) and Keith Waterhouse's *Mrs Pooter's Diary* (1983), rewritings including Christopher Matthew's *Diary of a Somebody* (1978) and new epistolary writings such as Sue Townsend's *Secret Diary of Adrian Mole, Aged 13 3/4* (1982). In the 1960s, the term 'Pooterish' became a recognizable shorthand for someone who is 'self-important', 'mundane or narrow-minded' – a definition that was established by the word's inclusion in the *Oxford English Dictionary*. More recently, the original text (inclusive of illustrations) has become a daily weblog which viewers can read online or receive via email with entries beginning at the appropriate calendar date.[47]

Charles Pooter has become emblematic of the many qualities associated with the class, in part, because he shaped how people viewed the clerk from the outset. For this reason, Pooter begins every commentary on the office, the suburbs or middlebrow culture. The Grossmiths' use of comedy is synonymous with a particularly British approach to humour that would later become a core part of the sitcom form. Despite his social *faux pas* and indelicate awkwardness, the reader is invited to cringe at Pooter's behaviours, and to laugh at him, without ever being encouraged to wholly dislike him – key also for an audience that watches a character on a weekly basis on screen. Like the sitcom, which is predicated on a cyclical structure and an episodic resolution, Pooter has his own happy conclusion – his boss gives him ownership of his suburban home in a moment that the reader should join Pooter in enjoying.

The lower-middle-class sitcom character played an important role in the democratic feel of new visual media: a platform, like *Diary of a Nobody*, through which to chart the everyday, the suburban and the quotidian lives of the rising number of white-collar workers. Roger Silverstone remarked on the 'interrelationship between television and suburbia' as a threefold development that rests on its position as the 'heir' of radio, as a 'constant mastication' of suburban dilemmas and as a space to come to terms with the 'ambiguities of modernity'.[48] It is on television that Dickens's legacy, in many ways, has been both continued and refined by writers as varied as David Nobbs, Jimmy Perry, David Croft, Bob Larbey, John Cleese, Connie Booth, Nigel Williams, Simon Nye and Ricky Gervais, many of whom likewise come from lower-middle-class backgrounds. Larbey, for instance, the sitcom writer famous for penning some of the most popular suburban sitcoms of the 1970s, the 1980s and the 1990s (*Ever Decreasing Circles, A Fine Romance, As Time Goes By*) followed in the footsteps of Arnold Bennett by being first a grammar school boy, and then working in an insurance office after leaving school.

Comedy, then, plays an important role in the construction of the lower middle class, just as it has come to create an aura of amusement around the lives of those who are socially on the cusp. It is used to give quiet satirical bitterness to characters like *The Office*'s Tim Canterbury, who understands the pathos of his clerical anti-career, and to Richard Bucket, whose wife's desperation to climb the suburban social hierarchy in *Keeping Up Appearances* (1990–5) gives him little peace. Comedy is similarly critical to the relationship between class and nationhood – inherent, as Andy Medhurst says, 'in the construction of cultural identity'.[49] As Stephen Wagg has argued, the 'successful sitcom in Britain has almost always hinged on ideas of authenticity and pretention in class identities'.[50] The focus of many British televisual exports is exactly this type of socially conscious comedy, reinforced, as Brett Mills identifies, through the unique positioning of the British Broadcasting Corporation as a public service broadcaster which has a long-standing reputation for comedy in various forms.[51]

Television comedy that focuses on the lower middle class invariably picks up on what are seen as the embarrassing behaviours of pushy social climbers – following in the footsteps of literary depictions such as *Diary of a Nobody* and Barry Pain's *Eliza Stories* (1900–13). Instrumental to the 'classic' British sitcom remains this crucial conflict between the middle and lower middle classes, articulating the many subtleties that are portrayed as separating them. And as Wagg argues, television comedy classics are a manifest exploration of 'what we are, as a society'.[52] The humour in these social tensions, often the most minute and banal of behaviours, form a stalwart expression of British comedy, and while shows like *The Office* and *Keeping Up Appearances* are widely exported to Europe, there are very few sitcoms that have been played on American networks without extensive adaptation. Many British sitcoms (including iconic series such as *Dad's Army*, *Fawlty Towers* and more recently *Peep Show*, *The Inbetweeners* and *Outnumbered*) have been rewritten or adapted and still fail to make it past the pilot stage on American screens largely because of these underpinning class dynamics that are not easily translated. Even the first series of *The Office USA*, which stayed closest to the script of the original, had references to class rewritten because they were based on interpretations that are largely meaningless in a transatlantic context.

Following in this vein, British screen humour is heavily based on what Jeffrey Richards called the 'comedy of character'; as Mills argues, it is the 'gap between how [characters] wish to be seen by others and how they actually appear' that gets the laughs.[53] Mills suggests that this is one of the key differences between British and American humour – while British audiences are encouraged to laugh at characters, in American sitcoms audiences are encouraged to laugh 'with' them. This implies that British comedy is more aggressive, in certain ways, but there is a nuance to this type of humour that prevents it from being cruel. As J. B. Priestley put it in *English Humour* back in 1930: 'We laugh at those we love. … Because we have come to know them so well, that certain traits or habits, as familiar to us as their faces, seem peculiarly absurd'.[54] In this sense, it is 'tender mockery', rather than angry or vitriolic laughter, that recognizes in attributes associated with the lower middle class like pomposity, social insecurity and awkwardness, reflections of our own national obsession with class.[55] This sits with Martina Kessel's approach to understanding humour as a 'cultural practice that both organized social order and revealed shared assumptions about society and politics'.[56]

These modern renditions of subtle class warfare owe much to a tradition that was established in the Victorian music hall and has translated well onto the small screen. David Brent's painful telling of half-remembered jokes and his ability to misread the social environment are reminiscent of Basil Fawlty's social awkwardness. Further back, this ineptitude was at the heart of Charles Pooter, who so often noted in his diary the underwhelming quips and puns he made across the course of his day, always accompanied by references to what the reader suspects are misinterpreted 'fits' of laughter by those around him. This low-key self-aggrandizement has become institutionalized in British culture and particularly on television – as examples of the lower-middle-class 'loser' from Captain Mainwaring in *Dad's Army* (1968–77), Reginald Perrin (1976–9), Martin in *Ever Decreasing Circles* (1984–9), Hyacinth Bucket (pronounced Bouquet), Mr Bean (1990–5), Inspector Raymond Fowler in *The Thin Blue Line* (1995–6) – or nearly any character played by Rowan Atkinson – demonstrate.

As Michael Hogan put it, in a recent review of *Colin's Sandwich*, aired first in 1988, Mel Smith's depiction of Colin as 'the gaffe-prone, anti-hero with thwarted ambitions' makes him the successor of Tony Hancock, Basil Fawlty and predecessor of David Brent.[57]

There are multiple positions on the relationship between class and comedy. Many of these rest on one area of humour theory: the notion of superiority that charts the 'triadic relationship [that is] negotiated'[58] and renegotiated between the teller, the butt of the joke and the audience. The premise of superiority, while seemingly straightforwardly focused on the feelings evoked in the audience by the poor behaviour, awkward situations or simply bad luck of the character towards whom the joke is directed, is rather complex in a lower-middle-class context. Superiority theory works much more straightforwardly when considering attitudes of the middle class when viewing programmes that make fun of the petite bourgeoisie. Many of the television shows under discussion in this book, however, have a wider audience, often in line with their status as British comedy 'classics'. In part, comedy in this guise performs a function as an 'invitation to belong', as Medhurst puts it;[59] it is both potentially inclusive and simultaneously gains much traction from the differences that mark the characters as 'other' to the audience. The lower-middle-class figure is, as Wagg establishes, so often the target of humour in the sitcom, but this is complicated by the multifaceted approaches to comedy which rest on the interpretation of the audience as much as the intended humour identified by the writer/s.

In *Comedy and the Politics of Representation* (2018), Helen Davies and Sarah Ilott argue that the 'way that a joke is understood – as aggressive, self-deprecating, or inclusive' – is a core aspect of the representational power of comedy performances.[60] While comedy so often invites a positioning that should 'encourage audiences to identify with or against the joker/and or the butt', which evokes a dichotomy between 'others' and 'ourselves', lower-middle-class comedy often poses a more complex positioning.[61] When excruciating or embarrassing consequences befall the many lower-middle-class sitcom characters across the latter half of the twentieth century, comedy rests not merely on the social differences that co-opt superiority theory but equally an empathetic response that, as Glyn White and John Mundy suggest, provokes an equally powerful relief that 'those particular mishaps have not happened to us'.[62] In this sense, lower-middle-class comedy can often be read not only through the lens of 'superiority' but also as 'incongruity', the other comedic theorization that rests on the potential pleasure in 'respite from the mundanities and certainties of everyday life' through incongruous acts.[63] In the type of sitcom covered by this book, ordinary and everyday settings and scenarios are frequently turned into slapstick, farcical or physically humorous events through this type of incongruity. Feelings of audience superiority are not, then, the only aspect of the sitcom that shapes our view of the lower middle class – it is often the hilarity by which the same class structures are parodied and inverted that defines instances such as snob Hyacinth Bucket (*Keeping Up Appearances*) emerging from a greenhouse with tousled hair and her skirt askew, a result of the upper-class 'Major's' amorous attentions. As Mills suggests, comedy on screen can often simultaneously be 'one of the most powerful ways in which unequal social distinctions remain upheld' whilst 'demonstrat[ing] the tenuous and artificial nature of social norms'.[64]

Cringe comedy, such as is so often found in the millennial *The Office*, pushes exactly these buttons; the scenario is painfully close to the lived experience of many, but the audience are outside of the situation in the moment of viewing even though they may recognize the setbacks and humiliations of the familiar office environment. It provokes more complex reactions than superiority alone, and while we can distance ourselves from the most objectionable views of characters such as David Brent or Gareth Keenan, there is a deliberate discomfort to how far we can deconstruct the more subtle tensions and petty behaviours of the office place. It might not be happening to us right now, but it could.

Julian Dutton argues something similar about the role of visual comedy across the twentieth century. He identifies the empathy that can be evoked through physical manifestations of the 'truth' that is that 'we all pretend to be able to operate successfully in the adult social world, but inside, none of us are actually doing so'.[65] In this sense, the physical comedy of moments like the dumping of a lorry load of manure on Martin Bryce's drive in *Ever Decreasing Circles* or Alan Partridge's loud staccato attempts to get the attention of 'Dan' before conceding that he will speak to him later remind us of the social perils that are always present. While superiority theory can imply a 'a malicious sense of superiority' and the 'sense of self-satisfaction',[66] this model suggests that the distinction between looking down on the 'other' and identifying with them is less polemic than may appear. The 'self-satisfaction' in this instance is immediate – I am not currently making a fool of myself – rather than suggestive of a long-term and deeper construction of difference.

Gender, politics and pathos

Alongside these discussions of class and comedy, this study is interested in variously gendered depictions. It was the male Victorian clerk in his top hat and suit, dyspeptic and sedentary when compared to his rural working-class counterpart, who first caught the eye of nineteenth-century commentators and novelists. In contemporary television, the lower-middle-class man has retained his position as a key comic force (Hyacinth Bucket, as a character, is perhaps the only well-known example of the lower-middle-class comedienne). While the late nineteenth century saw the beginnings of the 'white-blouse revolution', with women entering the clerical workforce in huge numbers, there was little change in the ways that men and women of the lower middle class were represented. Even now, and as the title of 'administrator' etymologically situates the gender neutrality of office work, depictions in popular culture and particularly comedy return to traditional tropes: the male mid-life crisis, the sexualized secretary, the power play between the middle manager and the ordinary employee.

Part of this focus on men in the office came about because of the way that the visibility of the lower middle class centred originally on male clerks. At the time, the clerk was marked out as being feminized by both his work and his position in what were seen as the heavily domesticated suburbs. Critics like T. W. H. Crosland picked up on what they saw as the feminization of suburbia, viewing family hierarchies within the suburban villa as shaped by a domesticity that was essentially inward looking, particularly when contrasted to the model of the lauded working-class 'community'. As a symbolic example of this, Medhurst talks about the prevalence of daughters over sons in British comedy films set in suburbia in the 1940s, the 1950s and the 1960s.[67] The shift from the communal living of the urban working class (in close terraces, public houses and in intergenerational cohabitation) to the reclusive interior of the suburban semi continues to be defined in terms of the closed-off family unit, uneasily headed by a patriarch who is sequestered into a traditionally feminine sphere. Even contemporary comedies such as the BBC's *Motherland* (2017) site the father away from the suburban home (in an endless parade of stag dos, business meetings and team-building 'away' days), while the now-career-driven mother struggles with the responsibility of running an orderly household and working full time.

White-collar masculinity continues to be a topic of debate in the press, literature and in film and on television, and it has not strayed far from the 'parodic discourse of littleness' that Bailey identifies in Victorian literature.[68] Equating white-collar work with characters who were small, insignificant or diminutive began as a comedic device that both feminized and undermined the Victorian clerk. This discourse quickly became associated with the wider lower middle class and continues to manifest in contemporary culture. This 'littleness' is used both metaphorically but also in a literal sense, with the constant reiteration of members of the lower middle class as being somehow physically diminished. As a result, lower-middle-class masculinity is particularly contested as a construct that is so easily reduced to parody – turned into a physical manifestation of social anxiety felt by a class that is construed as being 'below' the middle class.

The image of the short clerk came not only from the pens of the scathing middle class but also from the imaginations of those who had worked in offices themselves. Shan Bullock, an Edwardian novelist who published two novels loosely chronicling his experiences as a clerk in London, referred to his character Mr Ruby as a 'poor, troubled, homely little man'.[69] Likewise, H. G. Wells's draper Mr Polly is a 'short, compact figure', and Edgar Finchley, prolific clerk-author Victor Canning's creation, is abruptly described as 'forty-five, short'.[70] What is clear is that former clerks were happy to refer to this parodic shortness, if it meant that they could draw attention to the crisis of masculinity that was enveloping the white-collar world. And particularly, if like Bullock, they could promote empathy for the desk-weary clerk who wanted not mere condescension but to be more of a man.

In the 1950s, R. F. Delderfield's Avenue series (chronicling the lives of families in a close-knit London suburb) were populated by little clerical types: Mr Frith, a small-time antiques dealer, is described rather ruthlessly by his wife as an 'undersized little nonentity'. He is 'over forty, short, balding, and wearing pince-nez spectacles'.[71] His neighbour, Harold Goodbeer, is a solicitor's clerk who manages to woo a pretty young widowed client despite being 'spare, eager, bespectacled, and physically frail. He was also fussy, pedantic, and inclined to be pompous'.[72] Harold fulfils many expectations of the clerical type; he is even, for instance, 'at thirty-five ... still virginal'. The association between the single, male office worker and virginity was made significant in the BBC's 2018 Christmas adaptation of Agatha Christie's *ABC Murders* (originally published in 1936) when young, attractive waitress Betty Barnard makes fun of Alexander Bonaparte Cust, callously calling him a virgin when he tries to give her silk stockings (a taunt not used in the original novel).[73] Despite these seemingly damning depictions, however, Delderfield, like Bullock before him, demonstrates understanding of the approach to writing the lower middle class. He keeps the reader on the side of Harold and Mr Frith, and they are, in their way, heroic. Delderfield even goes so far as to remind us that Harold was part of a 'breed of clerks and shopkeepers who had recently defied the Prussians in the water-logged fields of Flanders'.[74]

Perhaps the best-known example of this type of lower-middle-class masculinity is Captain Mainwaring from 1960s BBC sitcom *Dad's Army*. Set in a Home Guard platoon in the Second World War, *Dad's Army* is iconic for being, as Mark Lawson called it, 'the BBC's single most durably valuable programme'.[75]

Following a music hall tradition, and while negotiating fears that veterans would be offended, it became more overtly a comedy about class and social status. It is still aired on a regular basis (in the same Saturday night slot on the BBC that it made its own long before my childhood memories of it) and is frequently discussed as an epitome of the sitcom form. In recent years, it has formed the basis of new adaptations (the 2016 film of the same title and *We're Doomed! The Dad's Army Story* (2015)) and documentaries (the most recent of which was a four-part series called *Saluting Dad's Army*, shown in 2018 on satellite channel UK Gold).

Mainwaring was, in many ways, the head of Jimmy Perry and David Croft's ensemble cast. Each of the early episodes begins at the bank where Mainwaring works, reinforcing the centrality of the captain to his platoon. Mainwaring is stereotypically lower middle class; educated at a grammar school, he works his way up from bank clerk to management. Mainwaring's class-consciousness and his precarious sense of social position are the butt of many a joke across the series (largely centred on the perceivable tension between Sergeant Wilson – a member of the upper middle class – and Mainwaring, son of a draper). Both his values and neuroses are pitched as typically lower middle class; his work ethic, sense of duty and desire for social betterment are often marginalized by the comedic potential of his unquestioning patriotism (tending, at times, to xenophobia), his snobbishness and his fervent attempts to keep others beneath him. Even the way Mainwaring speaks is echoic of the many *Punch* cartoons that picked up on the clerk's tendency to add a gratuitous 'H' in a desperate but misguided attempt to convey a higher status.

Enhancing these characteristics is a physical conformity to type that simultaneously exaggerates the comedy of his personality and normalizes it. Mainwaring, like many lower-middle-class figures both before and after him, is self-conscious about his thinning hair, for instance. Comedic in value, particularly when he wears a toupee (a trick still used as a comic point of reference about the lower-middle-class male in sitcoms – see Inspector Grimm in *The Thin Blue Line*, the police chief in *People Like Us*, Stan in *dinnerladies*), it also symbolizes an inherently sensitive concern, disproportionately played out as a lower-middle-class issue. It is even mentioned in *Diary of a Nobody*, when Charles Pooter writes 'my hairdresser tells me I ought not to brush my hair too much just now' (interestingly, Lowe played Pooter in a radio version of *Diary of a Nobody* later in his career).[76]

Mainwaring's position as Captain is predicated on a justification of military methods for social reinforcement within the community (seen, for instance, in the assertion that the village hall is needed for military business over church or social requirements in episodes such as 'The Love of Three Oranges'). In this, he is very similar to another character developed in the 1960s – Mr Banks from Disney's 1964 film *Mary Poppins*. Based on the books by Australian author P. L. Travers, but set in London, the film presents Mr Banks as a pseudo-military figure, in a homage to Edwardian Imperial ideals of masculinity. Just as Banks marches to work and returns expecting his children to be arranged in an orderly fashion by a Nanny who can act as 'gen'ral' to his private 'dominion', Mainwaring happily conflates the necessity for operational precision and the ordering of the social hierarchy under a military guise. Without 'precision', 'discipline', 'tradition' and 'rules', as Mr Banks puts it, there is nothing but 'disorder', 'catastrophe', 'chaos'.[77] In both examples, military authority shapes and moulds a controlled hierarchy that gives reassurance to the lower-middle-class clerk who has worked his way up to a level not necessarily commensurate with his more tenuous position in the wider world of class.[78]

These tropes are perpetuated in the physical form of the characters. Upright Mr Banks (David Tomlinson, at six feet one, should tower above his banking colleagues) is hunched, and snivelling around his senior Board members, all of whom have white hair or balding heads. Their stiff and formal short dance when Jane and Michael visit the bank captures a stifled social position, and the eagerness with which Mr Banks defers to their views places him at odds with his own children. Grown-ups in the film are of two types: those who are creative and those who are not. In an assimilation of Travers's books, and her own memory of her father – who was variously a bank clerk and a bank manager in her native Australia (as featured in the biopic film *Saving Mr Banks* (2013)) – bank workers are certainly *forced* into the latter category. Mr Banks must strengthen his tenuous position by unquestioningly conforming to the establishment. Only Mary Poppins can reanimate the stifled petite bourgeoisie, giving Banks the confidence to act as an individual.

Captain Mainwaring endlessly attempts to reassert his position through his stance. Arthur Lowe's physique was instrumental in creating the parodic element to the pomposity of Captain Mainwaring. In this, the height of Sergeant Wilson (played by John Le Mesurier – who at nearly six foot was several inches taller than Lowe) was an additional physical reminder of the suspected class differences and military experience between the two characters. In an interview, Le Mesurier mentioned that the original idea had been for Lowe to play an NCO whilst Le Mesurier himself took the role of Captain, but Croft and Perry hit on a much more successful comedic scenario in having the shorter man play

Mainwaring. Reinforced through a catalogue of references to Mainwaring's background (his father's poor-quality tailoring, his brother's wastrel behaviour, his grammar school education and rise from clerk to manager, marrying a woman whose family considered the match beneath her), Lowe's height became a crucial aspect of the reiteration of social neurosis as anything he said or did. In this, the character was slotting into a tradition of lower-middle-class slightness in circulation for a hundred years or so by the time *Dad's Army* was made.

Height is also a trope played with in *The Office* (2001–3) in order to parody stereotypes surrounding masculinity and office hierarchy. Alexia Panayiotou discusses 'man'-agement as a discourse of office masculinity in popular film in the late twentieth century and picks up on the trend towards 'macho managers' that are codified through 'dress, manner, appearance, language and in their actions and practices'.[79] David Brent's choice of high-heeled boots when speaking alongside his rival, the calm, suave and collected Neil Godwin, draw attention to his shortness whilst confirming conventional expectations surrounding 'masculine' stature. This is just one example of Brent's attempts to fit in with a managerial culture that is predicated on 'macho' behaviours; for instance, his choice of faded jeans and a t-shirt when acting as a 'motivational speaker' (dress) as well as his attempts to join in with Chris Finch's sexist and homophobic jokes (language).[80] During their battle for the role of branch manager, Brent's behaviour is constantly in opposition to Godwin's composure, his ability to tell jokes that are inclusive and not bigoted, and even his prowess as a dancer.[81] Godwin's self-assured manner and easy social skills situate him within the comfortable middle class in comparison to Brent's awkward pomposity and emulative behaviours.

In many ways, ideas around feminization and domestication became equally prevalent when considering the wider ideology of the class. Politically, in Britain if not elsewhere in Europe, the lower middle class have been seen as cautious supporters of Villa Toryism, symbolically moderate, prudent and vigilant in the protection of values such as home ownership, a risk-averse economy and policies that both promote ambition and limit social movement. There is an assumption that the lower middle class, particularly those living within suburbia, are often keen to preserve a status quo.[82] As part of this, suburbanites are often associated with the phrase 'property-owning democracy', which gained traction during the Thatcherite era. David Howell wrote about the origins of the phrase – Anthony Eden credited Noel Skelton back in 1929 – but he also talks of its earliest context, as a counter to Socialism and the beginnings of what Howell calls a 'de-collectivised, *petit-bourgeois* society on which Conservative leaders have set their sights all down the decades'.[83] By the 1970s, when Thatcher was making references to the 'Basildon Man' – the type of aspirational lower-middle-class figure who was seen as a potential swing voter – the political tie between Conservatism and the suburban lower middle class was, once more, front and centre, even if the need to woo the aspirant petite bourgeoisie was evidence of a rift between social conservatism and suburbia.

It is perhaps assumptions around petit-bourgeois voting patterns that have limited their political agenda in Britain. Indeed, their position as part of the electorate has, as Tom Jeffery argued, been historically overlooked, for the same reasons that their history is ignored, because of the 'contemptuous image of the lower middle class as mean little people, languishing between the collective strength of the working classes and the saving graces of their supposed betters' – characterized best in Sidney Strube's 'little man' cartoons in the *Daily Express*.[84] As a result, as Jeffery examines in the 1930s, they were a social group courted neither by the emergent Labour party nor particularly the Liberals or Conservatives.

Likewise, the Communists were equally uninspired by the potential of lower-middle-class support; Eric Hobsbawm referred to them as 'a sullen army of the suburbs and massive supporters of right-wing and anti-labor newspapers and politicians'.[85] Despite this, it is a mistake to fall into the trap of seeing the class in two-dimensional terms, as 'isolated and reactionary' suburbanites, because of the 'potentially damaging limitations'.[86] Jeffery looks, like Susan Pennybacker, to the membership, cultural affiliation and support of the lower middle class in organizations such as the London County Council (LCC), the Left Book Club and as consumers of Penguin and Pelican books and the *News Chronicle* as evidence of the growing interest in political activities in the run up to the Second World War.[87] Equally divergent are representations of socialism in middlebrow fiction of the early twentieth century and associations with jingoism and fascism within clerical histories.[88]

Regardless of these nuanced readings of political ideologies within the lower middle class, impressions of suburbia as a backbone to conservatism in the 1930s has, in some ways, led to a wider disenfranchisement that was part of a self-fulfilled prophecy which damaged lower-middle-class political confidence. As Crossick argued, the 'caricatured treatment' that the petite bourgeoisie endured became related to 'the reality, for it seems that from the middle of the nineteenth century there was little distinctive or coherent about the voice of the *petite bourgeoisie* in British political life', particularly when compared with the 'increasingly organised working class'.[89] British political parties continue in their attempts to lure working and middle class voters, while the centre ground in class terms are underevaluated because, as Jeffery puts it, 'the derogatory image of the lower middle class has been among the most resilient of all social stereotypes, surviving not only over time but in quite different political quarters'.[90] If, as this study suggests, we have become a substantially lower-middle-class nation, this represents a serious proportion of the electorate that are unnoticed, or as one lower-middle-class Mass Observation participant put it in 1939: the lower middle class has 'less power, and more opportunities for power, than any other class in the modern world'.[91] Following the results of the 2019 general election, and the Conservative majority, commentators and analysts have spoken widely about the changing affiliations of the formerly industrial working-class heartlands, but, once more, very little has been said about a conceivable lower-middle-class silent majority that are ignored by both major political parties and which represent a substantial subsection of the population.

While in the wider world of politics, the lower-middle-class voter has been projected as having few opportunities, in popular culture, the voice of the disgruntled and disaffected petit-bourgeois suburbanite has become perhaps not politically significant, but certainly popular. In 1975, David Nobbs humanized the struggle of the ordinary suburban man trying to bring about a personal revolution in his character Reginald Perrin. Following Nobbs's success on the page and the small screen, a new generation of suburban TV shows of the 1970s, the 1980s and the 1990s, by writers such as Brian Cooke and Johnnie Mortimer (*George and Mildred* (1976–9)), John Esmonde and Bob Larbey (*Ever Decreasing Circles*, *The Good Life* (1975–8)) and Roy Clarke (*Keeping Up Appearances*), kept the lower middle class on television, reiterating nuances amongst and between them. Core to these depictions was a narrative of pathos – of lost voices and cries that cannot be heard, personal crises and silenced ambitions.

As Felski drew attention to, the values and markers of the lower middle class are in evidence all around us. Most of the population now work in offices, commute increasing distances to work and dwell in twentieth-century suburbia or sprawling new housing estates; the 'everyday' of our nation has become subsumed within so many of those traits and characteristics traditionally preserved for the lower middle class. Michel de Certeau talks of the 'quotidian' as the routine patterns that shape our identity and many of the practices he identifies are those which were first aligned with the clerk – commuting, paperwork, bureaucracy, suburban living. As Andy Medhurst puts it: 'to inhabit a nation state is to live amongst countless, daily, unavoidable images of that nation's ideas of itself'.[92] Popular culture is thus a crucial site through which we both create and absorb attitudes and values that promote our understanding of self. Much of Western life is now shaped around these 'clerkly' behaviours and routines and while it is clear that these trends affect all Western countries, rather than just Britain, there is a validity to the suggestion that Britain's particular response to class, identified as a distinct aspect of our socio-cultural make up, evokes certain national rather than Western responses.

Lower-middle-class topographies

In order to structure such a diverse range and breadth of material into a coherent focus, this study takes several sites historically associated with the lower middle class and geographically situates key topics. The core argument of this book is that these spaces, once evocative of the lower-middle-class clerk, have now become emblematic of 'ordinary' or 'everyday' life. In postulating this idea, this study draws from the work of sociologists like Simon Gunn, who comments on the historical associations drawn between 'physical environments' and 'the identity of collective groups', but also Mike Savage, who argues that 'place is [the] basis for class formation'.[93] This structure allows examples from a wide range of media to be explored across an extensive chronology, making clear the continuities and the developments that have occurred from 1850 to the present day. Each chapter will find space to focus on important historical shifts (for instance, Taylorism or the development of suburbia) or significant cultural texts to situate an awareness of chronology, further establishing the sense of a wider history of the lower middle class. While some of these spaces have been previously theorized by historians, literary critics and within cultural studies – suburbia, for instance, has received more widespread attention in the last decade, particularly from the viewpoint of Victorian women writers – this study gives a reading of them as sites of lower-middle-class culture more specifically.

The first space under discussion is the office. Ingrid Jeacle and Lee Parker rightly called the office 'a ubiquitous feature of daily life', drawing attention to the unconscious impact of this space in which we spend a 'disproportionate amount of our waking hours'.[94] This chapter begins with early office culture and the development of the office as a distinct working space with particular tropes, many of which offer a convincing and long-lasting impression of a depressing, mundane and uninspiring environment. Through cultural texts as diverse as Arnold Bennett's *A Man from the North* (1898), Frank Swinnerton's *The Young Idea* (1910), E. M. Forster's *Howards End* (1910), Norman Collins's *London Belongs to Me* (1945), B. S. Johnson's *Christie Malry's Own Double Entry*

(1973), David Nobbs's novel *The Fall and Rise of Reginald Perrin* (alongside the two television adaptations), *Men Behaving Badly* (1992–2014), *People Like Us* (1995–2001), *The Office, Absolute Power* (2003–5), *The IT Crowd* (2006–10), Martin Knight's *Barry Desmond is a Wanker* (2010), *Twenty Twelve* (2011–12) and *W1A* (2014–), the chapter examines the historic entrenchment of uniform dreariness that remains dominant within cultural representations of the office as well as exploring assumptions that are commonly made about office workers on the basis of the perceived futility of office life.

In Chapter 2, the focus shifts from the office as a physical space to study several of the psychological aspects of bureaucracy often discussed in popular culture. Following discussion in Chapter 1 of the changes that have shaped evolving depictions of the clerk – from the competition of female workers to the mechanization (and latterly, computerization) of bureaucratic processes – this second chapter examines the impact of these developments on the representations of office workers. Much of the focus of this chapter is an assessment of late-Victorian rationalization and the impact that this continues to have on perceptions of clerical duties. This includes anxiety-inducing features such as competition and routinization (symbolized in the relationship with the ticking clock), as well as the poignant career markers of redundancy and retirement. At the same time, this chapter argues that the office becomes a site of reassuring familiarity despite the pathos and uncertainty within these tropes. Crucially, the cynicism of figures like Reginald Perrin or David Brent rest more easily with modern audiences than the unlikely optimism of Victorian Charles Pooter in fulfilling our cultural expectations. This chapter additionally explores the role of comedy in shaping our understanding of office life (in British culture post *The Office*) and the careful alignment of the self-deprecating clerk with a broader, national sense of reticent humour.

Chapter 3 examines the site of the commute, charting changes across the last two centuries, from the early days when travelling into the city was the premise of the wealthy middle-class businessman to the almost universal everyday migration of workers from across all industries. There is, in contemporary society, widespread acceptance that travelling to work – via rail, road or public transport – is an expensive (and often uncomfortable) yet essential part of working life. In 2016, the average commute time reached a new daily high and continues to grow (rising from 52 minutes in 2013 to 55 in 2014 and 58.4 by 2017);[95] more than 3.7 million commuters now travel for over two hours per day.[96] In the south-east corner of England, in particular, the number of daily commuters travelling into the capital has pushed public transport and road networks far beyond capacity.

And yet, this daily migration is not a new phenomenon; nineteenth-century railways joined the dots of the emerging suburbs to the heart of the financial and bureaucratic nation. By 1900, over a million commuters were travelling into the city of London from the new suburbs every day.[97]

Building upon the analyses of Tim Edensor and Joe Moran, both of whom focus on the contemporary commute by car, this chapter examines the office worker in the transition from home to work and back again across the late-nineteenth, twentieth and twenty-first centuries. Beginning as a site of concern for the earliest of train commuters – with suburban wives and doctors discussing their worries about so called 'suburban dyspeptics' – the chapter considers the commute as an ultimate contemporary symbol of the quotidian, a dimension made clear in the targeting of the transport network by terrorists during the 7/7 attacks on London.[98]

As new garden villages are being planned and debates surrounding the national housing shortage reach a peak not seen since the post-war period, the fourth and fifth chapters examine the cultural position of the suburban home. Building upon, and updating, the social histories of the 1960s, the 1970s and the 1980s by H. J. Dyos, F. M. L. Thompson, Kate Flint and Robert Fishman, and the more recent cultural explorations of Roger Webster, Mark Clapson, Lynne Hapgood, Robert Bueka and Roger Silverstone, the final Chapters 4 and 5 explore the rise and, often posited, fall of the suburbs. They look at shifting cultural opinions of suburbia (and the associated negativity that comes, as Clapson points out, as frequently from within academia as outside of it) and changing attitudes to suburban living. The first of these twinned chapters dissects the wider position of suburbia in society. It examines the ways that suburbia has been mocked, derided and undermined from almost the very beginnings of its development. By challenging the assumptions made about suburbia as an architectural, social and cultural blemish, the chapter puts forward the innocuous semi-detached dwelling – that very symbol of suburbia – as a key part of our British identity.

By examining the popularity of the suburban sitcom in the 1970s–90s, using television programmes like *The Good Life* (1975–8), *George and Mildred* (1976–9), *Terry and June* (1979–87), *Ever Decreasing Circles*, *Keeping Up Appearances* and *One Foot in the Grave* (1990–2001), the chapter also explores the position of the sitcom as a prominent vehicle for lower-middle-class comedy on British television. As Medhurst puts it: 'the suburban sitcom represents British comedy's most sustained attempt at *embourgeoisement*, its plots often concerned with the maintaining of genteel values against threats from outside'.[99] This makes the sitcom essentially preoccupied with the concerns of the lower middle class. More significantly, the cultural synchronicity of this type of subtle class interaction has become symbolic of national tropes. Patricia Routledge's portrayal of socially emulative suburban, Hyacinth Bucket, has, for instance, made *Keeping Up Appearances* the most exported British television show – outperforming such iconic programmes as *Doctor Who*, *Sherlock* and *Top Gear*.[100]

Using middlebrow fiction and popular television, Chapter 5 demonstrates the sense of opportunity that underscores works like Charles and Weedon Grossmiths's *Diary of a Nobody* and Arnold Bennett's *A Man from the North* and the comfort and stability of the suburbs that gave confidence to the new lower middle class in sitcoms from *The Good Life* to *Keeping Up Appearances*. It also explores the creativity that comes from within the suburban semi, arguing that the connotations of suburbia as soulless and uninspiring gloss over the ways that writers often conceive of suburban culture.

These sites – the office, the commute and the suburbs – began as distinctly lower-middle-class spaces, the environments where the Victorian clerk worked and lived. Key to this study is the idea that we have become a lower-middle-class nation – not only in that we are a nation of office workers but because our dominant cultural identity is a 'clerkly' one. In a sense, therefore, the nation is a metaphorical office and we are all clerks. The values and lifestyle of the office worker have helped to draw the parameters of modern cultural and social meaning, which have become, in some respects, an embodiment of Western identity at its broadest, but Britishness too. The familiarity of the tedious nine-till-five existence, compounded by what is often viewed as a retreat into the suburbs, remains a well-recognized narrative well into the twenty-first century. Modern audiences, who work in offices and live in suburbs, can continue to relate to the comedy of characters such as the late-Victorian Charles Pooter.

There remains, indeed, an appetite for mocking the clerical character, as seen in the popularity of Ricky Gervais and Stephen Merchant's award-winning series *The Office*. The show demonstrates many aspects of this modern attitude that, I will argue, began with the Victorian and Edwardian treatment of the same class. *The Office* was set in Slough – the modern suburb berated by John Betjeman in 1937 as not 'fit for humans now', with its 'bald young clerks' who have 'tasted Hell' – and Gervais's characters are supposed to epitomize the daily grind in a way that, at times, becomes too close for comfort.[101] While the clerk is Victorian in origin, he is a figure that remains almost unchanged until at least the 1930s and who, in a variable form, remains relevant in contemporary society. The wider implications of lower-middle-class taste and culture, viewed particularly in the continuing ambiguity toward suburbia, shows how deeply the clerk and his characteristics have penetrated British identity in a way that makes us uncomfortable still.

This book seeks, then, to bring the lower middle class to the fore by examining a wide array of cultural sources from the mid-nineteenth century to the present day. It aims to provide an overview of popular and widespread representations that have shaped the way that we continue to view the class. In teasing out the threads of continuity in those depictions and the changes, it explores the relevance of two ideas first raised in the nineteenth century. The first of these, mentioned by Victorian commentators, was that the clerk was a symbolic figurehead of a new lower middle class. Across the twentieth and twenty-first centuries, this has developed into a recognition that the office-working, suburban-living, lower-middle-class individual has become synonymous with modernity, representing the concerns, values and lifestyles of wider society. Taking this as a starting point, the overarching question is this: does it follow that British society is, or at least has been, at its core, a lower-middle-class society? It is this that the book takes as its motivation, providing an analysis of the clerk (later, white-collar/office worker or administrator), which is critical to understanding lower-middle-class identities and consequently key in shaping much wider representations of class, gender, comedy and even Britishness, itself.

1

The office

As the white-collar workforce expanded throughout the nineteenth century, the clerk went from being a semi-professional personal assistant to entering vast bureaucratic halls filled with row upon row of identical desks. Later the male Victorian clerk would face increasing de-skilling and mechanization as well as competing with a new generation of female secretaries. The Victorian lower-middle-class clerk would move from humble residences in unfashionable areas of the city to newly built suburban dwellings on the outskirts, forming a first generation of rail commuters as the tracks stretched further into Metroland. By the mid-twentieth century, white-collar work would no longer be confined to vast urban areas, as bureaucratic processes began to spread across all industries, centred not just around London but growing into fledgling industrial estates and suburban outposts. Across nearly two centuries of change, however, many of these daily details remained the same. The office worker continues to characterize the humdrum and the everyday in media and cultural representations. Even individual traits ascribed to the lower-middle-class clerk in the 1850s prove powerfully long-lasting: popular associations between the clerical type and a series of physical and temperamental characteristics became embedded in cultural memory, enduring into the twenty-first century.

Christopher Baldry suggests there are 'three aspects of "the office"' in social constructions: 'the office building (for most people symbolized by its exterior), the office space within the building and office work within that space'.[1] This chapter explores each of these realms within popular representations arguing that they are equally significant in a cultural sense. What follows is a second office chapter – 'The Desk' – which turns to consider a range of social, emotional and psychological features of working within this environment. What Baldry asks, when examining the office, is that we consider why it is that 'an office looks and "feels" like an office' – or, as this chapter posits – how is the office recreated through image, text and dialogue so that it feels authentic for the viewer or reader? This chapter addresses some of the ways in which the office functions within architectural semiotics, considering the ways that, for instance, exteriors and interiors perform as a simultaneous signal both to potential customers and clients but also to a company's staff. How do details that form the office interior instruct the ways that we view their 'status and appropriate behaviour'? And how are these communicated in popular representations?

The almost exponential growth of office work in the late nineteenth century saw one of the most impactful shifts in social structures in modern terms and a turning point for the development of the lower middle class. This relationship between the office space and class became fundamental and is astonishingly long-lasting. As Francis Duffy suggested in the 1980s:

> The clerks are gone now. Lupin as well as Mr Pooter is dead. But the office buildings which were designed to meet their need and foster their fantasies still exist and still contain their ghosts.[2]

Examining these spaces, in all of their forms – large, intensive halls of industrial clerical work through to tiny offices and cramped conditions – can offer us an insight into society more widely and the white-collar, lower middle class, in particular. Duffy calls old office buildings the social historians' equivalent of an archaeological dig: in Manchester, the city where I work, there is evidence all around me of this rich – and largely untapped – history of the many thousands of clerks who passed their working days in these buildings across the twentieth century. And, as Duffy observes, in many ways, despite their relative recentness, we know very little about why these offices were built in the style that they were; records of commercial buildings are few and far between making it difficult to draw conclusions about whether they were designed with efficiency, communication or comfort in mind. More fascinating still is just how many of those buildings are still offices; renovated, converted, made open-plan, contemporary office workers live with these 'ghosts' every day.

Significant, too, is the preference for privileging in modern memory the run-down office, ill-fit for purpose, rather than the grandly designed architectural pinnacle. This is not, it appears, just a contemporary trend; it is hard to find positive descriptions of office spaces in literature at the end of the nineteenth century, just as modern texts continue to place emphasis on the flaws of even the plushest of gleaming glass and steel office buildings. Cultural architectural impressions – or, rather the process by which we remember certain tropes over others – are negative and reinforce a perception that is constructed as much by the ways that office work is conceived, as they are any kind of reflection of the reality of the environment. The attitude towards clerical and administrative work thus shapes our collective understanding of the office as a space and vice versa.

In part, this scepticism towards office work evolved because, as Michael Zakim discusses, from the outset it complicated an Anglo-American tradition that 'identified labour as the source of value'.[3] As a result of this, manual labour has long been romanticized, particularly in a gendered context and most visibly in ideas embodying masculinity in the Victorian period.[4] In 1886, one commentator in *The Spectator* wrote about the position of the clerk in these terms: 'in a country where education has become universal, mere clerk's work is not skilled labour; and the man who uses the pen has, in the nature of things, no better right to expect high pay than has he who uses the chisel or the trowel'.[5] By this account, the office worker was neither specialist nor viewed as being particularly useful – in a context where the working class were at least respected for their ability to create something tangible. In the same way that the loss of British industry in contemporary analyses is considered irrevocable in the nation's decline, the rise of a bureaucratic, white-collar replacement has long held little weight in notions of worth. Indeed, much of the scepticism directed at the European Union rests on its conceptualization as a mechanism for needless bureaucracy.

Treated largely with suspicion, office work corrupted notions of Britain as a producing nation and destabilized associations imagined between physical labour, honesty and integrity. One manifestation of this – found most commonly within the banking sector – is the association between office work, fraudulence and theft. Recurrent mentions in the press of clerks who had absconded with sums of money highlight the way that white-collar workers had responsibilities that were above their moral station, a feature that filtered into genres such as crime writing where plenty of suspects are in dire need of money to replace misappropriated funds.[6] At the same time, the white-collar criminal is perceived in quite interesting ways; the details of criminal behaviour at a commercial level are rarely viewed with the same fascination or given as lengthy sentences as more visceral crimes, despite the consequences of this type of theft being potentially much more widespread in terms of the number of victims.[7]

Beside the more extreme association connecting white-collar work and corporate crime, there are a series of broader impressions of daily toil that continue to dominate popular representations. As Carl Rhodes and Robert Westwood draw attention to, popular culture is resplendent with images of working lives, nearly all of which are 'explicitly critical of work and its organization'.[8] Alexia Panayiotou expands on this when she writes about depictions of men, in particular, within representations of 'man'-agement in contemporary film, adding that

> Popular culture is imbued with images of managers, employees and organizations from the novels we read to the music we listen to, daily life is filled with images of blue collar heroes, ruthless bosses and bored office workers – typically male.[9]

These consistent attitudes to work, more generally, and office work as a specific site of tedium, continue to idealize or romanticize aspects of manual labour while highlighting the psychological, intellectual and creative monotony of the nine-to-five job. While, as Panayiotou argues, film and other visual sources are not straightforwardly related to everyday practices, their 'wide appeal and large accessibility' make them crucial instruments of influence – both in shaping our view of work and in having the potential to challenge 'dominant discourses'.[10] The gendering of this discourse is also significant; while the administrative workforce in contemporary British society is made up of more women than men, the typical characterization of the office worker who captures our attention is, as Panayiotou makes clear, a successor of the fictionalized Victorian male clerk.[11]

While organizational studies – both historic and contemporary – are important areas of critical attention (accounting history, in particular, provides the basis for several journals), the office as an environment that is shaped as much by those who work within it as it is by managerial aspirations (towards greater efficiency, robust output, cost effectiveness) is less frequently given attention. Aside from the important work by Jeacle and Parker and other historians on the physical layout of the office, and the implications for surveillance and mechanization, there is another strand of office dynamic that can be viewed through popular culture – the attempt to articulate the lived experience of the office space. This is more critical when considering that, as the wide array of popular cultural examples that Rhodes, Westwood and Panayiotou draw upon show, there has been a coherence in the representations of the office across the nineteenth, twentieth and twenty-first centuries. This chapter – and the one that follows it – examines in detail representations of the office space that range from the architectural to the emotional, exploring the ways that the office has been both designed, conceived of, and imagined from the perspective of those who work within.

The first of these twinned chapters takes physical descriptions as the focus, exploring the ways that space and personality conflate, creating a recognizable office-worker 'type' situated in a 'typical' office. Architectural historians like Duffy have tried to make use of the limited surviving records to offer a thesis about the ways that offices were designed and the potential implications for those who worked within them. Duffy takes as a starting point that office buildings are central to not only office history but also modern society. His argument raises interesting ideas about the under-considered ways in which work shapes our lives, forms our social groups, the basis of our personal finances and reflects our values. Much of Duffy's persuasive chapter on office design focuses on questions that need to be more rigorously asked of office buildings for us to understand their place in contemporary society. For instance, Duffy queries how we might read social relationships through office interiors, to understand the types of interactions around which they were designed. In this, cultural portrayals can play a key part in helping to translate the social dynamics that shaped the office environment.

The following chapter moves on to consider the psychological impact of this stereotype, engaging with portrayals of features such as feminization, mechanization, clock-watching and key moments including redundancy and retirement. Taken together, these recurrent tropes characterize much of what we assume about office life, but they also hold a wider meaning. The office has become key to the Western everyday, but in popular culture in Britain it remains tethered to the lower middle class in a way that should be no longer tangible through the persistent comparison in popular culture between the conditions of Dickensian clerks and contemporary administrators. In part, an association is reinforced between the mundane, the tedious and the office and the same attributes are assigned to the lower middle class – recalled in Panayiotou's description of the bored male office worker and the intertextuality with the early Victorian clerk. While the modern office is the occupational centre for a much wider cross-section of society, from executives to call-centre temps, to those working for the police, the NHS and in education, the continued depiction of the 'office worker' in television, film and literature as uniformly dull, uninspiring, boring and bored is often connected to the ways in which we collectively conceive of the office as a space. As Jeacle has surmised, these assumed attributes equally influence the modes of representation, thus continuing a cycle of the comically pathetic administrator in popular culture. Jeacle focuses on the epitome of these stereotypes – the accountant – describing the longevity of the 'dominant image [that] remains essentially that of socially stunted misfit, who provides a ready vehicle for satire and comic amusement'.[12] These chapters trace the connections between depictions of the weary, browbeaten clerk of the nineteenth century and the contemporary office worker and consider the ways that these attributes and assumptions about white-collar labourers more generally continue to shape popular discourses around value and worth of work traditionally associated with the lower middle class.

Landscapes of bureaucracy

From the 1850s onwards, offices underwent a revolution that matched the growth of the workforce inside them. As Gideon Haigh charts in his tome *The Office: A Hardworking History*, the office began as a home study – the space designated within the private house of the small businessman for doing the books – but soon became instrumental to the documenting and recording of the processes of trade and manufacture.[13] This style of private office was replicated in the business place, tucked away from the shop floor but crucially separate from the home. These neat, often elegant, rooms with their desks and fireplaces were appropriate for an individual accountant or bookkeeper, but once the paperwork involved in running a business increased and a couple of office boys as well as a clerk were required, they were no longer practical. The shift to using cellar spaces, with enough tall desks to suit the needs of an increased number of copyists and clerks, marked the beginning of a dismal era for the white-collar worker. Considered lucky not to be on the shop floor or the manufacturing plant, clerks were fitted in where it was convenient (and not for them). Charles Dickens captured the unfairness of this new focus on the efficiency of manual production that neglected to consider the needs of a collar-wearing workforce. His many basement offices, cramped, damp and often impractical, heightened this sense of a new class of workers who were being treated badly.

The earliest purpose-designed commercial office buildings began to appear in the 1840s, but there was an accelerated period of building at the turn of the twentieth century – particularly in cities like Manchester, Liverpool, Glasgow and London that saw an administrative boom. These grand new buildings turned clerical work from a small-scale operation, housed often in ill-equipped cellars and warehouses, into an industrial process that deserved specialist facilities. Historian Gregory Anderson describes vast dining rooms, kitchens and even in-house barbershops in wealthy businesses in Manchester and Liverpool.[14] Some clerks were lucky enough to work in these carefully planned and even innovative offices – in Liverpool, for example, were the impressive Oriel Chambers, designed in 1864 by Peter Ellis to make use of light in ways that later influenced the design of American skyscrapers. In Manchester, the imposing Refuge Assurance Company building (now a glamorous hotel) housed, at its peak, some 1900 clerks in vast open business halls.[15] It had a grand dining hall for its workers – with separate spaces for men and women – and waiter service. Holborn Bars, the Prudential building that Timothy Alborn talks about in some detail, was – like the Refuge – another project by famous industrial architect Alfred Waterhouse, who had designed libraries for Oxbridge but who also created, in his iconic Gothic Revival style, many of the office buildings in major cities around the UK. These 'palatial mills of insurance', as Alborn puts it, were fitted with all the technology required for efficient bureaucracy – 'pneumatic tubes and telephones' – as early as 1879.[16] Despite the efforts that were made to improve the quality and purpose of office buildings, narratives continued to focus on the dissatisfying aspects of office life, with audiences more receptive to empathizing about miserable conditions than being envious of innovative building design.

In 1992, Chatto published an anthology of literary depictions of the office (*The Chatto Book of Office Life: Or Love among the Filing Cabinets*) that captured the timelessness of many aspects of the office environment from Antony Trollope to Muriel Spark to David Lodge. Jeremy Lewis, the editor, begins the collection by talking about the ways that the office has stayed the same across the previous hundred years, arguing that while the office 'as most of us know it should soon become a thing of the past', it seems to be 'flourishing as never before'.[17] Lewis also talks at length about the love/hate relationship we have with our workplace and the ways that we both resent working but also struggle to exist without it. More stridently than John Lanchester, who wrote in 2009 that very few contemporary novelists tackle the 'complex realities' of office work, Lewis suggests that the lack of modern novels about the office environment helps to explain why 'the novel has become a matter of some indifference' in contemporary society.[18]

Whilst there has been, perhaps, a shift away from focusing on the white-collar workplace in contemporary fiction, this has not necessarily rendered the office redundant in creative depictions of modern life. Rather than struggling to find innovative ways to express the commonplace realities of the work environment, fiction has more readily given over to the small screen to capture the banal and every day in an equally expressive but visually geared format. This is also a British response: there are, as the *New Yorker* made clear in a response to Lanchester's article, American authors such as Joshua Ferris, Ben Marcus, David Foster Wallace and Ed Parks who write the office space.[19] British writers seem less eager to engage with the work environment, which, as Lanchester notes, is largely unrepresentative of how much our working identity is at the core of our understanding of self. Perhaps it is this shift away from writing about the everyday in the office that led to the widespread acclaim that Gail Honeymoon's recent novel, *Elinor Oliphant Is Completely Fine* (2017), received. The portrayal of the type of incessant routine found so frequently in the workplace – particularly in the type of generic office role that Elinor talks about having – and replicated in the customs and habits of private life, spoke to the wider reading public.

Where the office does feature in popular representations, merely giving an indication of negativity is not enough. Thompson talks of the 'poetic and meticulous' detail of Bartleby the Scrivener's office (in Herman Melville's famous short story), as symptomatic of the importance of the 'mapping of [office] space'.[20] In Victorian fiction, this occurs in the variety of details that are listed at the first visit to the office wherein these visual parameters are carefully drawn. Listed from the 1880s onwards are features such as uninspiring décor, tensions between colleagues, meagre facilities (cold, grimy canteens and later underequipped and dirty kitchens) and the cruel practices of middle managers. A brief survey of these descriptions in literature and on screen makes clear the many continuities that remain when offices are concerned.

Like Melville, Dickens goes into detail about the inadequacies of his many fictional offices. There is too little room in, for instance, Jaggers's office in *Great Expectations* in 1861, which is so small that clients leave grubby marks where they have leant against the wall. Jaggers has only a skylight in his office, which is 'eccentrically pitched like a broken head', while the office in *Dombey and Son* (1848) has 'vapid and flat daylight … filtered through … black sediment'.[21] The general 'grubbiness' and lack of natural light give a 'dismal' impression that gets picked up by later authors as part of an inventory of office depictions. In Arnold Bennett's first novel, *A Man for the North* (1898), for instance, young office worker Richard Larch talks about the poor conditions of his minor civil service post: 'the carpet was thin and shabby, the hearthrug worn through in the middle'.[22] His building has a 'large drab-painted hall' with 'long, narrow, gloomy' passages; a result of the ill-designed conversion of grand old buildings as state bureaucracy grew.[23]

In a similar vein, former clerk Shan Bullock gives his semi-autobiographical character Robert Thorne in 1907 an office that is equally 'small, poor lighted by one window and needed cleaning'.[24] In another of Bullock's novels (*Mr Ruby Jumps the Traces* of 1917), he evokes an 'atmosphere of stale tobacco, dust and stuffiness, with … three windows diffusing a soiled light'.[25] Around this time, other writers such as Frank Swinnerton and Edwin Pugh were also weaving narratives about the wider plight of the office worker, those who were stuck in their 'dusty wilderness[es]' that became unbearable particularly in the summer as 'the office grew hourly more close and stuffy though we opened the windows wide'.[26] These sort of descriptions appear in David Kynaston's history of London, *City of Gold* too; he gives examples from clerks in the 1920s who talk about 'gloomy building[s]', 'black dust', 'piled dog-eared papers', with lights obscured by 'fly droppings' in their 'scrappy old offices'.[27] Very few literary descriptions in the early twentieth century mention conditions that counter these; there is a widespread acceptance that the working environment of the office was – if not quite as dangerous as those of the working class – nonetheless uncomfortable. As the workplaces of manual labourers began facing further scrutiny in terms of workers' rights and a growing discourse around safety and risk, these authors express frustration that the, often poorly adapted or converted, office space was receiving very little attention.

By the mid-twentieth century, little had changed in literary depictions. P. D. James mentions the 'dusty and ill-lit room[s], insulated by tiers of filing cabinets' in her 1969 short story 'A Very Commonplace Murder'.[28] The story, a violent pastiche of the routine and the everyday within the office, turns the now expected dreariness of this environment into a macabre and voyeuristic sexual fantasy. Poor working conditions corrupt Gabriel; his violence comes from the stifling monotony of his life and his inability to feel like a 'somebody' within the cloistered office space. Texts like Lynne Reid Banks's *The L-Shaped Room* (1960) equally demonstrate the ways that the mundanity of the office space is a given. By this point, while the office space might be carefully sketched out, these details equally serve to reinforce the universal features of all offices. The office is at once a site of particularity and an every-space with which all readers/viewers can be familiar. As Reid Banks puts it:

> It was a very ordinary, dull [office] in a block in Shepherd's Bush, something to do with death duties; the usual thing, long lino'd corridors with thick ageless girls in grey flannel skirts and cardigans walking along them, and doors leading into outer offices with names scratchily painted in glass panels. The outer offices were too small to turn round in and littered with very tattered copies of government handouts. And the inner offices, which led in and out of one another like a rabbit warren, weren't much better.[29]

The space replicates the low-key dinginess that Dickens evoked a century earlier, and the featureless women who work in the offices are predecessors to Elinor Oliphant, who talks about how no one asks her what she does when she tells them she works in an office:

I can't decide whether that's because I fit perfectly with their idea of what an office worker looks like, or whether people hear the phrase *work in an office* and automatically fill in the blanks themselves – lady doing photocopying, man tapping at the keyboard.[30]

Reid Banks talks about 'the usual thing' but still feels obliged to sketch out the details – her illustration of her father's workplace is, like Honeyman's description of Elinor's status, gesturing towards certain universalities of the office – and by extension, the office worker – while including little details that the reader can connect with their own experience.

There is also, in all these accounts, a clear parallel between the office space and the type of person who accepts these conditions. Reid Banks implies that Jane's father is dull and narrow-minded because these are the working conditions to which he is best suited. Elinor too appears to have internalized certain behaviours because of her bureaucratic, and therefore, it is assumed, soulless, employment. This connection between environment and personality continues into the 1970s in the novels (and later television series) written by David Nobbs. The 'threadbare green carpet' in Reginald Perrin's office stands as a significant metaphor for the sort of low-level dissatisfaction that Reginald feels towards both his career and his life more widely.[31] In the 1980s suburban sitcom *Ever Decreasing Circles*, Bob Larbey and John Esmonde take this even further. Martin Bryce is a pompous, pedantic, pathetic, 'little' man, whose position at the head of various community groups and committees is an outlet for his officious (and often tedious) approach to life, as well as a mechanism to offset his wider social and career failings. In the workplace, Martin is put upon, insignificant and symbolic of the type of lower-middle office managers who were so often mocked in the late twentieth century.

While the office space is a less significant part of the series – most of which takes place in the cloying suburban social-scape, one episode focuses explicitly on Martin's career and takes the office as a symbolic part of Martin's wider character. Martin's office at Mole Valley Valves is predictably (given what we know of Martin as a person by this point in the series) mediocre, with bland walls, a broken telephone, a bare bulb hanging from the ceiling and a hook on the back of his door that spins around, dropping his carefully hung coat to the ground. Worse still, one morning Martin arrives at work to discover a decorator ready to take out the wall that connects his office to the one next door, rebuilding a new partition so that it effectively halves the size of Martin's office (Figure 1.1). This act of vandalism provokes Martin into recognizing that Mole Valley Valves has long abused his compliant nature, lamenting the Christmas Eves that he has

Figure 1.1 'Half an office' in *Ever Decreasing Circles* (1987)
© BBC

spent covering the switchboard and the endless health and safety roles that he has held. Martin's new office, complete with irritating decorator, mismatched paint and a still broken phone, epitomizes his time at the company and signifies the little respect that Mole Valley Valves offers him. Like Gabriel in James's story and Reginald Perrin, these conditions push Martin into action, and he eventually marches to the office of Mr Beavis, Managing Director, and demands the room be put right.[32]

Martin is by no means the only disaffected employee of the late twentieth century. In the novel *The Wimbledon Poisoner* (1990), for instance, Nigel Williams refers to his protagonist's 'cupboard' because ' "office" was [too] grandiose [a] term'.[33] At the turn of the twenty-first century, in his novel *Mr Phillips*, Lanchester comments on the same claustrophobic seasonal defect that was referred to by Edwin Pugh back in 1908: 'At the offices of Wilkins and Co., . . . the windows can't be opened and the air-conditioning doesn't work properly.'[34] This reiteration of a lack of air and space becomes an important symbol of restriction, constraint and compliance. In 2010, when the BBC made a new adaptation of Nobbs's story (this time as *Reggie Perrin*), the office is similarly blankly corporate, with windows that are painted shut and a company policy that dictates no deviations from the oppressive lack of individuality. The air conditioning, while working, controls the office air so rigidly that a small potted plant would threaten the entire ecosystem, both in an environmental sense and a psychological one.

Reggie Perrin is a marker of the shift from text to screen that Lanchester lamented in his article. While Lanchester's own novel and the recent success of the tale of Elinor Oliphant have attempted to refocus the novel on the office space, arguably seminal performances and the British preoccupation with realist and naturalist modes of representing the workspace on television in recent years – in evidence since *The Office* – have formed the basis of popular cultural references. The notoriety of *The Office* and the general impression that it encapsulated all that was every day, mundane, humdrum and depressing about work has, perhaps, restricted the ways that we can experience a fictionalized office. What is particularly interesting about how television has developed the office narrative is that the type of descriptions that culminated in *The Office* were shaped by characteristics that had already been seen across the previous one hundred and fifty years of literary representation. These descriptions do not completely replicate the variety of office spaces that exist, but instead they create a composite sketch of what the audience expects of the office and the tone that the writer wants to enforce – which is usually negative.

Even as Britain was celebrating the pinnacle of corporatism in the 1990s, popular culture remained wedded to representing the type of dismal office environment that had long circulated. As Lewis puts it:

> Probably because most writers are more familiar with newspapers and old-fashioned publishing houses than with City solicitors or merchant bankers, and have grown up on a diet of Dickens, those offices that find their way into print tend to be dingy, decrepit places with dirty windows and scuffed carpets, in which every available surface is covered with cracked coffee cups and tottering mounds of bumph.[35]

The Dickensian repertoire continues to carry weight, as Lewis suggests, but it is not entirely divorced from the reality that office workers face, and that is why these connotations are so pervasive. Lewis also explores the ways that the depictions of the office come more frequently from those within the lower middle class – the journalists and writers and clerical assistants – than from middle-class professionals who have, perhaps, another class of office. In lower-middle-class offices, either space is at a premium (cupboard offices) or privacy (in open-plan settings), or both.

The territorial battles between Tim and Gareth in *The Office* are a clear marker of this. The careful positioning of files and staplers becomes symptomatic of the 'spatial signals' that are more commonly signposted through the display of photographs, post-its, personal mugs and other objects that Baldry suggests give a 'degree of control over the immediate working environment'.[36] In many ways, as Ben Walters writes, the issues surrounding the need for space are simply magnified in the open-plan workplace.[37] The first episode sees a new employee join the team, providing the perfect excuse for David Brent to lead the fictional documentary team (and by extension the viewer) on a tour of the space, orientating the viewer in the same way that the extensive realist descriptions often did in earlier literature. To preserve the depressing authenticity, *The Office* was shot in a disused office building, and Gervais and Merchant were keen to retain even the stained carpets and broken blinds. Within the contemporary televised office, lingering shots of mindless photocopying, drawn out scenes of colleagues absently gazing at computer screens and half-heard conversations on the telephone reinforce also the sense of futility.

In the open office all behaviour becomes performative, and television shows – particularly those made as mockumentary-style comedies like *People Like Us*, *The Office*, *W1A*, *Damned* and *The Tourist Trap* (2018) – make clear that the audience is not only off screen but on screen, in the position of colleagues and managers. In this sense, integrated into the office environment are the audience, which, because it is a site with which so many of us are familiar, is a crucial part of the appeal. We can picture ourselves in the space, not only as viewers of a television show but also as co-conspirators in the office narrative. Looks made directly to camera in exasperation by characters such as Tim in *The Office* show us that we are as much a part of the office setup. They must be convincingly real because so many of us know how it feels; we are not just peripherally familiar with the office, but we spend around 2,000 hours a year in this environment.

Following *The Office* (and this accumulation of a century of similar depictions), audiences can find positive portrayals unrealistic – the impressive art, personalized workspaces and kindly interferences by the genial boss in the charity office of Richard Curtis's rom-com *Love Actually* (2003), for instance, register as relentlessly and unrealistically optimistic. To the cynic, they are reminiscent of Keith Waterhouse's *Office Life* (1978), the Kafkaesque novel in which Clement Gryce, new employee of British Albion, is unnerved by the relative comfort of his new workplace; the space, lack of work and luxurious facilities render Gryce entirely suspicious. Likewise, the open-plan affluence of the office in Mark Tavener's *Absolute Power* (2003–5) reasserts the shallow projections of the PR world, glossing over the more familiar power imbalances, competitive behaviour and failures of the company. Audiences are suspicious in many ways of the office environment as a positive space, favouring the bland monotony of an environment that speaks to the assumptions we make about the work that takes place within.

In BBC comedy *W1A*, even high-tech systems designed as part of the building, which should showcase the ways that progressive design and creative methods can combine, actually cause deep irritation through unusable AI (the hilariously dysfunctional Syncapatico) and by being 'aggressively over-designed around the principle of not having a desk'.[38] Sabina Siebert reads *W1A* as a 'universal satire' that takes aim at 'mechanisms to facilitate communication, unlock creativity and promote transparency', which are so often encountered in the rhetoric of contemporary organizational cultures and leadership strategies but which actually result in Ian Fletcher (as an embodied metaphor) wandering round New Broadcasting House attempting to find somewhere to work.[39] Counter to the openness that should allow workers greater freedom, the demolition of clear boundaries actually heightens the lack of privacy, restricting employees in a greater measure than the physical divides could.

The script of *W1A* makes a clear parody of the endless creative emptiness of a PR world that promotes image over integrity, and this is echoed in the redesign of buildings that promote the status of a business over the attention to staff competence and commercial ability. The many comic moments in which the building itself fails to allow those within it to do their jobs is a reflection of the ways in which we perceive that offices never function as they should, regardless of how well or expensively they have been built. Another very recent series, Channel 4's *Damned* (2017–), similarly picks up on these inadequacies of contemporary office design, while reiterating the type of low-level annoyances that have been part of the office narrative for many decades. The boss is cold, merciless and speaks in managerial clichés; the staff room contains a fridge so pungent that it poses an immediate health risk; staff compete endlessly for perks and opportunities; and the impressive looking glass wall and secure door prove inefficient and limiting. The 'mapping' of the office overwhelmingly reports gloomy conditions and a disheartening environment that parallels impressions of the tasks undertaken within.

While the exterior and interior environments within which the lower-middle-class white-collar worker performs their role is significant – partly due to the uniformity and standardized negativity across these examples – what is also key is the effect of this repetition within popular culture. This is not to say that British businesses always ignored the needs of their clerical workforce. The beautiful Edwardian commercial buildings of Britain's major cities are a testament to the significance of commercial centres and the outward projection of business credibility and success. Indeed, many remain elegantly inscribed with their company name as a proud measure of the facilities offered to their workers. Regardless of this, across the twentieth century, and into the twenty-first, dimly lit and poky, substandard offices have continued to remain synonymous with the repetitive mediocrity of office work in popular culture.

Collectively, wide-ranging examples have formed a canon of office landscapes that now shape expectations about what the environment ought to be like. The way that the camera follows Tom's gaze up at his Orwellian workplace in 1980s sitcom *The Good Life*, for instance, captures not only the essence of its modern, functional architecture but the emotional response to the monotony of work. The stark exterior of the design firm embodies the capitalist life that Tom and his wife reject, as they turn towards self-sufficiency after Tom's mid-life crisis. The opening credits to *The Office* begin, like *The Good Life*, with the use of several pan shots that take in anonymous corporate buildings from 1970s Slough – famously characterized as an epitome of soullessness by John Betjeman (whose words are read in voice-over and ridiculed by Brent in episode five of series one). The concrete wasteland of Slough Trading Estate, the location of Wernham Hogg, captures over a century of negative connotations.

Duffy pointed out in 1980 that 'office buildings have changed our cities [and] office work has revolutionised our society' an observation that carries even more weight in the twenty-first century as cities continue to be defined by the development of striking and architecturally significant office spaces (the Gherkin building in London is a useful example).[40] Despite the sheer quantity of funds and effort engaged in redesigning and rebuilding entire sections of cities to accommodate the swelling numbers of office workers, and regardless of the magnitude of architectural success, in cultural terms, the first impressions of the office have certainly stayed closer to the cramped Dickensian cellars. Repeatedly and continually portraying office spaces in these ways is a dehumanization of the office workers themselves. As Reggie Perrin's boss, Chris, puts it when he makes Reggie remove his non-standard office plant: 'You are now genetically an office worker. Don't fight it.'[41] This reiteration of mundanity, expressed through the literary and media descriptions and visual mapping of the office space, is an important part of the way that office work, office workers and the wider lower middle class are portrayed. The simple use of an (often comically) unsuitable, inconvenient or dismal setting is a further reiteration of the powerlessness of the white-collar worker, incapable of affecting real change that might improve their working lives.

Paper-pushers

In the classic British sitcom *Blackadder Goes Forth* (1989), General 'Insanity' Melchett declares that his right-hand man and pre-war employee of 'Pratt and Sons', Captain Kevin Darling, is 'a pen-pushing, desk-sucking, blotter-jotter'.[42] Darling, who in one episode of the series is excited by an evening spent unloading two shipments of paper clips, is, to Captain Blackadder's irritation, usually to be found about thirty-five miles safely behind enemy lines. Darling is a clerk-type[43] – effeminate, weak-minded, weak-bodied and utterly subservient – and a product of a century of sneering at pen-pushers. George Orwell coined the phrase in 1936 in *Keep the Aspidistra Flying*, a novel often exemplified as being saturated with lower-middle-classdom and the protagonist's fear of 'pen-pushing in some filthy office'.[44] This type of imagery characterizes the ways that negative attitudes towards the office space have shaped impressions of the office worker. By the time *The Office* hit British television screens at the beginning of the twenty-first century, its low-key background shots of chuntering photocopiers and scruffy bland office interiors were an effective form of pathetic fallacy for the people working within. Against this backdrop, the characters played out typical roles assigned within the office space from Bennett's *A Man from the North* onwards: the unbearable middle manager, the career clerk, the frustrated youngster, a cast of anonymized extras.

This section focuses on the ways in which Captain Darling, and others like him, are reduced to comic stereotypes based on their white-collar work. This association between the office and the office worker transcends the boundaries of the workplace and continues to define an individual's identity beyond their daily toil. While this form of stereotyping affects other groups of workers, the white-collar worker has withstood decades of mockery that comes directly from the duties they perform. Certain behaviours, like Captain Darling's endless compliance with obscene orders and fascination with stationery, have become synonymous with an office job, proving difficult to decouple. Attached to these foibles are a series of associated characteristics: cautiousness, pedantry, lack of imagination, and while there have been various shifts in the specificities of stereotypes, they more generally conform to these behaviours.

In 1907, for instance, it was the physical appearance of clerks that drew the attention of commentators – sleeve protectors and finger stains hinted at endless copying – as Shan Bullock observed when he discussed his character Robert Thorne: 'many little pen-*drivers* – fellows in black-coats, with inky fingers and shiny seats on their trousers'.[45] For the clerk, often posited as being particularly self-conscious about dress (E. M. Forster made his office worker, Leonard Bast, exceedingly concerned about the poor condition of his clothing and belongings), these signs of menial work were another badge displaying their lower-middle-class status. T. S. Eliot faced gentle mockery from the Bloomsbury set due to his cautious bank-clerkly appearance; Virginia Woolf referred to his conservative 'four-piece suit' and Aldous Huxley called him 'the most bank clerkly of all bank clerks'. Huxley was also keen to point out that Eliot's office was: 'not on the ground floor nor even on the floor under that, but in a sub-sub-basement sitting at a desk which was in a row of desks with other bank clerks'.[46] They are a workforce that are at once both invisible (underground) and prominent in stereotype and caricature.

For the modernists the office worker encapsulated everything that represented the numb and mechanized masses, returning home each evening for their tinned food dinners and cheap novels. Modernist writings frequently mentioned the clerk, but the portrayals were not flattering, and most made use of the office worker as a desperate figure – Septimus Smith in Virginia Woolf's *Mrs Dalloway*, Leonard Bast in Forster's *Howards End* or J. Alfred Prufrock in T. S. Eliot's famous poem. At the same time, clerks-turned-writers like Shan Bullock, Frank Swinnerton, Edwin Pugh and Edwin Hodder stood up for the office worker, albeit exploring the same misery of bureaucratic automation and the sheer monotony of clerical work in their novels.

This was followed by a post-war shift in perspective which saw middle-aged office workers becoming a key focus in fiction – and later television and in film. Instead of the plight of the young clerk, negotiating a clerical career from the bottom of the ladder, it was this dispirited figure, facing retirement or redundancy – and reminiscent of J. B. Priestley's motley crew of office workers in *Angel Pavement* (1930) – that garnered attention. This proved a significant change in emphasis that would linger across the rest of the twentieth and into the twenty-first centuries; the career administrator (and particularly the middle-aged male office worker) continues to carry certain implications, whereas young clerks are merely on route to a 'proper' career.

By the 1970s, the middle-aged office worker was increasingly typed as pompous and self-promoting, while the growth of large corporations and the ensuing devolvement of responsibilities to the middle-manager led to a wider culture of self-aggrandizement, often amongst, once more, male administrators. Characters like Rex in ITV sitcom *The Squirrels* are bad-tempered, hen-pecked and often unscrupulous, and their immediate bosses are often not much better; in this case, the manager of the firm is mocked as part of the inept middle class, who in comedy is often in post through nepotism rather than ability or experience. In the 1980s, and with the growth of corporate culture, there was an assumption that the office worker fell prey to the language of endless and empty expansion (captured so comically in *A Bit of Fry and Laurie* sketches) – demonstrative of a serious lack of imagination. In late 1980s sitcom *Colin's Sandwich*, for instance, Colin endures a tedious monologue from a suited man about his commute on the M25. Outwardly, he fits the stereotype of the bland office worker; the punchline reveals, to Colin's surprise, that this man is in the Special Air Services (SAS).

Colin's reaction exemplifies the assumptions we make about the meaninglessness of paperwork. And yet, as American economic historian Stephen Mihm points out, there is a real paradox in the 'symbolic power of paper and promises' (upon which a capitalist economy is, or at least, was once so reliant), and the powerlessness of the individual clerk buried amidst the ephemera of the office.[47] Even as the status of the lower-middle-class office worker fell from skilled scribe to typing machine operator, ironically, the significance of administration rose. Society was more dependent on bureaucratic processes, its administrators, secretaries and clerks, than it had ever been before. Now, almost all of our public services rest on vast numbers of administrators who, despite receiving widespread abuse from the media, oil the hidden mechanisms of the state. The almost universal scorn for those who have become figureheads for officious paper-pushing – Human Resources – is characterized in Victoria Wood's *dinnerladies* (1998–2000) in the character of Philippa. Scatty, chaotic but well intentioned, Philippa's attempts to provide support to the canteen staff is constantly rebuked as an unnecessary intrusion of a white-collar nobody in a blue-collar world. Stan's criticism that Christmas lights, which should come under his remit as handyman/estates management, are being poorly handled by someone from Human Resources makes clear that her skills are of very little value: 'this is flex; it's not envelopes or rubber bands or anything else you might deal with in Human Resources'.[48]

Wood was not the first to parody the role of the administrator. In 1898, Richard Larch in Bennett's *A Man from the North* muses on the tension between the contempt levelled at 'meaningless' paper-pushing and the nature of a society that depends on bureaucracy: 'This little man with the round face dealt impassively with thousands of pounds; he mortgaged whole streets, bullied railway companies, and wrote familiarly to lords'.[49] The 'little clerk', innocuous and made fun of, was actually performing an essential duty that was required by each homeowner, small tradesman and the state itself. C. F. G. Masterman also draws attention to this conflict between the environment and the impact when he talks about male suburbans working in 'small, crowded offices, under artificial light, doing immense sums' in 1909.[50] Ninety years later, Bernie, hapless stockbroker in Richard Curtis's *Notting Hill* (1999) (played by Hugh Bonneville, who later also played everyman office characters such as Charles Pooter, Ian Fletcher (*W1A*) and Mr Brown (*Paddington*)), glumly announces at dinner that he 'Bollocksed up at work again ... Millions down the drain'.[51] Bernie cannot find a girlfriend, is portrayed as a slightly scruffy, unimpressive sort of person, but in his white-collar role he is actually handling vast sums of money.

These conditions belie, in many ways, the significance of what the office worker is doing. Conversely, for those who realized the importance of the 'immense sums' of the counting house clerk, the mundanity of the reality was a shock. In B. S. Johnson's *Christie Malry's Own Double Entry* (1973), the eponymous character craves power and is desperate to work in a bank. Once he begins, however, he realizes he is not in 'any sense that mattered' any closer to money.[52] In the romantic film *Girl from Rio* (2003), bank worker Raymond literally handles millions of pounds worth of bank notes, but equally the monotony of this work renders it as menial as the endless photocopying of customer complaints that Colin does for British Rail in *Colin's Sandwich* in the 1980s.

What many of these depictions of the mundanity of paper pushing imply, but do not directly confront, are the strains and stresses associated with repetitive or seemingly meaningless work. Skirted around, or performed as comedic elements, are issues suggesting poor mental health, work/life balance and damaging levels of stress and dissatisfaction. As Ali Haggett discusses, in her study of male psychological disorders, there are pervasive narratives after 1945 that foreground the unhappy male office worker who is deeply embittered by his job and unhappy in his suburban marriage, but while these 'themes emerge with regularity in popular culture', they are rarely given sustained academic attention.[53] Instead, depictions of disenchanted office workers tend to place emphasis on ways out, and alternative career paths, rather than dealing with some of the issues that seem to be deeply entrenched: poor management, repetitive tasks, uninspiring conditions, collegiate competitiveness. While these are by no means intrinsic to office work itself, there is an assumption within the white-collar world that these problems are endemic and irreparable, a feature that is openly discussed as part of many popular cultural texts.

More frequently confronted in fiction is the concern that the office environment is not necessarily benign in a physical sense. Late-Victorian anxieties over clerical ill health have perpetuated into the twenty-first century and often focus on the body as a site of concern. In Bennett's *Anna of the Five Towns* (1902), William Price, the clerk of the Edward Street works, is described as 'tall, thin, and ungainly in every motion ... [with] the look of a ninny' because he works in a 'long narrow room, the dirtiest Anna had ever seen'.[54] Like many, Price works in the office of a manufacturing business – in this case, a pottery – that saw him barely separated from the factory floor itself. Bennett's depiction draws attention to the similarities between two environments that are usually seen in opposition. He was not the only author to raise the issue; in his novel *Robert Thorne*, Bullock characterizes the office workplace as 'the Mill' that keeps on 'grinding':

> Clank went the great Mill, wheel inside wheel, levers and cranks and safety valves everywhere, and now it whirred madly, and now smoothly ponderously did it grind: and there sat I in the Clearing-room, knee deep in the wheat and the chaff.[55]

Here Bullock undermines the separation between manual and non-manual work, suggesting, of course, that the quantities of paper created and distributed by the Tax Office are akin to the manufacture of a product. In conflating manufacturing and bureaucratic industries, Bullock was raising awareness that vast office spaces hold their own dangers, which are greater than the manual/clerical divide would imply.

Indeed, the processes of paper pushing were, in some ways, more dangerous because it was difficult to recognize them as such. In Mary Sundstrom's discussions of American offices, she talks about how office workers in the 1900s were not a priority for accessing the sort of welfare programmes developed for factory workers.[56] One article in *The Times* in 1912 attested to the terrible conditions: '[one office was] 120ft. by 120ft. in which 150 clerks were packed'. In an environment like this, the journalist continues, 'consumption among clerks ... was two and a half times that of the miner'.[57] While there was clearly little by way of reckless adventure or physical risk involved in office work, in reality, implied by Bullock's use of 'pale face and uneven shoulders' when describing commuting clerks, office work could be surprisingly damaging to health. As historian Gregory Anderson suggests: '[the] incidence of phthisis among clerks was particularly heavy ... due to the damp and draughty conditions, inadequate sanitation and especially overcrowding'.[58] More significant was the way that ill health became part of wider depictions of the white-collar worker resulting in stereotypically hypochondriac clerks like George Gissing's Mr Brogden. Brogden has numerous unlisted 'internal troubles which seem to menace his mechanic health', most of which are centred on his stomach.[59] P. G. Wodehouse's clerk, Mr

Meggs, is equally 'a martyr to indigestion', a 'chronic dyspeptic' and a compulsive purchaser of 'patent medicines'.[60] More serious still, D. H. Lawrence writes only physically feeble clerks in *Sons and Lovers* (1913) – Mr Jordan is 'red-faced' and 'rather stout', there is an 'old [and] decaying' chief clerk and Pappleworth is 'thin [and] sallow'.[61] This stereotype of the fussing, hypochondriac office worker remains ubiquitous across contemporary culture, with jokes continuing to be made about men, in particular, who are weak because they are administrators – see, for instance, the narrative built around contemporary masculinity in the first series of Bear Grylls's reality survivalist show *The Island* (2014) and Ant Middleton's *Mutiny* (2017), both of which reinforce a model wherein the adventurer-warrior must leave the safety of the office and push himself to the physical limits as a test of both modern man and a confrontation against historical measures of masculinity.

While we often consider sedentary lives a product of the twenty-first century, particularly given that fewer workers are engaged in manual labour than white-collar work now,[62] it is interesting to note that these sort of concerns about office work began in the nineteenth century and have reoccurred at various points since. Michael Zakim cites a wide range of feared 'desk diseases' that included 'giddiness, liver problems, bladder and urinary infections, a swimming of the head, deafness, stomach and bowel disorders, piles and strictures', all of which were 'disproportionately ascribed to sedentary men' in the late nineteenth century.[63] Many of these so-called sedentary diseases were not 'noble' or masculine inflictions, however, and lower-middle-class men were castigated for succumbing to lesser illnesses. As Mihm articulates, it went without saying that 'haemorrhoids, flatulence, blindness, deafness, lethargy, pimples, pallor, and most alarming of all, "masturbatory insanity"' were not conditions affecting 'strapping young men felling trees in the forests or machinists crafting a steam engine'.[64] Cultivated across popular culture was the impression that 'only members of the clerking class [got haemorrhoids], or so people wished to believe'.[65]

Gregory Anderson quotes an extensive list of concerns from C. T. Thackrah, who, as early as 1831, discusses weakness in muscle tone, digestive health and bone structure, all of which were directly attributed to working in an office. At the turn of the century, one response was the rise of organizations such as the YMCA that looked to improve the health of the nation, and particularly that of the urban lower middle class. Clerks were chief amongst those using their new gymnasiums, pitches and other sports and leisure facilities, in a bid to overcome what was frequently projected as their vocational weakness.[66] Likewise, in 1912, Masterman made reference in *The Condition of England* to the 'life of Sedentary occupation' that most white-collar workers were trapped in: 'divorced from the ancient sanities of manual or skilful labour, of exercise in the open air, absorbed for the bulk of his day in crowded offices adding sums or writing letters'.[67] By 1914, the London Medical Office for Health continued to draw public attention to the 'sedentary nature of the occupation, the cramped position, the strain on eyesight and the tendency to loss of tone'.[68] To add insult to injury, when office workers did get a holiday, many of them overdid it, as one article in the *Daily Mail* commented on in 1922. Doctors were experiencing a rise in cases of those who had spent eleven months at a desk before audaciously embarking on epic mountain walking or cycling holidays and over-stressing their poor, unfit hearts.[69]

Following the Second World War, the Gowers Committee on Health, Welfare and Safety in Non-Industrial Employment was set up, which made recommendations about space, ventilation, lighting and other environmental factors for office and shop workers.[70] These recommendations, many of which intended adaptation of measures already in place for factory workers, were very slowly taken on board. It was not until 1963 that comprehensive legislation passed through parliament on the advice of the Committee. By this time, office workers were already aware of some of the dangers of sedentary work – a glimpse through the archive of the *Daily Mail*, often posited as the newspaper of the lower middle class, sees articles in the 1950s on the danger of constipation amongst office workers, for instance.[71]

In 1967, one firm advertised yoga positions to enhance the strength and fitness of 'sedentary office workers' and the 'beauty and suppleness' of the 'office secretary'. Men could, as the advert promised, improve their 'fitness, physique [and] manly strength' by following a course of yoga, while women could find 'good health and grace and beauty and the supple figure that men find so attractive'.[72] In the 1990s, the bad back was a deep concern, caused by the cheap office chair that caught the attention of designers and ergonomists – the ball chair, kneeling stool and move stool joined the market in a bid to combat poor spinal health.[73] Diets targeting the sedentary worker emphasized moving around the office, even if only to the photocopier and back to increase the base metabolic rate.[74] The office worker was not only pitied for working in a dismal environment, but one that would, as various health scares and media campaigns have made clear, shorten their life expectancy as a result. In 2015, the BBC drew attention to a campaign – On Your Feet Britain – that aimed to get people moving more in the office following evidence that sedentary office work is creating a public health crisis. Heart disease, type 2 diabetes, cancer and poor mental health have all been linked to a sedentary lifestyle, and the article suggests that some of the problems stem specifically from behaviours in the office workplace. Even those who are fit outside of work (using the gym, cycle commuting), the research suggests, are at risk if they do not regularly move around at work.[75]

John Lanchester's eponymous *Mr Phillips* (2000) meanders around London contemplating (or rather, not confronting) his recent redundancy. As a now-former accountant, he muses on the dangers faced unconsciously every day from the terminal illnesses that 'can jump up and whack you' to those which are the 'more stealthy killers'. In his role as a 'reasonably kind-hearted, randy nonentity', as Nicholas Lazard put it, Mr Phillips represents a certain type of underplayed or everyday mortality.[76] As Lanchester writes: 'he has lived with the same proximity to death as any other sedentary man in his fifties with a white collar job'.[77] Recent articles in the press have focused on the links, for instance, between white-collar work and suicide, Parkinson's disease and diabetes, which, in contemporary society should affect both women and men equally. In representational terms, however, there is a long-standing association between middle-aged men, office work and poor health – a trend borne out in a study such as the one conducted by Edinburgh University in 2017, which claimed that middle-aged *male* office workers spent more time sitting than those over the age of 75.[78] Women of all age groups spent less time sitting than old age pensioners, implying that this is a particular concern for white-collar men, despite the fact that women make up a large proportion of this labour market. Of course, what these intimates is that office work alone is not the defining factor, but rather behaviours outside of the office are equally key in shaping activity levels.

Back in 1907, Shan Bullock romanticized working-class manual work when his titular Robert Thorne contrasts his life as an office clerk in London with the healthy, simple lives of the rural working class in Devonshire, those who he imagines working alongside wholesome seasonal rhythms. In his terms, clerical work is all about an inferior masculinity – as he says to his wife: 'we aren't real men. We don't do men's work. Pen-drivers – miserable little pen-drivers ... No wonder bricklayers and omnibus drivers have contempt for us. We haven't even health.'[79] At the close of the novel, he gives in his notice and tells his boss he is moving to New Zealand to farm, following in the footsteps of the many willing clerical recruits historian John Tosh talks about who emigrated to Canada, leaving office work for a rural life.[80] Thorne's simple equation between rural, blue-collar labour and ideal masculinity is perhaps less explicit in contemporary society, but still there remains a penchant for representing the male white-collar worker as susceptible to ill-health and the perceived ravages of middle age.

Whilst this undercurrent implies a certain vulnerability of the office worker, the suggestion that deskwork involves physical peril is generally a source of comedy, and even contemporary recognition of occupational health issues tends to be taken less seriously in the white-collar workplace. Instead, the office is a parodied site of danger, demonstrating the mundanity of office work and by extension the office worker. The comedic attitude directed at workplace health and safety inspections make clear the lack of seriousness that is attached to the welfare of those who sit at a desk – a feature made fun of in *The Office* when Gareth gives an extensive tutorial on drinking coffee near a computer and handling small, empty cardboard boxes to new colleague Donna.

Steve Coogan's 2001 film *The Parole Officer* equally makes explicit the inability of clerical types to face unsafe environments, when in one scene Coogan's character, Simon Garden, a naïve and honest social worker, attempts to fight off two thugs in a court office. Threateningly brandishing a desk fan and later a stapler, Garden triumphantly shouts 'never mess with an office worker', before pulling too far from the fan's socket and losing power to his weapon, to the glee of his adversaries.[81] The office worker, then, is not a threat, he is a joke, and his ability to deal with the type of danger faced by police officers is non-existent – a fact reinforced in the frequent taunts made by the police towards Garden ('we can't stand around, we're not probation officers').

Likewise, the comic peril of the office environment comes up again in the 1990s sitcom *Men Behaving Badly*. In one episode, clerk George suffers a head injury after a precariously stacked box falls on his desk, a result of his Scrooge-like manager Gary subletting the security firm's warehouse to pocket extra money. *Men Behaving Badly* simultaneously reinforces that the middle-aged administrative staff are not safe from warehouse conditions once corporate greed becomes involved, whilst satirizing the idea that the office is a dangerous space. It is George's muddle-headed middle-agedness and his clerical weakness that make him a victim as much as Gary's selfish actions. Gary's attempt to 'feed' a cock and bull story about a book that fell off the back of a bus, knocking George unconscious, is only slightly more ridiculous sounding than a head injury occurring in the office.

The office has been, for a long time, projected as an uncomfortable or even an unhealthy environment, whilst additionally holding a reputation as a space that is both physically unappealing and ultimately demoralizing. While John Carey, in particular, takes issue with assumptions about clerical work as degrading or mechanical, arguing that the office cannot have been such a universally negative environment, there is an overwhelming sense that cultural depictions tend to favour dispiriting attitudes.[82] In this sense, it appears that texts from *Robert Thorne* to *The Office* are aimed at office workers, many of whom seem to want a window into the office that feels authentic. This chapter has focused on the external facets of the office – the space, rather than the emotional or psychological responses – but there is clearly a consistent narrative about office surroundings that, despite widespread changes in office technologies, layout, work-force composition, has remained negative, and often while focusing on very similar complaints – space, privacy, conditions, light, poor health.

In terms of social class, these depictions are instrumental in building up a picture of the kind of conditions with which the lower middle class were associated. If the clerk was willing to accept long working hours in a dimly lit cellar, then a series of assumptions could be made about the type of person that he was: submissive, pliant and feeble. Later, in the nineteenth century, the worn carpets and shabby hallways of office buildings were equally symptomatic of the status of the white-collar worker, housed cheaply without much concern for revolt. The mid-century depictions of tedious office interiors into which multiple typists were squeezed similarly lowered the expectations of lower-middle-class families keen to get their daughters into secretarial work. Taken together, these strands of representation that consistently reinforce the office as neither important nor impressive have become symbolic iterations of the type of person who works within. Iconic scenes like those of the office in Tony Hancock's *The Rebel* (1961) make clear the way these representations work (Figure 1.2). The

Figure 1.2 Desk duties in *The Rebel* (1961)
© Associated British Picture Corporation

row of desks with identical office workers repeating a carefully choreographed series of repetitive tasks is a striking visual illustration of the ways that lower-middle-class office workers are automatons who accept their conditions and return dully each morning to their offices, compliantly hanging their matching umbrellas and hats on identical pegs.

2
The desk

While the previous chapter explored the environmental aspects of office work as well as simple stereotypes connecting spatial mediocrity with certain characteristics, this chapter takes the desk – or more specifically, the duties of the desk – as its focus. The desk, in this instance, is symbolic of the toll that office work takes on the psyche, from the endless routines, the jumping through managerial hoops, the desperate clock watching and waiting for the end of the day. This chapter will consider the many structural and ideological changes that have occurred since the late nineteenth century which have become stalwart features of literature, film and television and which substantiate the feelings of despair and frustration captured by the conditions.

It begins with the mechanization of office work and the immense impact of Frederick Taylor's theories of 'scientific management' in the white-collar workplace before examining related developments involving the policing of the clerical body, both through surveillance and time management. In doing so, this chapter explores the common thread through multiple cultural forms representing control as deeply dehumanizing, offering some reflections on the questions that Mihm raises about the psychological experience of growing mechanization:

> Did [office workers] not suffer some measure of alienation as their work became ever more routinized, ever more standardized, and ever more monotonous? The answer, I would argue, is a resounding 'yes', but the historical profession's lack of interest up until now suggests that not everyone agrees.[1]

Popular culture rewards readers and audiences that can relate to this essential part of their everyday, but it also must present a redemptive message: Why do we do it, *The Office* asks? Why do we continue to put ourselves in this environment? The answer is twofold: economic necessity, of course, but also collegiality – the shared daily experience that brings people together. It is this more positive aspect of office life that this chapter additionally explores, for instance, in the community that develops in the workplace and the collective responses that challenge the daily tedium. From this perspective, the office is viewed as a collegiate space – a site in which people develop friendships, relationships and communities, an act which counters some of the issues around monotony and routinization.

This chapter considers also the ways that gender has shaped office work across the last two centuries, reflecting on the drastic changes in the composition of the labour force during what Gregory Anderson has called the 'white-blouse revolution', and the long-lasting effects of this shift from the Dickensian male clerk to the gender-neutral role of 'administrator' in the twenty-first century.[2] Finally, the chapter finishes by considering redundancy and retirement, aspects of office life that are not frequently given academic consideration but which hold a poignant position in popular cultural references of the white-collar worker. Indeed, there is a powerful thread of representation that examines the end of the clerical career, which spans from the Victorian novel to contemporary office comedy. Perhaps it is the office worker, more so than any other, who is repeatedly pitied in cultural depictions at the moment of retirement. The image of the clerk, rigid and mechanized, and unable to envision a world without work, has proved powerfully long-lasting in popular culture.

Mechanization

From the beginning of the twentieth century, office workers were the target of a drive to increase output. In part, as Lee Parker argues, this was symptomatic of a wider 'discourse on national efficiency', but it was also a response to both state and commercial sector demand for further bureaucracy. Even where logistics made things difficult, clerks were not immune to theories such as Frederick Taylor's *Principles of Scientific Management* (1911), which provided a way of streamlining the white-collar mass whilst facilitating further growth.[3] Designed for the assembly line in manual industries, devotees such as W. H. Leffingwell quickly adapted Taylor's ideas for use in a white-collar world, rendering the office environment by the 1930s akin to the 'factory layout, with serried ranks of individuals positioned like cogs in a well-oiled machine'.[4] As Ingrid Jeacle and Parker discuss, this was as much about the 'identification of standard methods' as it was about setting out 'standard times for accomplishing office tasks'.[5] Individual practices that demonstrated the employee's skill and innovation were replaced, in many ways, with the standardization and piecework that shaped so much of white-collar work following Taylor's publication of his *Principles* and which still appear in contemporary management studies research.[6]

Taylorism was not the only driver of office mechanization. Earlier novelists, such as Arnold Bennett, had raised issues around automatization in clerical work from the late nineteenth century onwards, often as part of a wider discussion around increasingly poor working conditions and meagre career prospects. In *A Man from the North* (1898), Bennett's character Richard Larch moves from Yorkshire to London to work as a clerk for 'Messrs. Curpet and Smythe' and recognizes that he has 'become part of a business machine'.[7] Clerks were increasingly acutely aware of the parity of their position with that of the factory worker. In a similar fashion, in 1907, Bullock's Robert Thorne sees himself as merely part of a bureaucratic operation: 'One day was much like another ... I felt sometimes like a machine, grinding out its daily portion, mechanically turning leaves with cold grimed fingers'.[8] Thorne is truly an automaton; he fears he has lost all humanity, becoming simply a cog in the wheels of business. Comparisons can easily be drawn between Thorne's 'cold grimed fingers' and T. S. Eliot's 'dead' crossing London's Bridge in his centrepiece of Modernist poetry, 'The Waste Land' – those who spent their day as 'eyes and back / turn[ed] upward from the desk'.[9]

While Taylor's theories could never be as fully implemented in the office as they could on the factory floor, the general tone thus became part of wider clerical culture, with the consequent deskilling being written about at length in the pre-war period. Writers such as Victor Canning (who wrote also under the pseudonym Julian Forest) recognized the ways that Taylorism fundamentally affected the psychological experience of office work:

> He was a clerk, one of a hundred in a huge rambling building where individuals were not represented so much by their personalities as by their tasks. To his director he was less Francis Jago than the servant of the scholarships system, he was the file that held all the information about the scholars, he was a reference that could produce at a command the dates of committee decisions, and he was an instrument which with pencil and shorthand notes could suck in a letter or a report and an hour later produce it typed and neatly paragraphed for signature.[10]

By viewing Francis Jago as a series of skills or actions, Canning draws attention to the dehumanizing rhetoric of new office language. The novel was written in the 1930s but is set in the First World War as a reflection on the rapid changes in the industry in the period just before 1914. Jeacle and Parker categorize 1900–9 as a key period in the visibility of the record as a substantial part of bureaucracy, with record systems developing rapidly between 1910 and 1920.[11] They also refer to the ways that the office worker became 'subservient adjuncts to the record' itself around this period, reflected, too, in Canning's reference to Jago as a 'servant' of the record-keeping system.[12]

As Alexandra Lange suggests, much of this mentality highlighted the ways that mechanized bureaucracy logically implied that the 'paper record could become a useful substitute for the man himself'.[13] As might be expected, those who portray office work (and particularly those authors who had been or remained clerks, like Bennett, Bullock and Canning) see Taylorist bureaucracy in these terms rather than as a useful function for greater efficiency. The expectation that efficiency would be internalized was met with antagonism from workers who were increasingly concerned about a deep sense of dehumanization.

Writers like Canning identified this wider association between piecemeal office work and an impression that clerks and other office workers were simply automatons. Commentators in the press focused on dehumanization as a core concern, but they also discussed developments in efficiency and cost-effectiveness that affected career progression and power structures. Historian David Lockwood cites the 'International Labour Review' of 1936, which stated that 'in the old-fashioned office, even the office boy felt that he was *somebody* ... but the invoice clerk who now works a book-keeping machine all day is nothing but an impersonal unit'.[14] A write-up of the Review in an Australian periodical drew attention to the psychological consequences of the new 'organisation methods' in office work, particularly when viewed in the light of an 'instinctive desire for importance'.[15] The author suggests that the introduction of machinery creates a hierarchy in which employees are aware of their status as either destined for managerial success or 'meant exclusively for [an] unimportant function' and attached to an 'inferior post'.[16] In this sense, as the Review suggests, machine workers need not be trained in anything other than the piecework for which they are employed, and therefore prospects for promotion are entirely limited. Gone were the days when clerks were merely undergoing a necessary apprenticeship in corporate methods and skills before rising to become manager of their own small business.[17]

There had already been, by this point, a generation of clerks and other office workers who had negotiated various challenges to status and skill. As well as Taylorism, clerical work was redefined with each new technological development that entered the market. Machines such as the duplicator (an early type of document copier), the Hollerith machine and the comptometer (similar to a calculator), alongside the typewriter, had already led to the separation of processes into the constituent parts, each one handed over to a machine operator. As Parker and Jeacle argue, the result of this was 'tedium of repetitive labour' while the individual tasks could now be monitored even more closely for efficiency and time-management.[18]

As Graham Lowe argues, male clerks were often protected from the impact of new technological developments by the creation of a 'stratum at the bottom of the administrative hierarchy' composed entirely of female workers, most of whom were employed with the explicit intention of working with the new machines.[19] In his preface to *Women in the Administrative Revolution* (1987), Lowe talks about his own experiences in office work in the 1970s in Toronto and makes the observation that female administrators were often the most vocal in their elucidation of the ways that they were treated badly.[20] He links this back to the historic use of women in the new mechanical office processes from the turn of the twentieth century and the implications for progression and salary in this substantial and growing section of the white-collar workforce. In this, he calls administrative work the 'contemporary prototype of a female job ghetto', arguing that the dehumanizing principles behind the piece work of new technologies – as Lowe puts it, 'sex-labelled as female' – is suggestive of the wider relationship between efficiency, mechanization, hierarchy and ability to challenge conditions.[21]

While I discuss the impact of female administrators later in this chapter, what is significant are the ways that technology and mechanization altered attitudes towards the clerical body. If we take typing as an example, the 'typewriter' quickly became a synonym for the operator as well as the machine. Likewise, many literary portrayals draw out a shift in attitude towards male clerks, many of whom were not working with new technologies, but nonetheless faced a transition towards piecework. McKinlay and Wilson suggest that because of British cautiousness towards full mechanization – the direct replacement of men with machines – levels of control and surveillance *increased* because 'the clerk's body was the technology upon which the bank's efficient functioning depended', and, consequently, 'control of the body' or the human-machine became essential.[22]

As late as 1945, Norman Collins's novel *London Belongs to Me* explores some of the tensions between the modern and mechanized workforce and the old-fashioned manual processes. McKinlay and Wilson discuss this type of hybridization that occurred, often in smaller businesses, who were keen to follow Taylorist principles but did not have the technical wherewithal to achieve them; instead, they suggest that clerks were expected to increase their output in order to cope with demand by effectively becoming 'large scale data process[ors]' who 'performed in *manual* bureaucracies'.[23] Embodying this, at the beginning of the novel, Mr Josser still sits on his high stool propping up the unyielding ledgers 'with a piece of blotting-paper and a lump of rubber' – fundamentally operating as clerks had done for the previous century. At the same time, he is also mechanized to a degree. Twice in the novel, at the beginning and again at the end, Collins describes Josser as a walking ledger (once as 'four large ledgers with a pair of striped trousers underneath them' and later as 'the ledger walking towards him [that] had suddenly become human'), suggesting that, in fact, Josser survives because he has allowed himself to be dehumanized.[24] He also demonstrates the ways that the traditional clerk complements modern technologies, as witnessed by the young women who operate clerical machinery around him.[25] His retirement early on in the novel signifies his redundancy in an environment largely peopled by the young.

This cycle was repeated with the arrival of computer technology at the end of the twentieth century and continues as developments are made. Early attempts to get to grips with stenography machines and typewriters and the changes in workforce that came partly because of these technologies were replicated in attitudes towards computers in the late 1990s. Portrayals of middle-aged office workers show them struggling with digital technology in the same way that Victorian clerks were reluctant to engage with early forms of mechanization. Examples on television include the estate agent's clerk in mockumentary *People Like Us* (1999–2000) who, despite professing herself 'good with new technology', struggles to input a postcode or Inspector Grimm in Ben Elton's police sitcom *The Thin Blue Line* (1995–6) who forgets to plug his computer in.[26] There are similar concerns about the possibility of artificial intelligence rendering the white-collar worker obsolete in the twenty-first century. Collin's Josser was able to continue at his high stool with his dusty ledgers while he prepared data for new technologies operated around him, just as analysts suggest that in the future, 'jobs' will be broken down into tasks that are AI-appropriate and those which require support from human workers.[27]

Mechanization was both symptomatic of the duties carried out, but it also impressed on office workers a certain state of mind. It is this internalization of the habits and procedures of bureaucracy that has become particularly prominent in cultural depictions, reinforcing a certain assumption about mindless compliance and unquestioned customs. Bullock's young fictional clerk Robert Thorne is unusually self-aware about his process, reflecting on the methods through which he is 'being moulded into a pattern … stiff and bloodless as an office ruler'.[28] Thorne watches his senior, Mr Cherry, who is almost obsessive in his behaviours and whose attention to professional duty makes him a model of Taylorist discipline: 'everything had its own place, green pencil beside red, and blue between red and black, scissors paired with paper knife, pins lying head to head, inkpots square to a fraction of an inch'.[29] Thorne can still recognize the symptoms of this submission to model efficiency but is powerless to prevent it happening to him.

In internalizing the principles of Taylorism, the dehumanized clerk becomes victim to what Georg Lukács calls a 'rational mechanisation [that] extends right into the worker's "soul"'.[30] Rather more extreme than Bullock's Mr Cherry, Wodehouse wrote a short story about a figure named Mr Meggs – an overtly clerical type, who plans to commit suicide but in a manner that fulfils expectations about the rigid and methodical behaviours of those who work in offices: 'a man cannot be a clerk in even an obscure firm of shippers for a great deal of time', Wodehouse writes, 'without acquiring system'. 'And so we find him', the passage concludes, 'seated at his *desk*, ready for the end'.[31] Mr Meggs spends his final moments fulfilling expectations about clerical workers, whose limited imaginations prevent them from performing outside of stereotyped patterns even when carrying out serious actions.

Notably, this co-opted language that draws from ideas around factory mechanisms remains in common parlance in later twentieth-century depictions of office work. The first episode of *The Good Life*, for instance, sees Tom lament that he is 'a grotty little cog in a whacking great machine'.[32] Tom's issue with this is twofold: that he has no sense of meaningful purpose (he designs the little toys that go in cereal boxes), but also that his employer knows and cares so little about him as an individual. These ideas around mechanization and dehumanization – and the sense that the office worker, like Tom, should liberate themselves from the routine work that takes place in the office – is part of a recurring trope that connects the white-collar worker with dreams of a more creative life. Tom wants to turn his hands to self-sufficiently in a bid, like Robert Thorne seventy years before him, to be in tune with the rhythms of the natural world. Others across the nineteenth, twentieth and twenty-first centuries focus on creativity as the counter to mechanization – a pattern established in texts from *Diary of a Nobody* (Pooter is, after all, engaged in life writing), the literary aspirants in Arnold Bennett's *A Man from the North*, George Orwell's *Keep the Aspidistra Flying* and through to Dawn's ambitions to be an illustrator in *The Office*.

Paul Jordan's *The Author in the Office* (2006) argues that the clerk has a relationship with creativity that stems from their original purpose as scribe. He talks about the ways that the '[the office worker is] poised between the creative and the routine [he] reflect[s] – and reflect[s] on – the fundamental conflict between individual autonomy and the need to survive within the system'.[33] This battle between the internalization of mechanization theories and the desire to express the self results in several instances of characters in popular culture who are torn between their ambitions and their routines. Jonathan Rose's reading of the office as a site of inspiration and education in *Intellectual Life and the Working Classes* (2001) has proved controversial, and while individuals who have moved from office work into successful writing careers are notable – see, for instance, Bennett, Orwell, Canning, sitcom writer, Bob Larbey and novelist Gail Honeyman – these should by no means undermine attitudes towards the impact of mechanization in white-collar industries.

Indeed, one of the most significant aspects of the writing produced by former office workers is that it usually concerns the office itself. While Rose is sceptical of the 'mechanized clerk' figure, claiming that he is merely a projection of the modernist conviction that 'the typical clerk was subhuman, machine-like, dead inside', the accounts of office life from many former clerks reinforce these ideas.[34] As Paul Attewell suggests, despite what contemporary historians argue, 'unflattering images' of 'dull, routinized, narrow and mind-deadening' work came, in fact, 'from the pens of clerks themselves' – they still do.[35] This creates a paradox in that texts written by office-worker-authors are themselves about an explicit *rejection* of the office whilst often focusing on this setting. In this case, like early Edwardian novelists, Bennett, Bullock and Pugh, balancing office work with authorship produces texts that are based on the experience of paper-pushing.

In the 1980s, this was the same format for Paul Smith and Terry Kyan's sitcom, *Colin's Sandwich*. Colin is a miserable British Rail employee desperate to escape his tedious job by becoming a writer of horror fiction. After failing to find a successful short story idea, he hits upon the obvious solution: to write a Kafkaesque story about 'a literary genius writing in some dreary little office'.[36] This new story-line fits a strikingly universal narrative about the tension between aspirations for a better life and the reality of achieving this while working full time – one that, as Colin puts it, has been a staple of fiction across the twentieth century: 'Franz Kafka went through the same, didn't he? Worked in legal insurance. Richard Adams scribbling another page of *Watership Down* in the civil service canteen.' Colin further argues that office work is actually more creative than the professions of two of his friends – an academic and a fashion photographer – because 'anyone can hold down a glamorous job. But the nuts and bolts of the daily round, that's another thing. That demands true creativity.'[37] As Michael Hogan puts it, in his review of the release of *Colin's Sandwich* on DVD in 2014 – following Mel Smith's untimely death – Colin is a 'timeless' and 'acute portrait of the aspiring writer' that captures the tension between the demeaning realities of the work place, the daily struggles in the suburban landscape and the desire to find fulfilment through creative pursuits.[38]

This recurrent narrative around the mechanization of working life, and the ways that it affects workers, continues to shape discussions around white-collar work in popular culture. Recognition that each employee became little more than a file number as companies grew heightened the disparity between the 'artistic and business worlds', as Jonathan Wild points out.[39] While office work had once been a temporary stop-gap for writers and journalists – and an easy opportunity to make some money for those from the educated lower-middle-class who were aiming higher – increasing automation threatened to demoralize the office worker and compromise their creativity. This, in turn, led to the 'crucial classif[ication of] the office as an environment hostile to art and the artist', which was first identified by Bennett when his clerk Larch struggles to write whilst working, but which also comes up in *Colin's Sandwich*.[40] While the demands of the nine-to-five day are a key factor in this despondent turn from would-be author to full-time office worker, this is not the only obstacle to overcome. In both examples, the most difficult challenge is resisting the type of deeply rooted behaviours that characterized clerks like Bullock's Mr Cherry. In addition, in both examples, Richard and Colin, must resist the stability and routine that is symbolized through the monthly pay check and which runs counter to the insecurity of portfolio creative work. Tempted by middle managers who offer wage rises and corporate bonuses, both are lured back towards office work through pithy pecuniary rewards. Mechanization – and the rewards of capitalist bureaucracy – are thus deeply ingrained and hard to override.

Surveillance

If Taylorism altered the nature of office work fundamentally, it also necessitated changes to the physical space of the office too. Parker and Jeacle describe a 'Taylorization of space' that is characterized by the 'open-plan layout, with desks often in regimented rows, no visual or acoustic privacy, designed for ease of visual supervision, with all control of space and its infrastructure subject to management prerogative', features that remain prominent in open-plan layouts.⁴¹ Indeed, much of the work of accounting history focuses on the relationship between contemporary activity-based working, as devised in the 1990s, and much earlier renditions that were encouraged by Taylorism. Parker connects historic scientific management theories to the type of practices that ostensibly see spaces 'tailored to suit different activities' as required rather than performing as private workspaces, arguing that both focus on cost-cutting – often driven by surveillance and micro-management of individual processes – and deep efficiency that Taylor promoted over a century ago.⁴²

Victorian clerks in popular culture focus on the negotiation of hierarchies involved in moving from one office to the next – working their way up the ladder from outer to inner offices. By the time Taylorism was making its mark on office culture, in the 1920s, these separate offices were becoming less usual; already, as Jeacle and Parker identify in their study of photographs of workspaces, the open-plan design began to dominate. Methods of mitigating these hall-like spaces, many of which were designed purely for functionality, captured the attention of mid-century designers, as a way of improving efficiency through positivity rather than by logistics alone. Innovation has focused on the low-level dividing of areas of work whilst continuing the flow of communication and processes. While individual offices encouraged depictions of lonely and isolated clerks, trapped in their cubicles, the open office fosters a variety of interpretations: from the cosiness of gossip and blossoming of friendship to acts that invade privacy and prompt bullying cultures.

In their extensive study of 145 photographs of accounting offices, Parker and Jeacle conclude that Taylorism organized space in order to exert power and control. Francis Duffy gives a similar example of this from the Larkin Company Administration Building, built in 1904 in Buffalo, America. The building hosts a vast hall in which clerks and secretaries sit in rows, under observation from their superiors – segregated and demarked by the dark suits of the men and the white blouses of the women. The interior is decorated with corporate slogans demonstrating the control that is exerted over not only what the workers do but also what they see. As in Orwell's *Nineteen Eighty-Four* (1949), surveillance is endless, and dehumanization of the office worker is essential. Like machines, these workers should perform a seamless routine of copying and communicating, completing small but repetitive tasks under the watchful eye of the manager. Terry Gilliam presents something very similar in his iconic Orwellian film *Brazil* (1985). As the camera moves towards the office of Mr Kurtzmann, which, on the first floor, has a view across the stream of workers, the paper-pushers weave effortlessly in and out of one another as they file, stamp and skewer the ephemeral papers of the Ministry of Information.[43]

Following a brief experiment with cubicle working, seen in American sitcom *Friends* in the 1990s and Disney's *The Incredibles* (2004), which attempted to both facilitate the ease of managerial surveillance and provide an element of individual space at extremely low cost, the open office became a site of almost relentless sociability. Geoff Plimmer and Esme Cleave have conducted a review of the scholarly material on modern office design and identify that one of the crucial downsides to the open-plan project is that 'unwanted noise, distractions and privacy infringements' actually 'strain[] social relationships' and counter the aim of 'interaction, innovation and flexibility' by reducing the efficiency of most employees.[44] There are certain status implications within the open-plan environment too which conjure up the historic sense of a 'pool' of interchangeable workers, each of whom is easily replaced. This is, perhaps, a significant reason why professionals tend to work in individual offices – and could help explain the reluctance of many, for instance, to convert to open-plan office work as businesses look to cut costs.

The latest office rhetoric – hot-desking – takes this to a new level. Sold as a dynamic practice that fosters flexibility and creativity rather than promoting a boring stability, recent television shows like *W1A* mock the practice as a method of dealing cheaply with a lack of space in the city (as Joe Moran points out, '"hot desk" sounds more exciting than … "no desk"').[45] More worryingly, it indicates a loss of individuality more akin to the earlier foibles of office design. In fact, the concept of hot-desking becomes a metaphor for the office itself that captures, as Alistair McKay puts it, the 'corporate fear, open-plan loathing and Kafka-esque manoeuvring that is both tragic and banal'.[46] Similar cynicism about the practice features in *Absolute Power* when Jamie claims to be hot-desking at his colleague's station, in an attempt, as Alison rightly suspects, for him to snoop at her computer.

This ability for widespread observation by one's colleagues as well as the manager is one of the ways that surveillance in the office environment is not straightforwardly hierarchical. Whilst most commentators draw on Foucauldian thought on the subject of surveillance and the Benthamite panoptican, this can complicate discussions of the office since, as McKinley and Wilson note, 'nineteenth century institutions did not all share the same social architecture as the prison, nor the same intensity of surveillance' – something which Foucault did not elaborate on.[47] In this respect, its omission demonstrates further the ways that the office is underplayed as a significant part of modern society. As Thompson suggests,

> The first thing to note about the office is that it is perhaps surprising that it remained outside the orbit of Foucault's attention in his studies of surveillance and the 'carceral city' ... against the clear facts that the office and its various functions are tied so closely into capitalist development.[48]

While in many aspects, the new arrangements of the office allowed for greater managerial oversight than the endless run of narrow corridors and inner/outer layouts of the earlier offices, white-collar managerial surveillance is not uncomplicated. Theoretically, while the days of P. G. Wodehouse's clerks Psmith and Mike, strolling between departments and chatting with their friends, are undermined by open-plan managerial intentions, there are many ways of subverting the official gaze in the open environment. Equally, while status dictates that the manager retains their individual office, this can equally make them a target of surveillance.

Safely in their own office, the managerial figure can theoretically oversee the performance of their staff. However, as programmes like *The Office* show, the window onto the private office is limiting in each direction. David Brent can watch those working for him, but they can equally observe his performance. When he nervously peers through his office window, Brent exposes his paranoia rather than inspiring fear or efficiency in his workforce. Unlike the panoptican, in which observation is one way, Brent is as easily exposed as his staff – indeed, he is more visible because he is not part of a mass; there are a dozen people looking in his direction and he cannot watch all of them at the same time. In the small, windowed office, there are very few places to hide; even the use of blinds indicates to the staff watching from outside that something private is happening.

In contemporary offices, the architectural trend for glass interior divides further complicates ideas about surveillance and voyeurism. On television, in the last few years, glass office partitions have featured across a range of genres as part of a commentary on architectural impracticalities. Reggie Perrin can see his subordinates' reactions through his transparent office divide when he rejects their ideas, as they despondently try to cheer each other up in the corridor outside. Rather than encouraging patterns of their behaviour, the visibility of their dejection forces Reggie to analyse his own performance. In TV drama *Bodyguard* (2018), Home Secretary Julia Montague conducts a series of highly confidential meetings with the heads of the police and the director general of the security service behind glass walls, under the gaze of her bodyguard, David Budd. The visibility of this type of sensitive information – which in this case includes evidence of a connection between an attempted terror attack and Budd's daughter's school – has become a recurrent plot device in contemporary drama, which harnesses the potential for leaks that are caused by an architectural rather than technological vulnerability. Similar high-profile glass offices feature in *W1A* as well as in the recent BBC remake of Sir Arthur Conan Doyle's detective stories, *Sherlock* (2010–), in a manner that raises questions about their practicality in contexts where sensitive or classified materials are under discussion. Of course, these instances equally reinforce the idea that paper-pushing is not always benign but can be of real significance.

While the contemporary penchant for glass as a building material (which has come under scrutiny as climate change draws attention to the practicalities of heating and cooling what is effectively a 'glasshouse' environment) is potentially flawed in terms of data sharing and two-way scrutiny, the ideology of Taylorism perpetuates. In Taylorist terms, architectural developments were intended to formalize policing of the behaviour in the office, and this has not changed. In the nineteenth and early twentieth centuries, these methods of control were accepted as part of 'clerkly culture' – an approach to managerial oversight that was perpetuated in many published guidebooks, which encouraged certain standards both within and outside of the workplace. As Zakim has suggested, many of these supported the conflation of 'business maxims ... [and the] character of general wisdom'.[49] These manuals covered not only the technical skills required in the office but they also offered a framework for good behaviour that drew on sound business sense as a core aspect of respectability – and the first generation of lower-middle-class clerks were an ideal market.

One example, taken from *The Clerk: A Sketch in Outline of His Duties and Discipline*, from 1878, gives this advice: 'To be quiet and unassuming in dress argues a becoming modesty of mind; the contrary extreme implies vulgarity.'[50] The author recommends young clerks demonstrate their humility through fashion at all times, evoking a respect for rank and status and proving their reliability and sound budgeting. Repetitive reference to these guidelines for office workers, along with the ambition for a career-long position, served to internalize many of these rules and regulations. Following these maxims was, as commentators in the press picked up, not without its difficulties. As Robert White put it, in his call for a 'Rowton' house for clerks: 'Though their pay is lower than that of the lowest class of artisans they are nevertheless expected to live well, to dress trimly, and generally to bear themselves as gentlemen.'[51] While employers had growing expectations about how their clerks should present themselves, at the same time, the lower middle class were equally liable to be mocked for attempting to dress like members of the middle class on a much reduced salary. Commentators like

Crosland called clerks dressing on a budget 'vulgar' and accused them of aping middle-class styles, particularly when, as White sympathetically draws attention to, they could not afford to keep up with London fashions. Along with authors like Bullock, the Grossmiths and Forster, White comments on the poor state of dress of many London clerks – their 'shiny black coat, the frayed collar, the shabby cuffs'.[52]

Worse still than the impoverished office worker is the dandified clerk, who ignores the rules around sober respectability, daring to follow the more extravagant of middle-class fashions. When H. G. Wells's character Mr Lewisham disregards these guidelines, flaunting his bright red tie and waterproof collars, he is refused work by a clerical agency. Crosland was entirely scathing of this type of expression of individuality by the suburban lower middle class:

> If it were a case of neglect or scorn of appearances, the male suburban might conceivably be pardoned. But there is something in the preposterous air of the man who convinces you at sight that, so far from being a scorner of appearances, he is a zealous, assiduous, and never-flagging worshipper of them. He believes himself to be the glass of fashion and the mould of form.[53]

Crosland sees the attempts to follow fashion as part of a damaging propensity of lower-middle-class suburbans to believe themselves to be of a better status. Scott Banville talks about the similar behaviour of floorwalker Captain Peacock in 1970s sitcom *Are You Being Served?* He draws comparison between Peacock and the dandy of the Victorian music hall, a figure who attracted ridicule for 'his aloof manner and pretensions to a status he does not have'.[54] Banville talks about this as a 'misguided and socially disruptive attempt to mimic' the styles and behaviours of the upper and middle classes,[55] but he also draws attention to the implicit concerns around interest in fashion and gender, a topic already sensitive for the white-collar worker who, as has been discussed at various points, was assumed to have a tenuous grasp on masculinity.

Outside of dress, many organizations and individual bosses deliberately encouraged their staff to consider the ways their behaviour reflected upon the company even when they were not working. In *Punch*, and as early as 1884, a satire of banking regulations includes the new commandment, 'thou shalt not marry on less than £150 a-year' – a ruling echoed in the more serious guide to 'Our Great Banks and How to Enter Them' produced in 1894 for *Boy's Own Paper*.[56] This series is significant because it encourages boys to accept unquestioningly the conditions of service that include behaviour outside of work. This type of restriction only added to the perception that clerks were closely controlled and thus without any serious autonomy. In *Pick-Me-Up*, for instance, a satirical sketch outlines an angry employer chastising a clerk for growing a beard: 'I can't permit you to grow a beard in office hours. You must do that in your spare time.'[57] The joke is, of course, that the body cannot perform this feat – the clerk is, once more, emasculated by his work.

In Bullock's novel, *Robert Thorne*, the eponymous figure, receives a copy of the 'office Regulations' on his first day, many pages of which are dedicated to 'expounding [his] personal conditions of service'.[58] A young clerk starting life away from the family that had previously formed his moral and social parameters, Robert is happy to take on board these rules. While young clerks seem to be fairly accepting of this type of involvement in their personal lives, what is more significant is that employers clearly believed that they had the right to extend the control of the body beyond the office. This was particularly noticeable in industries such as banking where reputation was so critical, and where, as Lowe discusses, 'bank clerks were subjected to army-like discipline'.[59] Victorian bank C. Hoares and Co. had, for instance, a long series of rules that forbade, amongst other things, debt, marriage, smoking and conducting business without a top hat.[60] While banking had a reputation for being both the best-paid clerical work but also the most highly regulated, there was a wider sense in commercial culture that business life and private affairs ought to complement one another. In the 1964 Disney film *Mary Poppins*, the children are offered up for scrutiny by Mr Banks to his superiors at the Fidelity Fiduciary Bank, and his small son's desire to donate tuppence to feed the birds on the steps of St Paul's Cathedral is considered highly insulting – by extension; this gesture is taken to mean that Mr Banks is not suitable for promotion. In television sitcom *Dad's Army*, Captain Mainwaring considers it within his remit as regional bank manager to assess the suitability of his clerk Pike's suitors. Mainwaring objects to the young girl that Pike wants to marry because he does not consider her of the right class. His obsession with the reputation of the bank carries more weight than any personal consideration of Pike's happiness, itself ironic given that the family of Mainwaring's own wife objected to her marriage when he was a lowly clerk.

As these examples show, the association between performance at work and behaviour outside of the office is a strong one. The formal dinner party held by the office worker for their manager or client becomes symbolic of the influence of corporate values in the private sphere. One of the more obvious markers of Reginald Perrin's breakdown in the original television series is his attempt to invite C. J. and Mrs C. J. over for dinner even though his wife is away (he serves no food, providing only vast quantities of wine). The implication that that family must perform in order to establish respect in the workplace is an indictment of the extension of surveillance and control. When Jerry, in 1970s sitcom *The Good Life*, refuses to entertain a client in his home because his wife Margot has an amateur dramatic society performance on the same evening, his boss sacks him. In a heated argument about the ethics of this, the boss maintains that his course of action was fair, because Jerry ought to put the needs of the company above those of his family, despite, as Jerry and Margot's friend Barbara points out, the many occasions on which Margot has successfully entertained clients. The suburban home is equally subject to company scrutiny in J. K. Rowling's *Harry Potter and the Chamber of Secrets* (1998) when Mr Dursley must host a potential client at home in order to secure a business contract. Terrified of his nephew Harry exposing his magical abilities, and thus debasing the Dursleys' carefully constructed 'respectability', Mr Dursley sends Harry to his room.

Some of the codes of behaviour devised for Victorian office workers are now considered overly restrictive (rules about marriage seem far-fetched in twenty-first-century society), but there are ways in which modern office workers continue to conform to managerial expectations outside of the office. Rather than the body being under surveillance, contemporary workers from all industries are monitored via social media, with many signing contracts that include provisos on the use of web platforms to make comments about the company. More subtle are the unspoken rules about office etiquette and the performance of working that continue to be pervasive in contemporary office culture. In David Nobbs's updated *Reggie Perrin*, Perrin's boss, C. J., calls him into the office to berate him for not having a briefcase because it undermines the aesthetic ethos of the company.[61] Perrin is becoming dangerous for questioning the strict and often unspoken codes of middle management that are at once meaningless and instrumental. In C. J.'s view, not carrying a briefcase is akin to undermining the very purpose of work, of the business or even the concept of commerce itself.

In a similar fashion, Hyacinth Bucket forces her husband to take his briefcase to work each morning despite him having nothing to put inside because '[management] always promote people who look as though they have something to carry'.[62] She believes in the same codes of conduct that C. J. promotes, demanding that Richard look 'more aggressively managerial' if he wants to move up the corporate ladder. While this is not a behaviour that is required by regulation, following the unspoken rules is equated with success, just as Richard later must learn to play golf in order to fit in with middle-class measures of social value. Leaving the briefcase behind (even though, as Reggie also admits to his wife, he has never carried anything in it) is a clear symbol that each is challenging the aspects of outward performance that are so critical to the workforce – and particularly middle management.

C. J. additionally repeats the threat 'I'm watching you' on several occasions, both recognizing the power of unchecked transgressions and reinforcing the hierarchical surveillance that should force Perrin to comply with these behavioural expectations. In *Keeping Up Appearances*, the audience does not know if Richard's managers hold similar views to C. J. but it is Hyacinth who embodies surveillance. The motto of both is outward conformism: Hyacinth wants Richard to look managerial because that is how she suspects those above him will judge him. In his rebuke to Reggie, C. J. argues that a briefcase is essential in order to preserve a status quo: 'An office is a delicate and fragile eco-system requiring a certain amount of conformity if it is to be capable of functioning in an effective and socially cohesive manner.'[63] Reggie's simple misdemeanour, as C. J. puts it, is in danger of compromising the behaviour of others around him, leading inevitably to chaos and disorder. The irony is that C. J.'s explanation makes the office sound like a carefully balanced social entity when, of course, it is intensely hierarchical. C. J. can get rid of symbols of conformity, such as his desk, without any repercussions. These examples demonstrate the ways in which control of the body occurred in various ways, often through more subtle internalizations of principles rather than outward surveillance of work practices.

C. J. expects his employees to follow his own principles (or lack thereof) and value systems. Likewise, many fictional office managers play a crucial role in setting the tone of the office space. In ITV sitcom *The Squirrels*, Mr Fletcher fawns over his secretary, enabling his employers to view Joan and the other female administrators as appropriate sexual targets. Stephen Fry's character Charles Prentiss, the ethically and morally bankrupt partner in the PR firm Prentiss/McCabe in *Absolute Power*, similarly encourages the behaviour of corrupt young employees like Jamie, emboldening them to use any tactics possible in order to get ahead. Likewise, because Ricky Gervais's David Brent is determined to bolster his position as an entertainer, his constant barrage of jokes, quips and silly performances result in a lack of seriousness in the performance of his staff. In response, his employees, as many white-collar workers had done before them, turn to subversions, be they collective or individual.

Tim and Dawn's playful antics in *The Office* – many of which are directed at their socially awkward colleague Gareth – are a deliberate attempt to undermine Gareth's stance as a disciplinarian, as well as a wider playful thwarting of ideas around work discipline. As Brett Mills observes, *The Office* is a 'sitcom about humour and power, where the latter is expressed through the former', making attempts to control the shared desk space through practical jokes and pranks a part of this dynamic.[64] What the outlandish behaviours captured in *The Office* more widely suggest are the ways that surveillance can be circumnavigated. Office narratives from the late Victorian period onward suggest that this type of subversion has long been a response to the tedium of the work.

In *Psmith in the City* (1910), Wodehouse's clerk Mike finds that while discipline is strict, his workload is not intellectually taxing: 'There was nothing much to do except enter and stamp letters, and, at intervals, take them down to the post office at the end of the street.' 'The nature of the work', as Mike continues, 'gave [him] plenty of time for reflection.'[65] Mike finds opportunities to chat to his friend Psmith during the day, whilst also admiring Psmith's more extreme dedication to avoiding any kind of work at all. Bullock's Robert Thorne, while generally erstwhile as a young clerk, does start to use the time spent at his desk to fantasize about his future with the girl who later becomes his wife: 'Even in my office coat', he muses, 'I could think of Nell.'[66] Many of these recollections are based on the fact that repetitive office endeavours can be enacted without intellectual engagement.

Poet Richard Church talks at length about the private musings that could easily fill the long and often tedious hours in the office in his autobiography *Over the Bridge* (1956):

> 'You must attend to your work in office time', said an acid voice at my elbow. It was that of the tiny invalid with blue, transparent eyelids and thin moustaches that drooped from beneath his nose like two stalactites. That statement was an axiom which I tried bravely to practice during the twenty-four years spent in the Civil Service; bravely, but with sadly intermittent success.[67]

While Brent's team are more overtly relaxed, enduring his comic turns, playing cricket, flirting with colleagues and rarely mentioning work, Church's account makes clear that there had long been more subtle rebellions. Office standards and various methods of surveillance force the body to comply, but the repetitive nature of the work often left the mind free to wander. Moments of self-absorption and indulgent daydreaming recur across representations of office work in the last hundred and fifty years. In *Girl from Rio* (2001), bank clerk Raymond sits in the office with his colleagues, but he is lost to the samba music in his head – the only indication that his mind is elsewhere is that his toes twitch out a beat under his desk. When questioned by his supervisor, Raymond argues that dancing is an attempt to remain sane in, as he puts it, 'the dullest job, in the dullest bank, in the known universe'.[68] The office can force clerks to dress in a particular way and perform duties by clockwork, but it cannot control their thoughts.

The technicians in *The IT Crowd* (2006–13) go so far as to have a pre-recorded voicemail message asking callers to restart their computers to save them even having to answer the phone, giving them time to engage in frivolous escapades. Mihm suggests that, historically, this type of refusal to pay due attention to mundane tasks was inevitable: 'given the monotony and tedium of these desk jobs, is it any surprise that clerks would fantasise about doing something else?' – a statement he substantiates with evidence of the many attempts made by clerks to steal money, using their time to imagine complex schemes for dishonesty at the expense of their employers.[69] In lots of ways, little has changed; much of the work undertaken in the office is repetitive and often tedious. Financial scandals still take place, perhaps not at the rate that they were perceived to be during the late nineteenth and early twentieth centuries, but, in the case of the financial sector, there is the potential for these to be on a larger scale than ever before.

Girl from Rio gives a traditional reading of the bored bank clerk who turns to theft to vent his anger and improve his quality of life. After discovering that his boss has been sleeping with his wife, Raymond steals a large quantity of money from the bank, using it to run away to Rio in search of his dream woman. This fits the well-worn trope of the embezzling clerk in the history of office work. If you type 'clerk' into the archive of *The Times*, it is clear how many of references are to court proceedings and news stories that cover a wide range from the opportunist theft of small sums to vast fraudulent schemes. In the crime genre, awareness of this wider cultural prevalence seeps into narratives, shaping multiple characters who are potential suspects because of their dodgy financial dealings.[70]

Subversions from office work take multiple forms, not just the downright dishonest – they cover a wider range from the innocuous lapse of concentration (*Robert Thorne*) to the playful attempts to avoid work (*The IT Crowd*), or even the simple social procrastinations that include gossiping (the premise of BBC sitcom *Office Gossip* (2001)) or talking about the weekend that occurs in all representations of office life. The last of these is still considered one of the weaknesses of the open-plan office and a detriment to efficiency; recent articles on a shift to a four-day working week make clear that spending less time in the office is achievable if social interactions are cut to a minimum. Equally, though, in literature and on screen, a culture of work avoidance is more obvious than it is, perhaps, in practice, because it provides the basis for more interesting interactions than pure professionalism would allow. In *Campus* (2009–11), for instance, a comedy series poking fun at university administration, the emphasis is on the burgeoning romance between the university's accountant (Jason) and one of his team (Nicole). The friendly dialogue that wraps itself around the business of the day is much more rewarding for the viewer than the nuts and bolts of financial accountability, even if it is that which provides much of the humour.

While the blossoming romance between Jason and Nicole is mutually consensual and provides a counter to the strange hierarchies of power present in the dual sexual attraction/repulsion of the two academic colleagues who are equally part of a long-run 'will they/won't they' plotline, *Campus* does conform to stereotypes around sex in the office. While Robert Thorne ponders his future with Nell, others use time in the office to consider much darker sexual possibilities. Mr Phillips, in John Lanchester's novel of the same name, states categorically that 'everybody in offices thinks about sex all of the time'.[71] He certainly expounds the vast number of sexual thoughts that fill his day, from the clichéd attraction to his secretary through to the sexualization of strangers on public transport. While Lanchester is parodying the perception of an overly sexed office space through the middle-aged accountant, this is a strand of representation that can be charted back to the work of Bullock and which adds another dimension to the subversion of office surveillance. In this sense, the office worker becomes the voyeur rather than the 'surveilled', and the inversion is not one which can easily be detected by management (although in some cases, the blatancy of these sexual appetites are visible to both management and others – see, for instance, the open leering of characters like David Brent).

Bob Godfrey's 1970 short animated film *Henry 9 'til 5* is an earlier example where voyeuristic acts are the method through which clerical monotony is subverted. At first, Henry conforms to stereotypes; he is short, round, middle-aged, jaded and speaks with a particularly monotonous voice. In this parody, though, Godfrey confronts assumptions about Henry's capacity for free thought and imagination. Henry copes with the tedium of the working day by imagining a series of explicitly sexual fantasies, and hearing him discuss his sexual proclivities in a deadpan monotone reinforces the uninteresting nature of the work. Like Mr Phillips' overt discussions about the role sex plays in everyday life, Henry gives an insight into both the sexualization of the office while countering assumptions about male middle-aged office workers as being inherently unimaginative and boring.

This was a thread picked up by Nobbs in the Reginald Perrin novels (and the following adaptation), both in the sense of his outlandish attitudes towards life and the increasingly lewd fantasies about his secretary Joan. In the later series featuring Martin Clunes, many of these dream sequences fulfil tropes of masculine identity: Reggie as Tarzan and Jasmine (no longer a secretary but now the provocatively titled Head of Balms and Lubricants) as Jane. In a very similar fashion, Mr Phillips offers a highly sexualized inner monologue that focuses on women's bodies as he travels his well-worn path across London. When he admits to a professional pornography maker in the park that he used to fancy his secretary, the response he receives is 'of course you did. Everybody fancies their secretary. That's what offices are all about'.[72]

'Companions in misfortune'

While sexualization of female office workers is deeply problematic – more on which later – positive social interactions in the office space are fundamental to the creation of community, allowing workers to vent and support one another through their various shared experiences. There are, and have historically been, large numbers of young people who work together in offices. The camaraderie created between a group of young clerks living in the city, and often for the first time, features in nearly all early clerical novels from the late nineteenth century and is a key trope of television depictions across the twentieth and twenty-first – including in series such as *The Squirrels* (1974–6), *The Office* (2001–3), *Absolute Power* (2003–5) and *W1A* (2014–). Junior clerks in Bullock's *Robert Thorne* warm themselves by the fire while they drink tea and gossip at an appointed hour,[73] evoking the sort of 'physical and social intimacy' that historians McKinley and Wilson also identify in their study of banking prior to 1914.[74] In Thorne's building, the basement serves as a luncheon room, and it is on his first day, when feeling 'depressed, lonely, small', that 'the laughter, the friendly badinage, the merry sound of knife and fork' of 'fifty or sixty' clerks eating together cheers him considerably.[75] In Richard Church's autobiography, recalling his early life as a clerk in the early twentieth century, he likewise talks about how the other 'new boy' to start working alongside him at the Land Registry becomes his 'post-prandial confidan[t]'; on their first pay-day, they go 'together to Denny's bookshop in the Strand and spend some of [their] earnings'.[76]

For young office workers, negotiating social hierarchies and making friends (and sometimes enemies) is a significant aspect of their early career development and a feature of many loosely autobiographical texts. Thorne relies on other clerks to help him understand which senior staff members tolerate tea and chat amongst the clerks and which are stricter about socializing in the work place. When Wodehouse's Mike starts work in a bank, his friend Psmith is a guide to the rhythms of the day. Towards his other colleagues, though, Mike is largely indifferent. He considers himself socially above many of the other clerks and as a result is willing only to view his colleagues as merely 'companions in misfortune'.[77] While Mike would not socialize with the bank's employees outside of work, this label does acknowledge the ways that the office reinforces collegiality, often focused on the sharing of negative experiences.

Mike and Psmith are part of a generation that saw certain shifts in the relationship between clerks and their managers. They work in the New Asiatic Bank, and Psmith's family ties and status are enough to keep him out of trouble. Increasingly, though, application replaced recommendation, and thus gone was the shared commercial interests between father and son and employee and employer that had characterized earlier clerk-hood. This connection had been, as Geoffrey Crossick suggests, one of the key reasons that unionization did not occur to any great extent within clerical work; early clerks were essentially loyal to their employer, in part, because of these family links.[78] In 1892, Lupin in *Diary of a Nobody* symbolizes a crucial late-nineteenth-century shift in attitudes towards the workplace that saw the notion of family company loyalty, the lifelong clerkship, leading through promotion to a higher position, and finally a worthy retirement as outdated. More specifically, he also demonstrates that this was as much of a decision made by the younger generation as it is by the employers themselves. Lupin becomes an early iteration of the type of character who identifies the problematic aspects of his father's chosen career and is determined to find something better.

The working relationship between father and son may have disappeared by the end of the nineteenth century, but older clerks nearly always make an appearance in cultural texts about the office. Many offer a mentorship that becomes pivotal in their young colleague's understanding of how their business works. They also become influential in a range of other ways, as a role model for life inside the office and beyond its walls. In Bennett's *A Man from the North*, Richard Larch's new boss, Mr Aked, takes him under his wing, inviting young Richard to his home for tea, introducing him to his young niece and encouraging an interest in great literature. In a similar way, Mr Hope offers an invitation to Robert Thorne for a potluck supper because, as a young bachelor living in lodgings, he feels he is likely to need some company.

Nearly a hundred years later, this relationship is still relevant to television sitcoms like *Men Behaving Badly* (1993–9). Gary Strang starts at Security Appliances Limited as manager of the London sub-office, but the middle-aged clerk George (who is largely useless in a business sense) is a paternal figure. Gary often asks George for personal advice, despite their incredibly different attitudes to most aspects of life; the act of asking, though, is symbolic, reversing the manager–employer relationship and offering alternative social hierarchies. More awkwardly, David Brent tries to perform as a paternal boss in *The Office*, but his attempt at fatherly interest (when he hires his friend's daughter and lodger, Donna) backfires when Donna shows contempt for his leering invasions into her privacy. In *Love Actually*, Alan Rickman plays an amiable boss whose attempts to show fatherly interest in one of his young female workers (Mia) similarly fails when she makes very clear her attraction to him, jeopardizing his marriage and family life. These latter two examples rest uncomfortably on the long-standing association between sex and power in the office that has formed the basis of a multitude of representations between the introduction of women into clerical work and the present day. They also reference the generational differences that are developing across the twentieth century that challenge the assumption of a hierarchy between those of advancing years and young people in the office.

In order to bring colleagues together, and to unite them towards company aims, businesses began to promote leisure pursuits as early as the 1880s. (Little has changed when considering that Mia first works closely with Harry because she is planning the annual company Christmas 'do'.) These were particularly useful for promoting good health amongst workers, as well as encouraging people's sense of collegiality. Channelling the youthful energy of new clerks into socially acceptable leisure and sporting activities could, as a useful by-product, help gloss over the increasing mechanization and growing monotony of office work. This top-down approach to the social dynamics within the office space built upon the more informal ways that workers had long been disrupting official business for fun. In 1865, an article on clerking in *Punch* talked about the various ways office workers could enliven their daily toil:

> The term 'recreation' does not necessarily apply to the time after office-hours, for in the absence of the principals the course of the day will furnish many opportunities for relaxation from the toils of business. The newspaper, for instance, expands the mind, and is easily put down when you hear any one coming; while in some offices, not liable to very sudden intrusion, a game at cribbage – which is a great quickener of the faculties – may be ventured on. Where the clerks are all on friendly terms, and particularly in a government office, leap-frog is an agreeable exercise; for it not only fills up the time, but obviates the chief objection to the employment of a clerk, on the ground of its being sedentary.[79]

Laurie Dennett's history of the Prudential Life Insurance Company refers to the 'really good pranks' that some of its clerks played, many of which were tolerated by senior management. Dennett cites one instance where a shareholder complained to the chairman in 1872, to which he replied: 'I fully admit that our clerks do read the papers and chatter; but I have yet to learn that human nature can go on all day without some little relaxation.'[80] This widespread recognition that repetitive work required some sort of release of energy is in evidence again in the open admission of the young, bored secretary in 1970s sitcom *Is It Legal?* that she has photocopied her breasts just to 'break up the tedium of office life'.[81] In *The Office*, David Brent positively encourages Tim and Dawn's constant plotting of jokes at Gareth's expense – laughing along at the now infamous stapler immersed in jelly prank, and even refusing to discipline Chris Finch when he produces an offensive image of Brent and circulates it.

While these are informal and not entirely sanctioned endeavours (Brent's immediate boss, Jennifer Taylor-Clarke, compels him to cultivate a more serious environment), there was a recognizable validity in encouraging social interactions in the workplace. Jerome Bjelopera discusses the ways that forming company-sponsored clubs, for instance, not only provided entertainment but also helped to distract clerks from the rise of mechanization in the late nineteenth century. Channelling energy towards company ends provided a useful way of encouraging collegiate cohesion and cultivating a shared purpose. Bjelopera's study of Philadelphia suggests that the social aspects of company activities could produce a 'solidification of friendships to compensate for increasingly impersonal offices'.[82] As a result, many companies, particularly around the turn of the twentieth century, supported sports teams, reading libraries, amateur dramatic societies and rambling and cycling clubs. The Prudential had its own clerk's society (later referred to as the Ibis), which focused heavily on social and sporting activities, as well as more academic pursuits from the 1870s.[83] Of course, much of the emphasis on sport coincided with the rise of Muscular Christianity at the end of the nineteenth century, giving male office workers chance to reassert a masculinity that was viewed as becoming even more tenuous, thanks to the rising number of female secretaries and stenographers and a perceived feminization of the office.

Consequently, the Ibis, like many other insurance companies such as the Pearl Life, developed swimming, tennis, cycling, running and gymnastics clubs, as well as chess, debating, singing and horticulture associations. Reflecting the aspirational class position of lower-grade white-collar work, and demonstrating a distance from factory teams, football was not pursued (one of the Directors of the Prudential had his arm broken by a clerk during a game which equally did not enamour him to the sport).[84] Teams played other company teams, building a sense of 'strong Prudential identity' in replication of the sort of bond that was created as part of the public school ethos. Management were also aware that sport was a 'health complement to the sedentary, highly supervised working environment'.[85] Often used to designate social position, performance in extracurricular company activities could also be connected in certain ways to promotion. References to important golf games, inter-office five-a-side contests, corporate 'away days' and competitive quiz nights, as well as the crucial 'dinner with the boss', recur across the twentieth century and into the twenty-first. As Jeacle's article exploring the recruitment of accountants at companies like Price Waterhouse Cooper and Ernst and Young has shown, this type of social and sporting activities remain key aspects of corporate life – and advertising these opportunities is a key part of overthrowing impressions of those working as accountants, in particular, as 'seemingly dreary characters'.[86] Attempting to lure graduates onto their employment schemes with reference to extracurricular opportunities continues the assumption that office work alone is without excitement or fulfilment. At the same time, this emphasis on social and sporting activities reiterates the ways in which Taylorist efficiency has become interwoven with practices that facilitate staff satisfaction, articulating the approach of the senior manager of the Prudential in 1872, who commented that staff who are free to chat and read newspapers at certain times are happier and potentially, therefore, more productive.[87]

This ethos rose to prominence in the power play of corporate culture in the 1970s and 1980s. Sunshine Desserts, the company for whom Reginald Perrin works, boasts a sports ground, amateur dramatic society and amenities room. Reginald must impress his boss at a dinner in his home early on, and his wife being away is crucial to his plan to disrupt the expectations of this well-recognized trope by refusing to prepare food and forcing the guests to donate money to charity instead. In Keith Waterhouse's *Office Life* in the 1970s, Clement Gryce is keen to join the incredibly exclusive amateur dramatics society, seeing the after-work drinks between two of his colleagues who are members as strategically important events to help him achieve this. Hyacinth similarly identifies an opportunity for Richard's career progression in *Keeping Up Appearances* when she encourages him to win over a potential new boss through a round of golf in series four. The corporate golf game carries complicated social implications as well as work-related performance management, as golf in sitcoms like *The Good Life* and *Is It Legal?* demonstrate (and likewise bridge in *Terry and June*).

The team at Wernham Hogg face quiz nights, charity fundraisers and dancing together, heightening tensions and unmasking desires through drunkenness and forced conviviality. These social interactions are, of course, the essence of the series, providing the human interest that sustains the narrative and the relationships that fulfil the audience's perseverance. The office itself is the backdrop against which familiar themes are carried out, but the social scenarios – particularly the Christmas party – instigate significant moments of universality. The drunken antics and catalytic relationship shifts that occur as a result of the annual festive bash highlights the fine lines between collegiality, friendship and romance that are distorted in an unfamiliar setting. The famous scene between Tim and Dawn happens when she opens his thoughtful Christmas gift; their sweet and low-key reunion contrasts with the drunken debauchery or reluctant sociability that has become symbolic of the office party.

Even Gary Strang, who struggles with commitment to his long-term girlfriend Dorothy, fosters a familial obligation to his middle-aged colleagues George and Anthea. Across the series, this relationship develops from his initial frostiness in series one to inviting them out to dinner (hesitantly at the end of the first series), then later to his stag do – where George nervously negotiates attending a strip club – and, finally, his wedding (as two of the only guests on Gary's side). In workplace-based sitcom *Kiss Me Kate* (1998–2001), the characters begin as colleagues, and the series increasingly expands the relationships that grow, moving further out from the office and into their personal lives. This has become a standard approach to workplace television shows on both sides of the Atlantic – work may well provide the setting, but the social interactions grow much wider in scope (see, for instance, comedies like *Scrubs* (2001–10), *The Mindy Project* (2012–17), and *30 Rock* (2006–13) in the United States).

Gender and the office

While social events on-screen give life to characters beyond their professional identities, they also demonstrate the complicated relationships that exist within the workplace. While in Edwardian novels like *Robert Thorne* and even (because it is set in banking) *Psmith in the City*, these personal interactions are focused on friendships between men – either, as we have seen, young colleagues or the paternalism of older clerks towards those beginning their careers – a wider variety of social interactions form the basis of representations from the 1920s onwards. From slow beginnings in the 1870s, when lower-middle-class women began to break into the clerical industries, the early twentieth century saw the number of female white-collar workers rise dramatically. Indeed, Anderson identifies clerical work as having the most rapid shift in gender composition between 1871 (when women formed only 1.1 per cent of the clerical workforce) and 1931 (where they comprised 43.1 per cent).[88] This trend did not subside in the twentieth century; in terms of numbers, this involved an increase from 179,000 in 1911 to 648,000 by 1931 and 1.5 million female clerks by 1951 (which was one-fifth of all working women).[89] This was a transformation that, as Anderson argues, was partly enabled by the comical feminization of male office workers from the Victorian period onwards.[90] White-collar work had long been seen as sedentary, not dangerous and tedious, attributes which had made the clerical career an object of some scorn and humour for the male clerk but which actually recommended it for lower-middle and middle-class women who were newly looking for work. Rising educational standards and a widespread female labour market that had basic administrative skills coincided with the much-talked-about surplus of women in the late twentieth century. Clerical jobs were indoor, safe and respectable, and in most respects better paid and less physically tiring than domestic service.

In addition, there was a series of technological advancements complementing the work of existing clerical workers but which required a newly trained workforce. As Stephen Walker argues, female labour in the office had been in evidence from the nineteenth century, and was not simply a product of mechanization, but these new technologies did encourage a division of labour that equally owed much to the effects of Taylorism and the efficiency of piecemeal work.[91] Women trained to use these specialist machines, thus not directly competing with their male clerical counterparts, who continued to perform manual tasks by hand. Lowe sees this distinction as a significant part of his claim that proletarianization of the clerk did not occur because, he argues, it was a new stratum of worker that dealt with the mechanized tasks – and they were trained from the start as piecemeal, machine operators.[92]

The Prudential Life Assurance Company took on its first female employees as early as the 1870s, with the managing director defending them to the shareholders in 1874 'as in no way rivalling the male clerks, but rather as "doing a class of work that they could not get satisfactorily done by the male clerks"'.[93] Images collected by Jeacle and Parker between 1900 and 1930 show mixed gender offices, but with the women performing separate roles: using the new typewriters to type up male phonograph recordings, for instance.[94] They argue that engaging with developing technologies does not necessarily simplistically mean 'deskilling' in the sense that is often discussed, because actually these machines needed 'intensive training and the development of a specific set of unique skills'.[95] What they did imply, however, was a separation of labour; the new wave of female workers, most of whom, at this point, were young and unmarried, could more easily be trained in these specialist skills, whilst existing clerks were redirected onto tasks for which they already had training and expertise, most of which additionally carried more responsibility. This ultimately resulted in the hierarchies of employment that saw work such as typing as 'lower skilled' than bookkeeping, for example.

In some businesses, new female recruits were segregated physically from their male counterparts, having, like the women working at the Refuge Life Assurance Company, separate dining facilities and entrance hallways.[96] These arrangements were dependent on when the office block was built, and the conservatism of those designing the layout. At the Prudential, for instance, it was not until the First World War, when two thousand female war workers were employed, that male and female clerks began to work alongside one another, and only then out of necessity, as women were, for the first time, expanding their repertoire of roles into more complex areas of administrative work.[97]

Sectors such as banking, which had always held an elite status within white-collar work, remained largely male for much longer.[98] See, for instance, in films set in banks like *Mary Poppins* (1964) and *Girl from Rio* (2001), evidence that the all-male workforce appears prominent in representations across the twentieth and into the twenty-first centuries. Even in *Sherlock* in 2010, 'The Blind Banker' episode features mainly men on the trading floor of fictional bank Shad Sanderson, while women line the reception desk. More significantly, the fraudulent banker Eddie van Coon is caught out because he buys his female PA (with whom he is having an affair) a gift from his recent trip to China. This takes us back to stereotypes about the secretary that cropped up in 1970s sitcoms like *The Squirrels* but which equally continue to pervade popular culture.

If historically female office workers did not undercut men, or force them from their jobs, but instead allowed for the rapid growth needed in an industry that was relied upon increasingly in a growing paper economy, little appears to have changed in contemporary banking. Social barriers (such as marriage) and grade segregation once prevented female workers from rising above their male counterparts, meaning there was a restructuring of office hierarchies and the creation of new positions that generally favoured men. Now, as the press have recently reported, London's banking culture – long and anti-social hours, in particular – continues to shape the gender makeup of its senior staff.[99]

While these general trends are important, what is more crucial for this study is the way that representations both kept pace with and became divorced from changes. In some ways, the strict hierarchical division of male and female workers is significant mainly because it is not the impression in circulation in popular culture. Male clerks continued to be mocked in the press as being ousted by female typewriters (a word which became synonymous with the operator rather than the machine), undermined by New Women and anachronistic in a modern workplace. In George Gissing's *The Odd Women* (1893), for instance, old clerk Edmund Widdowson is unable to sustain a relationship with his young wife Monica, who represents the new generation of women – radicalized by Rhoda Nunn and her secretarial agency – who are attempting independence through white-collar work. In *The Squirrels*, efficiency analyst April Smedley arrives at the office and starts a similar revolution, encouraging secretary Carol to start a college course (in business management, not, as her boss suggests, shorthand) and helping the wives of Rex and Harry to learn to drive. The men make multiple scathing remarks about women who try to 'compete in a man's world' (including comments about the consequences of Margaret Thatcher getting a ladder in her tights), but their wives, along with April, have the last laugh at the end of the episode. While the humour in the episode plays on the threat to patriarchy within the office, rendering it typical of its time, April does offer an alternative role model for women like Carol, challenging ideas around the inherent sexualization of the secretary.

As Julie Berebitsky's extensive study, *Sex and the Office* (2012), makes clear, female workers were sexualized from the beginnings of the 'white-blouse revolution'.[100] Initially, women's entry into the clerical labour market was treated with great suspicion, with commentators assuming nefarious intent. Women were posited as aggressors, desperate to find a husband and ruthless in their attempts to marry the boss. Male office workers, on the other hand, could leave their wives and families to run away with their secretaries and be portrayed as the innocent party. Berebitsky gives many examples of cases in America where women were treated with vitriol after having 'affairs' in the workplace that were referred to by the press as evidence of a decline in female morality. By the mid-twentieth century, women were less of a threat but more overtly represented as a sex symbol in the modern office, and whilst attitudes towards sexuality meant that this was less rancorous than previously, it was still a misnomer, which turned hard-working professionals into little more than attractive features of the office environment.

Figure 2.1 Introducing a new colleague in *The Squirrels* (1976)
© ITV

From the 1970s onwards, there was a definite shift towards open discussion of male and female sexuality in the office – albeit mainly as a method by which men could more overtly chase female colleagues. One episode of ITV's *The Squirrels* sees Carol, Mr Fletcher's secretary, dress provocatively for his birthday, angling for a dinner invitation. An attractive female colleague, Heather, comes over from personnel to request a file, and the men in the office joke that Heather is a birthday present. To the dismay of Carol, as well as jealous Rex, Harry and Burt, Mr Fletcher schemes to spend more time with Heather (Figure 2.1).[101] The episode results in various clumsy schemes from each of the male members of staff, resulting in a final chaotic attempt to eject Heather from the office once it becomes clear that her sweet disposition and flirtatious behaviour has proved the downfall of many colleagues at the London office, where she formerly worked. More significantly, the women in the workplace act like characters in a male fantasy – doe-eyed Heather (referred to by Carol as an infamous 'wrecker') and sensual Carol both throw themselves at a middle-aged boss, Mr Fletcher.

This open sexualization of female colleagues features in other texts of the 1970s; Reginald Perrin fantasizes without repercussions about his secretary, and the main character in Waterhouse's *Office Life* immediately fixes on Pam as a likely mistress following a brief examination of his new female colleagues. On the big screen is the iconic relationship between James Bond and Miss Moneypenny – which continues to be as highly sexualized as it was in the books, even in the latest films, particularly in *Spectre* (2016). The 1980s, the decade of power dressing and a female Prime Minister, saw the sexualization of the woman boss for the first time, whose position inverted gendered power play into a deeply masochistic male fantasy. Women's liberation at work, as shown in one *Punch* cartoon from 1981, was enjoyed by male colleagues but potentially dangerous to their career prospects. David Landon's 'audit clerk' cartoon features a drunken, topless, female office worker table-top dancing (at a company Christmas party), captioned with the by-line: 'it'll take some little time for me to readjust to her as an audit-clerk'.[102]

Sexualizing women in the office was one way of undermining their contribution to clerical culture. The notion of the 'sexcretary' was an effective device in continuing the segregation of the workplace that had begun in the 1870s as women joined the white-collar market whilst reinforcing gendered hierarchies. The eroticism of the power dynamic between the male boss and the female secretary has become deeply ingrained in literature, television, film, popular culture and particularly in forms such as pornography. Other sources refer to flirtations, attractions and (more often) one-sided lustful desires: Lanchester's Mr Phillips fantasizes about his secretary Karen, and Martin Knight's fictional Barry Desmond masturbates while dreaming of the telex operator on the third floor. In *Ever Decreasing Circles* (1984–7), when Martin moves up the corporate ladder at Mole Valley Valves, his secretary Mrs Ripper comes immediately into his office, declaring: 'I am all yours ... call me when you want me ... tiger', at which there is a great deal of laughter from the audience.[103] Even as recently as *The Office*, Brent immediately displays his misogynist attitudes towards female employees when first introducing Dawn with a crude pun about anal sex. Dawn's reaction makes clear that this managerial performance is predominantly for the benefit of the camera rather than a manifestation of Brent's daily comments, although his actions throughout the series make clear that these are entrenched views, if not always so explicitly put. This symbolic introduction nonetheless captures attitudes that have persisted since women first entered the clerical workforce in the 1880s, particularly where the power dynamic, as in nearly all instances, favours men.

When Judy, in 1990s sitcom *As Time Goes By*, complains about being 'knees and dimples', despite her increasingly managerial role in her mother's secretarial agency, she demonstrates the danger of a long-lasting emphasis on female administrators as decorative rather than fully functioning. More widely in *As Time Goes By*, the separation of typing and the 'brain-work' in the 'by-the-hour' secretary industry displays how long the segregation of labours, if not spaces, lasted. But why was it so essential to reinforce the idea that female administrative work was separate and inherently inferior to male administrative work?

In part, the cultural role of the secretary was a response to the concerns that had circulated amongst white-collar workers since the first clerks began copying documents for their middle-class managers: clerical work was not physical, nor particularly skilled, and thus, it was worryingly not conventionally masculine. The rise of the stenograph, the mimeograph, the addressograph, the typewriter and – alongside these developments – the female clerical worker captured the tone of much that had already been brewing in representations of office work since the mid-nineteenth century: a lack of control and independence identified as being essentially feminine. Had office workers not been undermined in terms of masculinity from the outset, there would perhaps have been less of an insistence on the absolute division between the way men and women worked in an office environment.

While there are clearly many changes that have had an impact on the role of women in the office, contemporary examples seem to return to the simplistic binaries of much earlier representations. Female administrative staff continue to be defined in sexual rather than professional terms. Donna shows very little interest in her work at the paper company in *The Office*, becoming merely a toy over which the men in the office crudely fight. Depicted as barely working, the scenes in which Mia features in *Love Actually* focus instead on her blatant flirtation with Harry. This aggressive pursuit of the married boss harks back to the assumptions made about young women entering the clerical workforce in the 1920s, but which leaves a palimpsest of representational assumptions. The secretarial agency in 1990s sitcom *As Time Goes By*, for instance, is run by attractive 'girls' who combine efficiency with secretarial good looks – indeed, like Mia in *Love Actually* and Heather in *The Squirrels*, typist Judith aggressively pursues a much older man (her mother's former lover, Lionel) in the first episode. While the female protagonist in rom-com *Bridget Jones's Diary* (2001) is a journalist rather than a secretary, the attitude of her boss remains alarmingly like that of Mr Fletcher and his secretary, Carol. Bridget must dress unprofessionally and provocatively at the request of her boss, Daniel, as part of their growing flirtation, whereas Daniel gets to act as normal, demonstrating how little has changed. *Bridget Jones* captured the continuation of the sexualized power play that had begun in the 1930s and that was such a feature of *The Squirrels* and, to a lesser extent, *Reginald Perrin*.

In *Ever Decreasing Circles*, Martin warns Anne away from office work, claiming that, in his experience, 'no woman is safe' from 'clammy-handed reps' in Sales.[104] Rather than addressing the dominant and aggressive male sexualization within the office, he simply refuses to let Anne be part of office culture. Likewise, in *Men Behaving Badly*, Gary openly complains that middle-aged Anthea, with her hand-knitted Tupperware pouches and floral blouses, is very different from the buxom young secretary he had in mind before he started working in security appliances. Each of these examples gives weight to the explicit foregrounding of sexuality, women and the office that has lingered for over hundred and fifty years.

Male office workers, by contrast, come in a slightly wider range of representations, many of which similarly function as stereotypes, but crucially these are not all articulated through their sexuality. Two-dimensional character templates continue to be used by writers, such as the relentlessly youthful and naïve clerk (see, for example, trainee solicitor Colin in *Is It Legal?* or bouncy Steve and Antony from *Reggie Perrin*) and the disgruntled and frustrated middle manager (Reggie is one, Carl from *The 7.39* another, Ian Fletcher in *W1A* too), but these tropes are not simply focused on their availability in the sexual market. Usually, it is the tension between these two types of male characters that gives the comedy to the situation; enthusiastic yuppies bring home to their middle-aged superiors their own rapid descent into a mid-life crisis or relentless middle managers make more excruciating the lives of their middle-aged colleagues.

Where there is reference to male sexuality (and where stereotyping becomes more prevalent), it follows the tropes identified in relation to women – in the voyeuristic leering of figures like Mr Phillips and Clement Gryce. These characters capture the unhealthy sex obsession that fits neatly alongside the other stereotypes that surround office work. Rather than the type of open sexuality associated with working-class figures, those who in literature flaunt their status as virile emblems of physical masculinity (following in the iconic steps of Oliver Mellors in *Lady Chatterley's Lover* (1928)), the male office worker is often portrayed as engaging in covert behaviours that include staring, fantasising and objectifying women. These behaviours are aligned more widely with other negative attributes associated with the clerk as a snivelling sycophant who has little imagination or personality. Many of these patterns focus on a stage in the life cycle of the middle-aged male clerk, who, following years of dissatisfaction and suppressed ambition, turns to unhealthy outlets for this frustration as part of what is typified as a 'mid-life crisis'.

The mid-life crisis

The mid-life crisis of Reginald Perrin in the 1970s was a key moment that has continued to shape impressions of male office workers. The opening credits of

The Fall and Rise of Reginald Perrin feature the slow walk down the beach before Reginald removes his clothes and steps into the sea, ostensibly to take his own life. This iconic moment was the amalgamation of a series of underlying issues for the lower-middle-class office worker that saw attitudes towards masculinity, the value of white-collar work and the restrictions of social hierarchies come together. Reginald was also not the first to face a deep sense of crisis: in 'A Freak of Nature', one of George Gissing's short stories, Mr Brogden snaps at his wife and runs off into the countryside rather than going to work. He plays an uncharacteristic game of 'knock-door-run' before faking his identity and staying with a country parson. On returning home, his boss suggests overwork is the cause and offers Brogden a short holiday as a solution in an attempt to lure him back to the office.[105] Also at the turn of the twentieth century, Bullock's Mr Ruby carries out a similar mutiny – taking a sea voyage in a bid to see the world before socially embarrassing himself and returning bashfully home. Both examples feature the clerk returning ruefully to their desk, having achieved, like Reginald Perrin, very little real transformation. Incidentally, the third series of *The Fall and Rise*, sees Reginald once more contemplating suicide on the Dorset coast.

On the big screen, in *The Rebel* (1961), Tony Hancock directs a similar outburst at his boss (played by John Le Mesurier). He shrieks: 'I've got greatness in me – I can feel it ... I'm being choked, crushed, bogged down in a sea of triviality.'[106] Hancock shouts and brawls and pushes the boss over, but he is still not taken seriously. Instead, Le Mesurier's character simply offers him an hour of two away from his desk and suggests that he channel his creativity into the company tennis club or the amateur dramatic society. When Mr Banks tells a joke at work in *Mary Poppins*, this simple act is taken as a severe statement of rebellion, resulting in his being sacked. A parody, in this instance, of the rigidity in the banking world – where caricatures like those performed by Dick van Dyke mock a century of rules and regulations around moral fibre and upstanding character – *Mary Poppins* nonetheless turns hapless Banks into a kind of outspoken lower-middle-class hero.

Similarly, an episode of 1990s sitcom *Men Behaving Badly* is dedicated to this type of mid-life moment. Middle manager Gary starts to question his career choices, lamenting the lost opportunities in his career: 'I wouldn't mind if I'd actually done things with my life ... I was an office junior, then I was a new office manager and then I joined the floppy knitwear scene.'[107] Gary references the woolly cardigans that his fifty-something-year-old colleague George has always worn and which Gary increasingly finds himself drawn towards. Gary's sartorial transformation turns him a very typical lower-middle-class icon; a middle-aged middle manager who prefers comfort over style. Upon recognizing this, Gary attempts self-reflection, throwing himself into an ill-advised spree of youthful spontaneity (involving a messy, alcohol-fuelled all-night rave) before returning to the cocoon of the office – this time, complete with boiled sweets and a game of chequers with George, to a soundtrack by The Seekers.

The Office also deals with this type of male-crisis moment – following an outburst in a training session, sales representative Tim resigns, determined to go to university and study psychology. His intention to follow this path is authentic, but David Brent soon convinces him to stay by offering him a small pay rise and a promotion to senior sales clerk. Tim relinquishes his aspiration for a university education when offered five hundred pounds per annum more by Wernham Hogg. What is carefully captured by the writers is the poignancy of Tim staying. In the script, this is particularly well signposted in the following stage direction once Tim agrees to the promotion: '*we see Tim back in the office, still trapped behind his desk*' (Figure 2.2). The camera dwells on Tim's expression as he glumly assesses the inertia inherent in staying.[108]

David Nicholls's romantic television drama *The 7.39* tells the story of Carl and Sally, two commuters who meet on a train and begin an affair. The narrative follows a typical formula for the male office worker's mid-life crisis: Carl loathes his job in an estate agent's office, his boss is tyrannical and unfeeling and his family life is characterized through dealing with tiresome teenagers and a loving yet preoccupied wife. Meeting a younger woman on the train during the monotony of the daily commute to work and forced into spending a night

Figure 2.2 Tim (Martin Freeman) back at his desk in *The Office* (2001)
© BBC

together by the inadequacy of their rail provider, the subsequent affair fulfils many clichéd expectations about the male mid-life crisis. Like Reginald's sexual fantasies about his secretary Joan, Tim's ill-fated attempt at asking Dawn out during his resignation speech (or even Richard Larch's fleeting experience with a prostitute in *A Man from the North*), the notion of 'crisis' is shaped by a sexual impulse.

In *The 7.39*, as with the other examples listed, this is a temporary rebellion; the resolution at the end of the final episode sees Carl back at home with his wife and family, but also back in the job he loathes. In short, the effects of Carl's infidelity are merely disruptive (and emotionally damaging) rather than life-altering. For Sally, on the other hand, the affair has much greater significance in that it instigates a series of real changes on the back of their romance; she has a baby, a new partner and a new life. There is a gendered difference, here, that reiterates the sense of the male mid-life crisis as a futile exercise, merely causing anguish and chaos, whereas for Sally – who is several years younger – the affair is not a 'crisis' but a moment of reflective redirection, and one which takes her away from her controlling fiancé and towards an idealized future.

Even in films directed at children, there are references to the male mid-life crisis. In the 2017 film *Paddington 2*, Mr Brown misses out on promotion to Head of Risk Analysis (itself a typically cautious petit-bourgeois role), bringing on a full-scale mid-life crisis, which is humorously evident in his new penchant for yoga and a series of desperately youthful fashion choices. His frustrations that he has 'peaked in the middle' leads to a period of deep self-reflection.[109] *Christopher Robin* (2018) similarly places the grown boy, of A. A. Milne's enchanting stories for children, in a tedious office job working for a company that creates luggage. Christopher is overworked, neglecting his wife and missing the childhood of his young daughter. Winnie the Pooh and the other soft toys reanimate Christopher, reuniting him with his family but also helping him to understand a revolutionary new way of promoting his company's interests: giving office workers holidays so they need to buy luggage. Like the other clerks who return to the office, *Christopher Robin* sees the main character have an epiphany, stage a short revolution, but ultimately also return to his role, this time at the special request of the director of the company.

More broadly, these cases represent a seminal mid-life crisis moment, a taking stock of life and worth at a time when youth is waning. This ties into another trope of the lower-middle-class office worker – and one that is made very clear by the actions of characters like Gary and Tony across *Men Behaving Badly* and Tim in *The Office* – that white-collar work encourages a 'Peter Pan' impulse. In

J. M. Barrie's novel itself, this is apparent in the behaviour of Mr Darling. Mr Darling responds to the disappearance of his children by stubbornly confining himself to Nana's kennel – having it carried to work and back each day. Mrs Darling sees this as a juvenile attempt by her husband to draw blame on himself in a manner that does little more than gain attention from his colleagues and neighbours.

Captain Mainwaring accuses Sergeant Wilson of a similar refusal to take on adult responsibilities in the *Dad's Army* episode 'War Dance', when Wilson is reluctant to have a paternal chat with Private Pike: 'You're not a middle-aged chief clerk', says Mainwaring: 'You're a sort of Peter Pan'.[110] The name becomes a key word across the episode, forcing Wilson to face his responsibilities towards Pike and reminding the audience that Wilson's bachelor life comes at a cost to others. Likewise, in 1970s sitcom *The Good Life*, the first episode sees Tom (upon turning 40) engage in taking stock of his life. His boss and neighbour Jerry gives him a pep talk early in the episode, telling Tom that he must start taking his job seriously. 'Damn it all you're not *Peter Pan*', he reprimands.[111]

Tim turns 30 in *The Office* and responds to Brent's awkward mention of a 32-year-old friend still living with his parents, by enacting a series of particularly juvenile pranks. At one point, Dawn picks him up on this saying: 'You're how old, thirty?'[112] In one of the interviews that make up the box set, Gervais talks about how the series is intended to emphasize the 'men as boys, women as adults' dichotomy as a fundamental flaw in the characters' working environment.[113] As Rhodes and Westwood suggest, the workplace starts to channel the 'characterization of male figures in [wider] British sitcoms as childish, childlike or even infantilized'.[114] This builds on the relationship that is already established in domestic comedy from the late Victorian period onwards – starting with the Grossmiths – and which forms the basis of the suburban sitcom.

As Jeffrey Richards says, there is also a key trope of 'eternal boyishness' embodying the 'irreverence and incompetence' of British men as 'overgrown schoolboys' that runs throughout British comedy – he gives, as another example, the high jinks of aged pranksters in the nation's longest-running sitcom, *The Last of the Summer Wine* (1973–2010).[115] *Men Behaving Badly* was clearly predicated on this dynamic, with the female characters representing adulthood while Gary and Tony run amok. While the series is a comic critique of the overt and open childishness of the new 'laddish' culture, the show also tapped into a longer-held view that there was something ostensibly 'middle-aged' about office work (see, for instance, Gary's colleague George, who is so unutterably boring that he has a favourite paperclip) that could drive the office clerk into crisis.[116] Gary's outrageous behaviour in his leisure time and at home is an attempt to create distance from the expectations of office work and the office worker. In popular culture, then, the clerk has disproportionately suffered from reactive mid-life crises that involve reverting to a pattern of immature behaviours as a response. It is more often, though, in the necessarily adult world of the work environment that these behaviours become most overt and at their most comedic.

In P. D. James's 'A Very Commonplace Murder', this piqued introspection takes a more sinister turn. 'Pedantic, respectable, censorious Ernest Gabriel', filing clerk, murders a woman from across the street that he has been observing from his office late at night, following a short tirade about his 'Sixteen years of the same job, the same bedsitting room, the same half-tolerant dislike on the part of the staff'.[117] The woman's young lover is hanged and, while Gabriel attends the court case and could save the young man's life by admitting that he saw him leave the woman's flat alone, he is concerned he will be sacked. Instead, then, Gabriel puts his own job ahead of the life of an innocent man. In a similar vein, B. S. Johnson's Christie Malry is another chilling parody of the clerk, driven to violence by the frustrations of office work. Malry takes the 'Double-Entry' system of accounting, repetitively reinforced in his bureaucratic labour, and turns it into a manifesto for karmic living; carefully balancing 'Aggravation' against 'Recompense' and issuing punishments and penalties that escalate from removing paper clips to the death of '20,479 innocent West Londoners'.[118] Both of these examples play upon the assumption that the male clerk is immutable, that even amidst the throes of a mid-life crisis he is considered a benign figure. They also draw attention to what Williams so carefully parodied in *The Wimbledon Poisoner*, that the little man is dangerous because he 'thinks the world owes him something'.[119]

Williams' own fictional rendering of the male mid-life crisis is more typical than those of James and Johnson. His main character, Henry Farr, makes a public declaration of the state of mind of the middle-aged office worker, who, he argues, lives in a state of perpetual existential turmoil. Farr's homily at Doctor Templeton's funeral is an attempt to 'destabilise bourgeois society' and, like Reginald's speech at the seminar on 'Fruit in Instant Puddings', Tim's outburst in the training event, and David Brent's talk on the philosophy of motivation, ultimately fails. Together, these examples form a collective of the harmless rantings of the disenfranchised, middle-aged, white-collar worker who is unlikely to cause any damage or incite substantial change. More radical actions, like those taken by Ernest Gabriel or Christie Malry, remain on the fringes of fantasy; they revel in the sheer unlikelihood of an accountant committing a brutal murder or a clerk poisoning half of the people living in a London suburb. As accounting historian

Jeacle posits, there are very specific behaviours and characteristics ascribed to office workers – particularly those who handle accounts – and they all remain wedded to the concept of the 'dull and grey suited bore', who, even at the point of crisis, is unlikely to affect real change.[120]

Retirement/redundancy

The mid-life crisis also signals the impending proximity of another stage of working life. Retirement – or in some cases redundancy – is posited in certain stereotypical ways in impressions of office work, many of which are connected to the characteristics ascribed to white-collar workers but also the lower middle class more widely. In early examples from literature, this often derived from the common reality that career-long posts were held with one company (thus implying that clerks were cautious, unambitious, unimaginative). Following this corporate devotion, the symbolic gift and arbitrary ceremony enacted upon retirement felt like a shallow symbol of a working lifetime. As such, and as Michael Heller discusses in his economic history of the clerk, resentment became an overriding emotion felt by many upon retirement. He refers to end-of-career reflections that focus on the 'potential failure to deliver promotion and social mobility, [thus] thwarting years of hard work and pent up aspirations'.[121] Charles, one of the characters in George Gissing's *The Odd Women* (1893), makes a similar observation:

> He commences life as an ill-paid clerk, his ambitions are never encouraged, all the hopes of his manhood are thwarted, his employer can get numberless others to replace him at even less than he earns; and so he continues at the only calling he is capable of following and with nearly every feeling soured by adversity – he dies: a hard-worked, ill-paid clerk from beginning to end.[122]

Gissing captured the sense of futility for many lower-middle-class clerks – the life of paper pushing was neither well-paid, intellectually invigorating nor respected by wider society. In the 1950s, as one journalist put it, little had changed: '[pen-pushing] invites contemplation of an elderly figure perched on a high stool in some Dickensian office condemned to copy, with hope and ambition long since dead'.[123] While middle-class professionals are protected from social disdain by qualifications, professional affiliations and pay, lower-middle-class office workers continue to be seen as 'trapped' by lower-grade jobs; having a 'typical' office job is considered a failure to do anything better.

This narrative is not only dismissive of the careers of older clerks, but it also deters young office workers, who view a career in the office as a poor one. Wider cultural references to an office job as something that is temporary – on the path to better – reinforce this sentiment. In contemporary crime drama *Shakespeare and Hathaway* (2019), undercover detective Lou Hathaway refers to herself as having 'just a boring office job' when she wants to avoid being asked further questions about her life. Eleanor Oliphant raises the same point when she says that no one responds to the statement that she works in an office, because it is self-explanatory, with further details being assumed uninteresting. Equally prevalent is a discourse around office work as a temporary fix whilst making space for something more creative.

On his father's deathbed, Colin's mother (in *Colin's Sandwich*) goes so far as to refer to her husband's life as wasted because it has been spent in the office. She challenges her son to leave British Rail rather than becoming trapped by indecision: 'Your father spent the first ten years at the Inland Revenue "thinking about it." And then the worst possible happened. The bastards made him district manager.'[124] She too refers to the way that the clerical world seduced the office worker into committing their life to a purpose that she views as meaningless (in shorthand, the Inland Revenue, like the Internal Revenue Service (IRS) in the United States, is at the very top of a hierarchy of overly bureaucratic institutions). Colin recognizes that there is 'no way out' and that the job will trap him until at least retirement and the 'whisky decanter' he will no doubt receive as a token of a lifetime's service.[125]

This reference to the decanter articulates another common trope in white-collar culture – the presentation of a symbolic gift that marks, however benignly, the years spent with one company. The tradition dates to the Victorian age, where often a clock was given as a present on retirement – it stood for time served as well as being a weighty gesture in terms of quality and cost. The metaphor of the clock in office work, however, can be traced back to Charles Dickens, when he writes in *Sketches by Boz* (1836) about a clerk working beneath a symbolic timepiece: 'There he sits till five o'clock, working on, all day, as regularly as the dial over the mantel-piece, whose loud ticking is as monotonous as his whole existence.'[126] For Dickens, the constant reminder of time passing serves as a reiteration of what is a futile countdown through career, retirement and ultimately towards death.

In Frank Swinnerton's novel *The Young Idea* (1910), clerks Hilda and Galbraith similarly feel the pressure of their youth slipping away as they hear the dominant sound of the office clock 'add[ing] to the flying seconds'.[127] The pressure of the same sound drives Tony Hancock's character to madness in 1960s film *The Rebel*: 'You can't crush me in a monotonous soul-destroying routine for ever!' he shouts at his boss, before waiting for the clock to strike five so he can leave.[128] The constant reminder of time passing is a recurring feature in novels by Bullock, Wells (who called 'clock-watching' 'a common failing of human beings at work'), Canning, Nobbs, and television series ranging from office sitcom *The Squirrels* to 1990s crime drama, *Jonathan Creek*.[129] As Ricky Gervais explains about *The Office*: 'A lot of it is watching the clock ... the boredom of it, the sense of the clock ticking on the wall'.[130] These 'trappings of a familiar world', as Ben Thompson puts it, are those which create a lasting impression of the wider existential meanings of work, rendered both poignant and comedic as fundamental and relatable aspects of the everyday.[131]

Bullock's *Robert Thorne* offers a typical representation of the ironic moment in which the office worker is finally gifted a ceremonial clock on retirement – where clock watching ceases to matter. When elderly clerk Mr Hope is forced to retire from the Tax Office after thirty-seven years of service, he receives a marble clock as due token of a finished career. After a lifetime in the same office, Mr Hope is distraught at the minimalism of his goodbye:

> September came, and one morning in it Thomas woke up an official no more. The previous day there had been a little celebration in the Tax Office – a gathering in the Principal's room – a fulsome speech by the Principal, and a presentation to Thomas of a revolving chair and a marble clock ... His career was ended.[132]

Following his usual routine, Mr Hope's first morning of retirement sees him '[sitting] down to breakfast at the stroke of half-past eight on the presentation clock'.[133] The clock symbolizes rigid punctuality – one measure of Hope's embodiment of Taylorist principles. The point at which the fictional clerk's career ends is, perhaps, the clearest example of the pathos of the office, and Hope's feelings of redundancy further the impression of office workers as fundamentally so deeply moulded by their role that they unsuited to anything else – even retirement:

> [W]hat Mr Hope was, as man and citizen, does not matter I think. Before everything, in everything, he was an official. He lived for the office. It had his heart, filled his thoughts. Through the most of thirty years he had slaved devotedly; had shaped himself and been shaped into an almost perfect part of the machine. He never made a mistake. He knew every strand of the ropes. He seemed tireless. He was order itself. Like a planet he moved in eternal routine. You might set your watch by his doings.[134]

Young Robert Thorne offers this narration of Mr Hope's final moments in the office, drawing a metaphorical connection between the presentation clock and the inner workings of the 'tireless' machine to whom it has been presented.

In Collins's *London Belongs to Me*, Mr Josser is also presented with a 'handsome marble' mantel clock to mark his retirement, reminding him of the forty-two years that have passed whilst he was a clerk.[135] His boss condescendingly remarks, 'no more waiting about in the rain for the same old tram to take you home again', a comment which the reluctant retiree resents:

> Why shouldn't he wait about in the rain for trams if he wanted to? Waiting for trams in the rain suddenly seemed entirely delightful and proper. It was part of the old order of things that he had wanted to go on for ever and ever.[136]

Josser is lost not only to public-time but public-space; he no longer needs to travel, to engage with city life, or to fit in with a scheduled day. Ironically, after an eventful trip home with his gift, it no longer works – just like Mr Josser:

> There it stood on the mantelpiece – handsome, dominating, useless... Something had gone wrong with the striking part. Every few minutes, the clock roused itself as though it were going to play a full carillon, then paused for a moment and uttered a single hollow boom before relapsing into silence.[137]

The clock is thus a powerful metaphor for the retired man. At the end of the novel, and as the war demands more workers, Josser's return to his office as a much-needed worker (and a 'somebody again') is marked by a detailed description of his joyful return to commuter transport.[138] The 'alarm clock' wakes him and he eats his scrambled eggs 'with one eye on the presentation clock'.[139] His earlier reluctance to retire and his regret at being a clerk for so long cause an uneasy paradox that seems to symbolize popular representations of office work. While not wanting to leave – and in returning at the end of the novel to his 'old familiar' desk – there is in that moment of exit, nonetheless, resentment directed at his career: 'It was no longer Mr Frederick Josser, retired, who was standing there. It was the ghost of Mr Josser, junior, the courageous young clerk who was getting married on twenty-five shillings a week and his prospects.'[140]

This removal from the world of work is symbolically more poignant than the employer recognizes, and it is something that continues to hold emotional weight. In J. B. Priestley's *Angel Pavement* (1930), Mr Smeeth's deepest fear is not having his job anymore because of how far it defines him: 'Once he stopped being Twigg and Dersingham's cashier, what was he?'[141] Like Mr Hope, Mr

Smeeth is a clerk by more than just career; his behaviour marks the conflation of personality and occupation so often found in descriptions of white-collar work. Retirement is thus more significant for the office worker than those who pursue other careers, rendering this a distinctly lower-middle-class problem. The type of mechanization that characterizes modern administration is often portrayed as becoming deeply internalized, making retirement deeply disorientating, particularly for the same lower-middle-class figure who is a bureaucrat both in employment and in personality. The clock, in many ways, epitomizes the routinization of this behaviour, acting as a reminder about punctuality and precision beyond the point at which it is required but highlighting assumptions about how the clerk will remain subservient even into retirement.

There is a deep irony in the act of providing the retiree with another method of watching time pass – particularly towards the end of one's life. In 1980s sitcom *Ever Decreasing Circles*, Martin comes home one evening and tells his wife: 'they're letting old Bill Tidyman go … They're giving him a watch but he wanted a Teasmade'.[142] Bill's age ('old') indicates that letting him 'go' is euphemistically somewhere between a retirement and early redundancy, but 1980s office culture insists, like its Victorian predecessor, on giving a timepiece as a reminder of the time passed and a life lost to the daily grind. The simple sadness of the man who wanted something useful like a Teasmade but receives an unnecessary ornamental trifle adds additional pathos to poor Bill's departure, as does the fact that despite giving his career to Mole Valley Valves, Bill is a mere footnote to Martin's day at work.

Where retirement can be reluctant, the company's decision to remove a worker brings deep resentment, anger and a sense of 'redundancy' in every sense of the word. Priestley captured fear of redundancy in *Angel Pavement* in the 1930s, as he reflected on the gloomy conditions of the period and the uncertainty of white-collar labour in a time of transition. His cashier, Herbert Norman Smeeth, gives an existential soliloquy on the desperation that seemed, for many, to sum up the precariousness of the white-collar workplace:

> All round them was the darkness in which lurked the one great fear, the fear that he might take part no longer in these events, that he might lose his job … sometimes at night, when he could not sleep, it came to him with all its force and dreadfully illuminated the darkness with little pictures of shabby and broken men, trudging round from office to office, haunting the Labour Exchanges and the newspaper rooms of the Free Libraries, and gradually sinking into the workhouse and the gutter.[143]

While redundancy in the 1930s affected workers from all industries, there is emphasis on problematic redeployment of the clerical type because office workers are depicted not as being 'ordinary' people who opt to work in a particular environment but are seen as synonymous with the values and attributes of bureaucracy; they are, as we have seen, paper-pushers beyond their official capacity. Priestley pauses when describing Mr Smeeth to examine the cashier as wider society so often cast him:

> He looked what he ought to have been, in the opinion of a few thousand hasty and foolish observers of this life and what he was not – a grey drudge. They could easily see him as a drab ageing fellow for ever toiling away at figures of no importance, as a creature of the little foggy City street, of crusted ink-pots and dusty ledgers and day books, as a typical troglodyte of this dingy and absurd civilisation.[144]

Priestley attempts to override impressions of the white-collar worker as a drudge, grey and inert, but what he achieves is to further entrench the connection between the pen-pusher and the duties of the desk. Smeeth thrives on the endless 'neat little columns of figures, entering up ledgers and then balancing them'[145] and is incapable of imaging a world without these daily tasks. Redundancy is terrifying because it threatens the essence of Smeeth both as a worker and a man.

Similar socio-economic factors were identified in the final series of ITV's long-running *Reginald Perrin*, filmed in the 1990s. *The Legacy of Reginald Perrin* took these ideas around redundancy, turning them into a wider discourse about the role of white-collar workers when faced with a future in which they would no longer be needed. The series takes place after Reginald's – and Leonard Rossiter's – actual death (Reginald is struck by a falling billboard advertising the Royal and General Accident Insurance Company, ironic, the vicar points out, as it was the company 'with which he himself was insured').[146] The focus of the series is the last will and testament of Reginald Iolanthe Perrin, read before his gathered family and friends, each of whom are desperate for money because they are, to various extents, redundant. In a literal sense, Tom, Reginald's former son-in-law, has been sacked from his job in an estate agency because he is middle-aged. Despite no longer employed in this field, Tom puts his lack of imagination down to his status as a former estate agent – he is, by personality, if not professionally, a rigid and monotonous clerical machine.

During the series, Reginald's former secretary Joan is replaced with a 'twenty-two-year-old bimbo', and her new boyfriend loses his job as a result of being 'too old'.[147] Just like Lanchester's Mr Phillips, who narrates his first day of redundancy, these characters underscore the changing economic landscape of the late 1990s. Like Mr Phillips, Tom and Joan struggle with the serious – and often underappreciated – loss of identity, purpose and self-worth that is often associated with redundancy. Reginald's legacy gives them a focus, encouraging them to join forces to enact a rebellion on behalf of the elderly and the 'occupationally rejected'. As Jimmy says, people are being made redundant earlier and earlier, severing the assumption that redundancy only affects the nearly pensionable, while blurring the lines between voluntary and enforced semi-retired. When the council offer Richard Bucket early retirement in suburban sitcom *Keeping Up Appearances*, he is only too aware that he is being encouraged to leave. His wife Hyacinth, however, labours under the misapprehension that he is being offered some sort of reward, proudly boasting that 'not everyone gets offered early retirement'.[148] Like many white-collar workers, Richard is mortified at the thought of leaving the office, in part because it will mean spending all of his time with his wife. Richard's behaviour becomes erratic across series three and four, as a response to the emotional and psychological trauma of giving up work before he is ready.

Like the middle-aged crowd at the reading of Reginald's will, Mr Phillips is preoccupied with the distance between the youth and middle age. Lunch with his son reiterates the changes in the labour market and the social-scape of the 1990s. It also offers a perspective on the thrusting yuppies that thrived in Thatcherite culture from the position of those who were 'thrust' out of the way. When Jerry loses his job briefly in *The Good Life*, he confides in Tom that he cannot just walk into another job because he is 'Forty two'. 'At my executive level', he continues, 'that's practically senile'.[149] Anthea, secretary in *Men Behaving Badly*, responds to Gary's query about whether or not their office is suitable for a 'thrusting young business executive' by retorting that 'too many young people are scrambling to get ahead at the expense of older people'.[150]

In 2001, rising fears about redundancy were at the heart of the first series of *The Office*. Both at the level of senior management and by David Brent, redundancy is used variously as a threat and a crude method of encouragement. From the first episode onwards, Brent fails to appreciate the sensitivity of potential unemployment, wrongly assuming that he will not be affected. When he plays a cruel joke on Dawn, in which he pretends that she is sacked for stealing Post-It notes, Brent demonstrates a worrying naivety about the economic context in which he runs the branch. His redundancy at the end of the second series is, on one level, a fair retribution for his behaviour towards colleagues across the series. At the same time, there is a clear pathos in what follows: just as Jerry

Leadbetter predicts in *The Good Life*, middle-aged middle managers like David Brent struggle to find work at their previous level (Brent ends up as a travelling cleaning-supplies salesperson). His redundancy is also a form of 'death' (both in career terms and his relevance to the documentary upon which *The Office* is supposed to be based). Brent is no longer a 'main' character of the office, and his removal is a reminder of the cycle of retirement parties, leaving dos and awkward terminations of contract that take place in the workplace and from which individuals are rendered forgettable. *The Office*, like *Reginald Perrin* before it, foregrounds the tragedy that the office does not care about individuals. As Joe Moran puts it:

> It is about the forgetfulness of office life, the way that its impersonal procedures do not acknowledge the finite trajectory of individual lives, despite the leaving dos and retirement parties that lamely suggest otherwise.[151]

The office does not care about Mr Hope and Mr Josser's dismay at their meagre leaving parties or Richard's turmoil at having to give up work; it does not want Tom Good back when he toys with earning money again. Typing and phone calls resume, gossip moves on to cover new topics and desks are quickly de- and then re-personalized by new occupants.

There is little optimism in ending this chapter on redundancy, but in many ways, it mirrors the lifespan of the fictional office worker. Other working groups are more commonly associated with the economic and social consequences of mass redundancies – many blue-collar workforces have had their cultural legacy shaped by the systematic dismantling of their industry – but there is a quiet thread of despondency woven into the clerical career across the twentieth century. In *The Full Monty*, the 1997 film that tackles the industrial downturn in Sheffield in the 1990s, the depictions of unemployment come not only from the steelworkers who are on the dole but the redundancy of their lower-middle-class foreman, Gerald, who has yet to break the news to his wife that he has no work. Like Mr Phillips, he cannot face the disruption to his suburban lifestyle; the loss of his garden-gnomed bungalow and holidays abroad are a deep blow to his sense of self. Redundancy reiterates the perilous position of the lower-middle-class office worker who can quickly lose everything once they have no income. The garden gnomes are an ironic symbol, like the aspidistra in Orwell's work, of the fragile social status of the clerk. Gerald's utter desolation at his redundancy is equally a marker of the deep association between the white-collar worker and white-collar work; like so many lower-middle-class characters before him,

Gerald is typecast as a boring bureaucratic figure who, as his working-class colleagues assume, would not be interested in their striptease plans.

The subsequent chapters on the suburbs explore these markers of status in further detail, but the office is hugely significant in shaping attitudes towards the white-collar worker that bridge the gap between work and home. The caricatured behaviour of the office worker informs stereotypes about the commuter and the suburban in popular culture, many of which take behaviours associated with mechanization, bureaucratic pedantry and hierarchical compliance as a starting point. This leads to assumptions about rigid, routinized and unhappy clerkly types forming the groundwork for impressions of the lower middle class. In this way, the historical connection between the rise of white-collar industries and the emergence of the lower middle class has retained its meaning in contemporary representations and cultural iconography.

3

The commute

Where once only those with very highly paid professional jobs would have commuted into the city from outside of its boundaries, now commuting up to an hour is a reasonable expectation for all types of workers. While flexible working patterns have allowed some white-collar employees to travel to work less frequently since the 1980s, the distances that are covered have increased over the last century, and particularly in recent years, which means the commute retains its significance, even if it is no longer a *daily* part of our lives.[1] Culturally, the commute has become particularly synonymous with the white-collar classes; images of suited pen pushers flooding out of railway carriages during rush hour are indeed symbolic of modern life. Despite this significance, the commute is a fascinatingly transitional space – or 'third space', as Gail Cunningham has referred to it – and one that, for that reason, often slips between the critical cracks of suburban and urban analyses.[2] Crucial as a growing border between home and work, the commute is essentially a site that blurs the boundaries of each. In contemporary society, laptop, tablet and phone users co-opt the journey on public transport into additional work time (if not as fully functional work 'space'), while as a site without managerial surveillance (and for which most are not paid) it can equally be viewed as forced leisure time suitable for little else but reading, streaming videos or listening to music. For those who commute by car, it is often considered 'dead' time, with increasing traffic jams and overcrowding on the roads rendering many commuters spending longer getting to work and cutting down on their time at home in order to compensate.

This chapter examines the commute from the perspective of the lower-middle-class white-collar worker. It analyses the various attributes associated with the commuter from the earliest days of suburban and railway expansion to the contemporary car share as a twenty-first-century response to environmentally aware practices. In doing so, the chapter posits that the commute is a complex site in which lower-middle-class workers are often portrayed as seething towards the urban centre, part of an indistinctive mass that signals towards the deep dehumanization that will take place in the office environment. It also explores the journey home, and the process through which the white-collar worker renegotiates status from employee to family figure and the reintegration into the domestic sphere that is often commented on, particularly at the turn of the twentieth century, where gendered depictions of suburbia as a deeply feminine space contributed to the undermining of lower-middle-class masculinities.

Rush hour

Certain cultural tropes have certainly dominated representations of the commute and the commuter. Many of these are connected to the urban and suburban development of the south-east, in particular – although, of course, commuting is now a core part of many British working lives. It is in the history of the structural and economic foundations of the capital that the roots of modern-day work-travel are most often studied, however, and from where most historical examples are drawn. The relationships between the commuter, the railways and London suburbs certainly form the basis of many analyses of contemporary travel, while the dominant imagery of the Tube as a form of common transport is, of course, disconnected from its limited geographical scope.

It was the railways above all other forms of travel that became synonymous with the contemporary commute, particularly as trains were part of a triumvirate of economic advancements that historically connected office work and the suburbs. The development of a regular commuter service by train, as Nick Barratt outlines, occurred once the new generation of white-collar workers started to look outside of the city for accommodation in the latter half of the nineteenth century.[3] Government legislation in 1863 encouraged rail companies to consider this growing market rather than continuing their expansion of inter-city networks.[4] A workforce that was professional and thus worked fixed hours in the centre of the city was perfectly placed to make the most of the regular commuter trains, and their desire to separate leisure and work, like the middle class, meant that they were keen to move their families further out of town. As Michael Freeman points out, the population of London's outer suburban ring increased by 'roughly 50 per cent every ten years between 1861 and 1891', a move dominated not by manual labourers, as in cities like Manchester during the Industrial Revolution, but bureaucracy.[5]

Suburbia was, in effect, a 'railway state', with seventy stations opening after 1919 in London alone as part of the development of various suburbs, most of which were subsidized by the companies that would pass through them.[6] The Metropolitan railway company even developed its own suburbs after the Metropolitan Inner Circle Completion Act of 1874, granting building licenses, taking ground rents and becoming the Metropolitan Railway Country Estates before promoting the famous Metroland in the 1930s.[7] The honeyed tones of the smart new posters that highlighted the space, light and vibrancy of mass suburbia lured potential new commuters with details of routes and travel times, as well as pitching features such as the new electric lighting and inside bathrooms.

Suburban train schedules dictated the rhythm of the day and led to the patterns of behaviour that saw the commuter community becoming widely recognizable. In particular, the railway station became more than a simple site of glamour and exoticism, connecting travellers with holidays, long-distance travel and adventure. Instead, the commuter crowd needed to negotiate the space at high speed in order to arrive at work punctually. Rather than the excitement of the long voyage or the emotion of the farewell, the commuter encountered the station as part of an intensely regulated and everyday experience. John Ruskin put it this way: commuters are those '[who], being in a hurry, are therefore, for the time being, miserable'.[8] Ruskin implies that the decorative aspects of railway architecture are thus lost on the worker who is primarily concerned about being on time.

George Beard took this idea further when he argued that the modern obsession with punctuality (cultivated once getting to work no longer occurs simply by travelling on foot) contributed to a 'neurosis of modernity' itself. In *American Nervousness* (1880), Beard 'blamed the perfection of clocks and the invention of watches for causing nervousness wherein "a delay of a few moments might destroy the hopes of a lifetime".[9] In the same year, pressure from the growing railway network encouraged Britain to standardize the use of Greenwich Mean Time (often referred to colloquially as 'Railway Time') in order to synchronize timetables.[10] One news article pointed out that a mis-intended side effect of GMT was that commuters arrived at the station only to find they had just missed their trains. Stations could no longer keep their clocks fast to help those travelling by rail stand a better chance of catching the train. Time was now the great regulator of behaviour not only in the office but outside of it.

As early as 1889, for example, one commentator in *The Times* went so far as to attribute ill-health to the obsession with the clock, calling many clerks 'suburban dyspeptics' because '[they] eat breakfast with time-tables in their minds and their eyes on the clocks'.[11] H. G. Wells commented on something similar when he had this to say about the clerk: 'I've seen hundreds of 'em, bit of breakfast in hand, running wild and shining to catch their little season ticket train'.[12] His commuters eat on the hoof, unable even to find time to partake in the family meal that should start the day. By the 1990s, as Joe Moran observes, eating breakfast on the go was so ubiquitous that food companies started marketing the breakfast bar as a solution to the morning rush.[13] While we have reconciled ourselves to breakfast *à la* commute, little has changed when it comes to the anxiety that rushing around in the morning brings. In *The Fall and Rise of Reginald Perrin*, Reginald embodies commuter angst with his 'body sloping forward in its anxiety not to miss the eight-sixteen'.[14] Given that his train is rarely on time, this description underscores the irony in the commuter hurrying towards the station only to arrive late to work. Webb argues that this type of anxiety disproportionately affects train commuters because, unlike those who walk to work, missing a train does not mean being a few minutes late to work but involves waiting for the next train.[15]

Nobbs's portrayal echoes *Robert Thorne* and the narrator who paints a picture of the thousands of clerks who 'time [their] rate of progress by the public clocks' as they walk to work.[16] In his history of railway stations, Richards talks about the fashion for featuring clocks in station designs (which seeped into popular romantic phraseology as 'meet me under the clock'),[17] but there are more quotidian implications. Vast clerical buildings such as the Refuge Assurance Company Building in Manchester – now opposite Manchester's Oxford Road station, one of the busiest in the country – were and are a prominent reminder of the pressure to live by a strict timetable. In another of Bullock's novels (*Mr Ruby Jumps the Traces*), it is this constant pressure that forces a revolution of sorts from the main character. Mr Ruby hears the clock striking ten; it should dictate the start of his working day, but in an act of defiance he deliberately ignores it, drifting away from the route he has taken twice daily for twenty-six years. Perrin's rebellion similarly begins when he takes the unorthodox decision to catch the 'eight forty-six' rather than the 'eight-sixteen'.[18] This seemingly underwhelming mutiny derives meaning from the cultural connotations of the rigid daily routine and the inflexible office worker. And, literature is full of office workers who are depicted as desperate to break the bonds of the commute.

Mr Ruby tests the waters by ignoring the clock but finds its pull too persuasive: 'linger[ing] a few minutes under the clock: [he] yielded to force of habit at last, and joined the stream of workers making across the Bridge'.[19]

Bullock captures the sense of frustration at being lost in a crowd in his works, and in doing so, he draws attention to what is a recurrent trope in the depiction of commuting, and which is ultimately epitomized in the title of Pooter's diary: *The Diary of a Nobody*. Cunningham talks at length about the ways in which the commute represented a 'daily signifier of the depersonalized mass' in Victorian and early twentieth century literature, with the journey into the city evoking the shift from personal/domestic/suburban to professional/urban that the term 'to commute' ('to change (for or into)') implies.[20]

In *Psmith in the City* (1910), Wodehouse talks about the disorientation that this transformation brings to a young clerk, taking part in his first London rush hour:

> Nobody seemed to look at him. He was permitted to alight at St Paul's and make his way up Queen Victoria Street without any demonstration. He followed the *human stream* till he reached the Mansion House, and eventually found himself at the massive building of the New Asiatic Bank, Limited.[21]

The passivity with which Mike approaches the bank echoes C. F. G. Masterman's words in *The Condition of England* (1909), when he famously describes the commuter as being 'sucked into the City at daybreak [and] scattered again as darkness falls'.[22] Masterman was very cynical about mechanization, and the commute becomes another platform on which the office worker performs as a soulless automaton. In one description he implies that commuters are deeply dehumanized: 'It is in the City crowds, where the traits of individual distinction have become merged in the aggregate, [that] the impression (from a distance) is of little white blobs of faces borne upon little black twisted or misshapen bodies'.[23] Masterman has no desire to become part of this distorted mass, but he views them from outside; he has no need to fit in.

Cunningham captures the use of watery metaphors to describe the movement of commuters when she refers to the 'passive flotsam on the twice-daily tide'.[24] These descriptions deny the commuter an identity beyond that of the mass, diminishing the individuality that was sought by moving out of the city and into the suburbs in the first place. By reducing commuters to a soulless form – the 'blobs' and 'misshapen bodies' of Masterman's descriptions – commentators were able to destabilize the individual, whilst continuing to connect the much-maligned suburbs with the dehumanized automaton who mindlessly followed the mass into the city centre. Writers like Bullock tried to re-establish the distinctiveness of each individual that made up the commuter crowd:

> There are thousands like him. There they go, hurrying for the bridges, each in his cheap black coat, each with pale face and uneven shoulders: thousands of then. Slaves of the desk. Twopenny clerks. And he is one of them, just a little higher in the clerkly scale perhaps, just a little superior in attainments and status maybe: but unmistakably one of them. A Twopenny clerk. Why, yes. Still he, with all the others, is to be respected. He is doing his best … Also he has a soul, this figure that I see in the crowd, and he has an ideal.[25]

Of note is that Virginia Woolf wrote a similar description of the commuter rush in *Night and Day* (1919). The novel deals with middle-class protagonist Katherine's complex relationship with a lower-middle-class solicitor's clerk. At first, her snobbishness prevents her from seeing Ralph Denham as little more than an automaton, but she later realizes that even within a cascade of clerks merging seamlessly into the rush-hour traffic, he is an individual:

> She ran as far as the Tube station, overhauling clerk after clerk, solicitor after solicitor. Not one of them even faintly resembled Ralph Denham. More and more plainly did she see him; and more and more did he seem to her *like no one else*.[26]

Woolf's depiction of Denham as distinctive ran counter to many popular references to the faceless troupe of lower-middle-class workers streaming into the city. In the novel, this passage marks a moment in which Katherine must also confront her own (and her parents') assumptions about the lower middle class, who, until this point, have been little more than on the vague peripheries of her own existence. Suddenly, Katherine wants to belong to the crowd, to be immersed within the white-collar class, rather than directionless and without purpose outside of it.

Like other literary texts at the time, Bullock and Woolf paint a picture of the crowd within which it was so easy to become anonymous and undervalued. As early as 1872, Paul-Gustave Doré and Blanchard Jerrold depicted London Bridge with its mass of suited workers surging across the river towards the city, just as Victorian and Edwardian postcards show sepia-toned scenes of bowler hats and dark suits. Magritte did something similar; his bowler-hatted figure (first in 'Golconda' (1953) as part of a rain-cloud of similarly suited and hatted workers and later with his face covered by an apple in 'Son of Man' (1964)) is a visual rendition of the anonymity of the clerical worker seamlessly merging into the mass. The persistence of this imagery long into the twentieth century demonstrates the few changes to the white-collar workforce. Even contemporary renditions depict rush hour as a seething mass of suits; individuals crossing

London Bridge are merely contemporary versions of their nineteenth- and twentieth-century counterparts. While fewer wear hats, carry briefcases (although these have their modern equivalency in the laptop bag) or are called 'clerks', they are, in essentials, the same. When Chris Moss wrote about his experience of commuting in 2013, he harked back to the lines of T. S. Eliot in 'The Waste Land': 'A crowd flowed over London Bridge, so many, I had not thought death had undone so many' – Moss even referred to himself as one of Eliot's 'zombies'.[27]

Contemporary artists like Mark Sanders continue to focus on this sombre tribe crossing London Bridge. Sanders talks about the influence of L. S. Lowry in the description to *Urbis* (2016), his free newspaper collection of photographs that capture contemporary commuting. He takes as his focus the 'human conveyor belt' that makes its way across London, harking back to the imagery of writers like Bennett who depicted the mechanized arrival of workers, spewed out by commuter trains.[28] This terminology is also deeply enshrined in attitudes to rush hour – the human conveyor belt is deeply associated with the white-collar workplace.

Contributing to this sense of uniformity was, and remains, the way that the lower-middle-class office worker dressed. John Betjeman's 1972 book *London's Historic Railway Stations* features a striking photograph by John Gay of the commuter crowd arriving at London Victoria station. Captioned 'ten to nine on a weekday morning', the shot makes clear the conformity of office dress on the commuter platform.[29] Taken from behind (as people walk down the platform towards work), men are, without exception, in suits or with dark, formal raincoats. Women are dressed, almost as uniformly, in skirts and jackets, carrying handbags in the place of briefcases. Sanders's twenty-first-century photographs offer a telling similarity, not only in the images of pre-occupied and weary faces but in also what his commuters are wearing. Office clothing has changed very little over the twentieth and twenty-first centuries, and while people often dress more informally (and women no longer only wear skirts or dresses), the suit remains customary, particularly in the city. What this continuity has shaped is a powerfully long-lasting visual synchronicity to the commuter crowd.

Sanders's images also draw attention to the subtle differences in the morning and evening commutes. On the way to work, commuters are collectively preened, prepared (or preparing on the train), coffee in hand and facing the prospect of the day ahead. Tie in hand as they race up the station steps to make the train home, individuals are dishevelled, exhausted and yet, strangely triumphant at the working day's close. The unarticulated space in between (the office) is responsible for this shift in embodied attitude, but the commute has its own psychological power. John Lanchester refers to this in *Mr Phillips* when he describes office workers entering central London as 'tired at the beginning of the day and febrilely energetic ... on the way home'.[30] This moment, captured also in *The Rebel* as a large crowd of city clerks charge through the streets and onto the waiting trains, is a significant marker of the various shifts in status that the commuter encounters across the working day – what author Julian Barnes refers to as the 'twice-daily metamorphosis'.[31] The commute is part of an endless cycle (home – commute – work – commute – home) that separates the private and the public, while not quite being either. Simon Webb talks about it as liminal – a space of acclimatization – which can prepare the commuter for each of these sites, but it must also have its own set of significations.[32] The commute is not merely a state in between but a space in its own right, and yet it remains difficult to articulate. What is clear is that a series of behaviours have become associated with the psychological state of commuting, which is deeply entrenched in both historic and contemporary assumptions about the white-collar commuter.

What is clear is that there are a set of conventions that accompany depictions of the commute, many of which have remained remarkably static across the nineteenth and twentieth centuries. One of the most cited literary examples is W. Pett Ridge's humorous depiction of commuter hoards leaving a suburban crescent:

> At about eight-twenty every week-day morning The Crescent dispatches its grown-up male inhabitants in search of gold. The adventurers set out, each with a small brown bag, and, excepting on rainy mornings, are silk-hatted, because there are many ways of getting on in the city, but none apparently in which a silk hat is not indispensable.[33]

Pett Ridge parodies the metaphor of the suburban commuter as an adventurer – the men return, sadly, as he writes, without any treasure or even measurable evidence of success. In many respects, these unheroic commuters are the predecessors to Mr Brown of *Dad's Army* theme-tune fame. Like the 'Well Respected Man' of The Kinks' song, Mr Brown is characterized as dull and unadventurous, sombrely following his daily routines. The Home Guard is semi-mockingly postulated as the answer to this tedious existence, offering Mr Brown a chance to prove himself as a man while trying something out of the ordinary. The reality, as the humorous escapades of the sitcom show, is that the Home Guard offers merely another opportunity for rigid behaviours and petty hierarchies.

In R. F. Delderfield's *The Dreaming Suburb* (1958), the author lists the morning departure times for each of The Avenue's commuters, giving the reader a sense of regularity. This implies that each character is moulded and shaped by the need for habit, a feature that becomes a comic marker of rigidity in, for instance, Captain Mainwaring's absolute insistence on opening the bank at exactly nine o'clock each morning – Mrs Gray observes that on the one occasion she thought he might be late, it was the clock that was wrong, and not Mainwaring.[34] These specific details add weight to the humorous image of the white-collar worker as an automaton who subliminally desires routine – just as David Nobbs mentions that Reginald stands 'at his usual place on the platform, in front of the door marked "Isolation Telephone"'.[35] In wartime texts like *The Dreaming Suburbs*, one of the sombre markers of the continuing everyday are the rhythms with which commuters leave and return to the suburb. This becomes particularly poignant as individuals start to disappear from the crowd on the platform as they are called up for service – in this instance, exchanging one set of routines and procedures for another.

Delderfield talks about the reluctance of commuters to make small talk on the platform once war is in full swing. After the flutter of excitement about what the war might mean, and the sharing of early gossip, the office workers waiting for the train become reluctant to converse, slipping back into their commuter behaviours: 'the train catchers took to spacing themselves out along the platform, and awaiting their trains in gloomy silence'.[36] Rather than the strategic positioning for a seat and the jostling to get on-board first, the tone has shifted to reflect the wartime context and the unwillingness to give voice to new fears. As well as heightening the impression of the commute as a silent space in which small talk is somehow painful, this new awareness of separateness along the platform demonstrates how the war has altered the everyday. Rather than using strategic placement to ensure a comfortable commute, the depleted number of figures making the journey into the city are hiding from each other. Joe Moran cites a returning veteran who writes in 1946 about the 'brief flowering of wartime community' and the 'return of English reserve' soon after;[37] Delderfield's novel marks the natural return to what has already been established as characteristically national reticence, once the initial interruption of the war becomes normalized. This association between the commuter and 'English reserve' has long permeated impressions of daily life, in a manner in conflict with the tactical aggression deployed in order to get a seat.

This short cessation of hostility when boarding the train is particularly telling; Delderfield captures the changing tone of wartime life and the reluctance

Figure 3.1 Fighting for a seat on *The 7.39* (2014)
© BBC

to engage in combative or aggressive behaviour. In contrast with Delderfield's commuters, in the 'Commuter's Sonnet' in 1903, the poet talks of how the 'people, like stampeded cattle, rushed/and, jamming one another, pushed and crushed' when the train arrived. This sense of a physical fight to get onto the train has been picked up again in contemporary depictions, particularly with the media covering rising overcrowding on commuter services in the south-east and north-west of England. In the 2014 drama *The 7.39*, Sally ends her mobile phone conversation so that she is prepared to 'fight for a seat'; the commuter beside her on the platform knowingly adds: 'here we go. Elbows out' (Figure 3.1).[38] Tom O'Dell addresses this in contemporary sociological terms as a distinct marker of the shift between the individual (walking to the station, waiting on the platform) and the moment in which the train arrives when the mass emerges, surging onto the train and fighting desperately for a seat. If victorious, the commuter can then return to a space of individual privacy (the opened newspaper, the headphones, with closed eyes).[39]

Early examples discuss middle-class commuters – with only six to a railway carriage – who spend their journeys in silence, respecting each occupant's right to read their newspaper in peace while preparing for the day ahead. When Aldous Huxley wrote about season-ticket holders in *Along the Road* (1925), he drew attention to the unforgivable sin made by the lower-middle-class suburban commuter, who was not acclimatized to the conditions of the commute:

> It is possible at a distance to feel the most lively curiosity about a season-ticket holder from Surbiton. His bald head is so shiny; he has such a funny waxed moustache; he gets so red in the face when he talks to his friends about the socialists; he laughs with such unpleasant gusto when one of them tells a dirty

story; he sweats so profusely when it is hot; he holds forth so knowledgeably about roses; and his sister lives at Birmingham; his son has just won a prize for mathematics at school ... One loves the little man; he is wonderful, charming, a real slice of life. But make his acquaintance ... From that day forth you take pains to travel in another compartment.[40]

Huxley imbues his observations with the sort of tongue-in-cheek satire that was so readily directed at the suburban class by this point. The season-ticket holder is 'little', like many of the lower-middle-class stereotypes of the period, but Huxley also draws on the type of social insecurity that makes his Surbiton commuter brash, awkward and sweaty. He neatly captures so many of the varying impressions about the lower middle class: nuances about baldness (middle age), gardening, political beliefs and educational aspirations further impressions of the clerk as someone for the middle-class commuter to avoid. Crucially, the Surbiton commuter threatens the social tenor of the railway compartment in his fundamental lack of respect for the vow of silence that has so often been a dictate of the successful commute.

In a more extreme example, in Raymond Postgate's *Somebody at the Door* (1943), miser Henry Grayling gets the suburban train home unwittingly in a carriage full of people who later each turn out to have a reason to kill him. In many ways a commuter-focused rendition of Agatha Christie's *Murder on the Orient Express* (1934), Grayling's brutal murder by gas poisoning takes the premise of the silent indifference of the carriage full of commuters and turns it into a deadly absence. Combined with the black comedy found frequently in fiction about the lower-middle-class – in works such as B. S. Johnson's *Christie Malry's Own Double-Entry*, P. D. James's 'A Very Commonplace Murder', Nigel Williams's *The Wimbledon Poisoner* and *The Rise and Fall of the Queen of Suburbia* by Sarah May – the innocuous commuter, passive and indifferent, is turned into an unlikely source of explosive violence.

Perceived British reluctance to make small talk has become a common feature in representations. In his *Compendium for the London Commuter* (2013), Chris Moss refers to 'the procession of silent spectres' that makes up the contemporary commute but his description matches both a comment in *The Railway Traveller's Handy Book* (1869) and a complaint raised in the 1970s to the *Daily Telegraph*.[41] As a result, the commute is often a space of overcrowding but simultaneously of silence, what Moran refers to as 'collectively experienced solitude'.[42] This is, in many ways, connected to ideas surrounding the anonymity that can be sought within urban communities, but it is also specific to the physical proximity that the commute can entail and the sensitivity of negotiating personal space. An anonymous 'Tube Chat?' badge campaign in 2016 – and the indignant backlash that it provoked – was one twenty-first-century marker of the communication complexities of a generation that are more connected digitally than ever before but who are increasingly suffering from a lack of face-to-face conversation. As an article in *The Guardian* reviewing the campaign pointed out, 'the perception of the London commuter as an unfriendly curmudgeon has been bolstered' by the response to the suggestion to talk.[43]

This is also an issue brought up by Martin Clunes as *Reggie Perrin* in the BBC's 2009 revamp. While updating David Nobbs's 1970s series, the revision puts the commute centre stage in the design of the opening credits – simple, animated figures appear on a screen symbolizing the arrival onto the station platform; a train moves in front of the commuters, stopping only to eject a lonely, suited Perrin on another platform. This replaces the live-action credits of the original series that showed Reginald Perrin walking down a beach, taking off his clothes and stepping into the sea. It implies that commuting is perhaps one of the most relevant connections between 1970s lower-middle-class culture and contemporary life. The style of the new title sequence also references the animated simplicity of Bob Godfrey's 1970 satire on British sexuality *Henry 9 'til 5*, which features simple black and white figures in identical hats reading identical newspapers on the train to work.

Early in the first episode, and faced with a crowd of zombie-like commuters, Perrin, who like Henry frequently indulges in fantasies, enters a dream sequence that sees him cutting the cord of the nearest passenger's headphones before shouting to the occupants of the train carriage, 'Let's all have a chat!'[44] Heads turn and a general conviviality erupts between passengers as they talk, joke and bond. For the viewer, the comedy comes from the sheer unlikeliness of the scenario, rendered ironic by a quick shift back to the silent carriage, full of rigid and unspeaking commuters (Figure 3.2). Across the series, Perrin offers an increasingly aggressive series of comments, questions and insults to his fellow passengers, all of which go unheard due to the headsets and determined passivity of the commuters. More dramatic still, Reggie even mentions one incident to his wife in which someone vomits into their laptop but refuses to admit it, preferring to continue typing 'stickily' rather than acknowledge emotion, vulnerability or weakness.[45]

Across the two series, this reboot makes the commute a more central part of Reggie's experience, and his rising frustrations are in line with a growing media dialogue about the poor quality of rail travel for the nation's commuters. Overcrowding is a source of much press attention; as people are forced closer

Figure 3.2 Enduring the silence in *Reggie Perrin* (2010)
© BBC

together, many attempt to enact a level of privacy that is hard to retain in packed conditions. In the heat wave of 2018, *The Independent* issued a tongue-in-cheek guide to travelling in the heat, in which it made clear that the usual rule of never 'making eye contact with strangers on the commute, especially in the capital' was even more significant when 'everyone on the underground is visibly melting'.[46]

O'Dell makes clear that the ultimate target for the railway commuter is the successful acquisition of a seat, or, failing that, a suitably private space (the areas near the doors are often desirable because they can be fashioned into closed-off standing spaces, whereas being wedged in between aisles should be avoided). In *The 7.39*, Carl suggests to Sally that people deliberately pretend to read a book so that they can avoid conversation; the performance of opening a book creates a symbolic privacy that can provide a social boundary. The strategic position of regular commuters gives them a better chance of winning these small victories, as the recent outrage at a London Underground decision to mark out the position of each carriage door in paint on the platform made clear.[47] Commuters were angry that infrequent users of the service would acquire tactical knowledge, losing them their edge gained through the experience of being a 'regular'. Considerable emotional investment alongside strategy and planning are directed at the temporary ownership of a tangible space, as Carl's outburst at Sally makes clear when she sits in a seat that he has visually marked out as his own. In his contemporary novel *Barry Desmond Is a Wanker* (2010), Martin Knight refers to 'personnel managers for Shell or Unilever [who] would so easily revert to playground aggression' in a bid to get a seat on the train.[48] The 'unseemly race' and physical altercations of 'grown men com[ing] to blows' reminds Barry of the damning juvenile violence of William Golding's *The Lord of the Flies* (1954).

In *Mr Phillips*, Lanchester uses his titular character's redundancy to encourage reflection about the behaviours that have been automatic for the 'twenty-six years' of commuting to Waterloo station.[49] Attention is drawn to the routinized actions that are at once so deeply internalized and yet recognizably problematic as soon as Mr Phillips is no longer a commuter. When he travels into London, on his first 'redundant' day, we read of this awareness of techniques that were previously unconscious:

> The platformful of passengers assembles around the doors, which wheeze open in a row, and a few dozen people hop out of their carriages, minding the gap, before a couple of hundred others surge onto the train. Like most experienced commuters, Mr Phillips has a variety of techniques for seizing somewhere to sit, sneaking in around the side of the door and sliding into one of the jump-seats or barrelling down to the far end of the compartment, through the thickets of passengers, briefcases, newspapers, out-stretched legs.[50]

These tactics are obstructive, selfish, bordering on aggressive: the dishonesty of 'sneaking', the violence of the 'surge' and the 'barrelling' of the commuters makes clear that the onus is on the individual at the expense of the collective. More important, is that psychologically, this is also an important moment in the day. Just as O'Dell talks about the commute as a space in which the commuter prepares for work – these days with coffee, laptops, mobile phones – there is also a groundwork laid for the battles ahead. Lanchester makes clear that this initial daily 'battle for a space' is effectively an 'allegory or image of, the daily struggle'.[51] The commute is, in these terms, a mental and physical preparation for the wider difficulties of working life or, as O'Dell refers to it, 'a very important corridor for ritualized processes of identity transformation'.[52] Outside of any need to transform, Mr Phillips can identify the patterns of behaviour that he used to engage with and recognize the uncompromising nature of the commuter.

What Lanchester draws upon is a relentlessness about modern working life that is seemingly not a new phenomenon. As long as people have commuted by train into work, and certainly once the suburbs provided local stations with a multitude of workers, all of whom were destined for their city offices, this type of behaviour has been commented on in popular culture. Arnold Bennett captures it as early as 1911 in *Hilda Lessways*, when he describes the repetition of commuter trains driving up and taking passengers away. Rather than placing the ruthlessness with the commuter himself, he depicts the train itself as mechanically unyielding, extracting the hoards and sweeping them along the suburban rails. Bennett makes this a part of an essential need to survive, calling it similar to the 'flight of some enormous and excited population from a country menaced with disaster'. The 'surge' represents the fear of being late to the desk, followed, in the evening, by the desperation to break free of the bonds of work:

> A dark torrent of human beings, chiefly men, gathered out of all the streets of the vicinity, had dashed unceasingly into the enclosure and covered the long platform with tramping feet. Every few minutes a train rolled in, as if from some inexhaustible magazine of trains beyond the horizon, and, sucking into itself a multitude and departing again, left one platform for a moment emptying – and the next moment the platform was once more filled by the quenchless stream.[53]

In this description, the commuters are passive, part, once more, of that 'stream' of commuters that was mentioned earlier in this chapter. The essential competition between commuters has an animalistic implication echoed in literature (see, for instance, George Orwell's 'ant-like men' in *Keep the Aspidistra Flying* (1936), who are commuting with the 'fear of the sack like a maggot in [the] head') and screen depictions such as the 1961 film *The Rebel*, where office workers jostle and fight to get onto carriages, whilst the 'rebel' – Tony Hancock – slips across the rails and through the back of the carriage. Bennett identifies something inhuman in the process of the rail commute that persists in popular cultural representations, and that perpetuates the notion of the commute as essential to *survival* itself.

In Steve Cutting's recent short film *Happiness* (2017), he depicts thousands of rats, suited and booted, waiting at the subway for trains headed to 'Nowhere', trapped on a treadmill of meaningless activity in a bid to work more, earn more and have more. Much of this drive is in response to fear; the twitching nose of the antihero rat and his increasingly agitated and anxious state reflects contemporary society as expressed across the twentieth century. Texts like H. G. Wells's *War of the Worlds* (1898) refer to the desperation of commuters and the 'fear they'd get dismissed if they didn't [make their train]'.[54] Like Bennett, who sees the arrival and departure of the trains as apocalyptical, Wells and Cuttings are connecting the essence of survival to the daily commute. In the 1970s sitcom *The Good Life*, the first day of Barbara and Tom Good's experiment in self-sufficiency begins with Tom turning down the offer of a lift to work from his boss and neighbour Jerry. Jerry is incredulous that they can survive as smallholders in Surbiton, but the rejection of the traditional narrative that sees the perpetual cycle of commute to work to earn to live disrupts the assumption that work is required for existence.

The Good Life makes the concept of survival very literal and tangible – if Barbara and Tom cannot provide for themselves in terms of basics like heat, water, light and food, there could be consequences beyond hurt pride and social embarrassment. In contemporary terms, the impact of the commute on mental well-being is equally a key concern, viewed as exacerbating the frustration, anxiety and loneliness of the commuter. The longstanding trend of depicting the office worker at crisis-point takes the commute as a manifestation of the metaphorical straw that breaks the camel's back. In part, this exemplifies one of the paradoxes of the commute: it is both an active word that implies movement and a journey that, as part of the ironically named 'rush hour', is frustratingly slow. This stasis is psychological, encouraging in popular culture an association between being stuck in traffic and being trapped in a rut in life more broadly.

In *Mr Phillips*, Lanchester talks about traffic as a 'cancer of stasis' using the metaphor of disease to explore the problems of 'immobile traffic', 'blocked-in vehicles', 'junctions clogging' and 'back flows building up'.[55] Mr Phillips imagines a city that is eventually totally inert, full beyond capacity and moving nowhere. This is another metaphor for Mr Phillips' career, which has, like the 'dying brain' of the city blocked with traffic, come to a halt. Frequently the commute, and frustration with the conditions and time that it takes, starts to foreshadow the wider complexities of life. In *The 7.39*, Carl's problems begin because he is getting tired of commuting, but this, in turn, starts to spread into dissatisfaction in his job, and with family life.

What is perhaps most pertinent is the way that the commute has become deeply symbolic of our modern lives. Ian Fletcher, the focal character of the tandem BBC series *2012* and *W1A*, is an interesting contemporary example of the ways the commute captures the relentlessness of the everyday. Ian spends the first series of *2012* getting to grips with commuting in central London on his new Brompton folding bike (with many near disastrous consequences), while negotiating an acrimonious divorce settlement with his difficult ex-wife-to-be and settling into a high-pressured job running the 2012 Olympics. Ian's minor cycling ineptitude (most of which centres on his hopelessness at folding the city bike) heightens his insecurities about his ability as a manager of a complex project. The conversations that occur during his commute, the tail end of which are witnessed by the audience, make clear that commuting is in many ways replete with its own problems as well as being a space that can envelop both work and private issues. These insecurities, anxieties and tensions come to a head in the final episode of the second series of *W1A*, where Ian arrives and coolly collapses his bike before his young (and generally incompetent) assistant and his boss nonchalantly arrive on what are new and superior models.[56]

Waiting at the garden gate

When Bullock's character, Mr Ruby, crosses London Bridge and dreams of embarking on a life-changing journey down the Thames, rather than slipping into the stream of commuters making their way to work, he is responding to a deep dissatisfaction with the office as well as the restrictions of home life that are exacerbated by the commute. Bullock's novel draws attention to a strand of representations that position the return commute as particularly emotionally fraught, as the shift from professional to domestic is renegotiated. Much of this discourse rests on particularly gendered imageries that position the hard-working, exhausted husband in opposition to the hen-pecking wife, who has her own expectations from her spouse once he returns. In Victorian and Edwardian representations, this contributed to a discourse around contemporary masculinity both in suburbia and the office – seen as at the beck and call of his boss and then his wife, the clerk was depicted as incapable of asserting himself in either sphere. As Mr Ruby laments: 'If he is ten minutes late at business he may suffer reprimand. Let him be half an hour behind time of an evening and Catherine is watching at the gate'.[57] Even Mr Ruby's daughter views this behaviour as problematic; she refers to 'poor father trotting off' to work each day, while her lover adds, 'toddling home each night as limp as flax'.[58] They see the perpetual routine of commuting and working as unfulfilling and deeply controlled.

In George Gissing's short story from 1899, 'A Freak of Nature', Mr Brogden uses the trains to run away into the countryside when work and his wife leave him feeling at the end of his tether. Mr Ruby takes a ship to Gibraltar to make a bigger gesture about his dissatisfaction, while in Nobbs' novel Reginald Perrin flees work and home life in a jelly-shaped Sunshine Desserts truck. Carl, in BBC mini-series *The 7.39*, finds his way out of a rut by having an affair with fellow commuter Sally, most of which takes place as they travel from central London back to their suburban homes. Like most of these male characters, Carl acknowledges that he is in classic mid-life crisis territory – indeed, these revolutions, however minor, are very short term, with each of the male characters returning to their suburban homes and the daily grind once they have experienced this flurry of activity. These flights from everyday life each take place through the subversion of the characters' usual routes and modes of commuting, offering a reminder that while the journey to work is seen as restricted and limiting, there is an implicit freedom in travel that is easily overlooked when it becomes part of a commonplace routine.

Cunningham writes about the early development of suburbia and the impact that widespread commuting had on the perceived feminization of the space during the working day because it was 'exclusively male worker[s]' who departed for the trains and buses, but the comments of Ruby's daughter suggest that the separation of business and domestic spaces was not enough to rescue the white-collar worker from condescension.[59] Indeed, the wife waiting at the gate and the expectant boss in the office are both represented as a challenge to the concept of the paterfamilias earning respect in either sphere. While Cunningham discusses the ways that the front garden becomes a complex site that often exists in literary examples as a frontier between the world of domesticity and the public sphere, the space of the commute can equally be read as a buffer between each of these aspects of daily life. Cunningham cites texts such as Ella D'Arcy's *Modern Instances* (1898) and H. G. Wells's *Tono Bungay* (1908) as examples where crossing the threshold at the end of the commute is fraught with emotional turmoil (in *Modern Instances*, the wife awaits to convey bad news, and in Wells's story, the philandering protagonist faces a rejection of suburban domestic values). In both examples, the front garden presents a significant site from which the commuter must renegotiate their position.

While we would expect to read mainly of male rail commuters in mid-nineteenth-century literature, it is perhaps more surprising that in a 2017 survey, men are still more likely to use a train to get to work – with, as a causal outcome, men also making two-thirds of commutes lasting more than an hour.[60] Equally of note is that, of the 9 per cent of workers who live in a different region to their workplace, 65 per cent of those are men (with this rising to 77 per cent in Scotland).[61] This perhaps explains why we continue to find more representations of male commuters particularly on the rail networks than we do those of women who are travelling to work. Indeed, there are several more recent examples that still foreground the very traditional nineteenth-century depiction of the wife who sends her husband off to work in the morning and awaits his return.

Hanif Kureishi's 1990 novel *Buddha of Suburbia*, for instance, refers to the suburban wife awaiting the return of her commuting husband – a factor that makes son Karim incredulous that his father could begin an affair given this constraint. As Kureishi writes: 'Life for commuters was regulated to the minute', implying that there is as little freedom at the end of the day as there is on the way to work.[62] Contemporary television series perpetuate this particular gendering of the commute, often placing greater emphasis on the psychological and physical effects of commuting on male characters, rather than working women. While Reggie's wife (in *Reggie Perrin*) is also a professional (a teacher), there is no reference to her journey to work – equally, while roughly half of the BBC management team portrayed in *W1A* are women, only the men are shown arriving in the morning. This is partly because the perceived trauma of the commute contributes towards the type of mid-life crisis often experienced by male office workers. When Reggie Perrin attempts to take back control of his commute, for instance, by driving to work rather than taking the train, he becomes even more frustrated, marking another stage in his rejection of office work. The car journey is straightforward, but he is twenty-seven minutes late, as usual, because a futuristic and nonsensical car-parking system confounds him upon arrival. Reggie's journey home is even less successful, and he resorts to driving through a field, arriving home so late his wife is already in bed. Even his later move into corporate management – where a chauffeur drives him to work each day – becomes poignant as the extensive hours he is working result in his wife no longer noticing (or caring) when he returns home – itself a significantly gendered depiction. Nicola's affair with his best friend becomes a just response to Reggie's tardiness underscoring the ways that, even in the twenty-first century, there are assumptions about gendered marital obligations; the wife as waiting, the husband returning promptly.[63]

Brief encounters

While people travel to work in a variety of ways, on screen there has been a tendency to place emphasis on the railway as emblematic of this experience. This leads to a number of key distortions in popular culture: the typical commuter is often represented as being (a) male, (b) working in central London and (c) travelling by rail or the Tube. While the etymological roots of the very term 'commute' are connected to the historical name for an American railway season ticket holder, rail services make up only 10 per cent of all contemporary commuter journeys in the UK.[64] The London-centricity of popular depictions is equally a factor which gives a misleading impression that trains are a majority form a transport.[65] In reality, two-thirds of commuters travel by car.

Peter Kay's *Car Share* (2015–18) is a rare example of a text that places emphasis on driving to work, in doing so drawing upon the sometimes-unlikely alliances between colleagues who might have little more in common than a shared route and a desire to help the environment and to cut costs. It picks up on the brief view of neighbourly co-commuting in *The Good Life* in the 1970s, when Jerry calls by to pick Tom up for work (he declines, having decided to quit his job). In *The Good Life*, Tom's rejection of the working routine marks out a new period of neighbourly friendship – the next time Tom gets a lift from Jerry, they are transporting a goat, symbolic of the shift in Tom and Barbara's priorities. What Kay gives voice to in *Car Share* is a similar reinvigoration of human interactions. Rather than being merely co-workers (or, as in the case of Tom and Jerry – and not the cat and mouse but the suburban draughtsmen – neighbours and co-workers), the car sharers discover a new depth to their relationship that goes beyond professional status.

The audience of *Car Share* is privy only to the two journeys at each end of the day that John and Kayleigh take together; events in the middle are recounted to highlight the disparity of each character's experience during the working day. Likewise, the home life of each is dissimilar – Kayleigh talks of her former drug dealing ex-boyfriend and moves in with her sister, while John supports his Nana and reluctantly explains his fear of commitment. All that initially unites the pair is the simple need to travel to the same workplace and a shared enjoyment of Forever FM. The commute exists as a significant 'third space' in which the two characters can build their relationship (which later turns into a potential romance), highlighting the potential for the commute to function beyond the parameters of both domestic and professional surveillance.[66]

At times reminiscent of a 1950s romantic comedy, *Car Share* rehumanizes the commute, giving the audience an intimate close-up of the interactions between the two characters. Filmed mostly from the front of the vehicle through an interior dashcam, the figures counter the narrative of the commuter as indistinctive. Rather than the gaze of the outsider, commenting on what is seen as a frantic mass or seething crowd, the viewer of *Car Share* is encouraged to feel part of a scenario which they should be able to recognize as familiar. Equally, *Car Share* subverts impressions of the journey to work as being tedious or monotonous. Through a series of dream sequences, the mundane becomes the romantic and the spectacular. The daydreams of each of the two characters are encouraged by tunes like Jane Wiedlin's 1980s 'Rush Hour', with Forever FM pumping out romantic anthems that reinvigorate negotiations of traffic on the familiar route.

Rather than the silent world of the train, the car commute involves the negotiation of personal relationships in a much more communicative space.

While there are silences, particularly in the early days of Kayleigh and John's car sharing, there is pressure to negotiate a greater familiarity or face what is an excruciatingly reserved journey twice a day. In a similar way, in Richard Curtis's rom-com *Love Actually* (2003), the lift home that Jamie offers his Portuguese cleaning lady, which is by necessity quiet (neither speaking the language of the other), is filled with awkward noises that are bilingual – half remembered songs, inarticulate hums, and incomprehensible gesticulations. Unlike on the train, however, Jamie must attempt to connect across the language barrier, and this communication – however flawed – leads to romance.

What *Car Share* also draws our attention to, with its fictional radio station Forever FM (and particularly songs like Wiedlin's), are the cultural implications of commuting: the rise of 'Drive Time' and 'Rush Hour' genre radio shows in the 1970s is a key marker in the growing significance of time spent on the way to and from work. An earlier equivalent was, of course, the rise of the W. H. Smith chain of railway bookstores, which recognized in the rail traveller a ready market to be entertained on route. As Marsha Dunstan explores, as part of her BBC Genome blog, technological developments occurred alongside a need for 'aural companionship' either on the solitary car journey or through headphones on the tube, train or bus. This concept of 'companionship' is complex, again, when considering the density of the commuter crowd on public transport.[67] In tension is the need for privacy versus the basic craving for company and human interaction. In focusing on a relationship that blossoms in this unusual site, Kay draws attention to the potential of these commuter interactions. Interestingly, despite the general impression that commuting is a silent world, and in many ways, a lonely one, there are a surprising number of screen romances that take meeting on a (usually) commuter train as their starting point. In many ways, this makes sense, when considering, as Carl puts it in *The 7.39*, that, by his calculations, 'thirty-seven days a year [are spent] on this train with these people'.[68]

Many modern renditions have developed from Victorian and Edwardian impressions of the commute as a space for potential romance. Shan Bullock's character, Robert Thorne, spies his future wife Nell in the commuter rush and follows her along the streets until she turns and spots him. The thrill of the chase amongst the surging throng of workers is almost erotic in a poem titled 'Sonnets of a Commuter', featured in the *Shields Daily Gazette* in 1903. In the poem, a commuter, angry at missing his train, is soothed by seeing the 'deep and soulful eyes' of a beautiful woman who he blushingly watches during his commute.[69] Part of the deep and appealing romance of the scenario is that by gazing surreptitiously around his newspaper, 'the ride that oft had seemed so long' felt brief. Equally, the commuter-poet is struck by the depth of communication in the 'deep' eyes of the young female rail user, which is heightened against the expressionless crowd. Fantasy pervades the routine and renders it a site of excitement, just as it does in Thomas Burke's work, which, as Cunningham argues, demonstrates the potential sexualization of the commute.[70] As Cunningham suggests, we consider only our view of the commuting crowd from the outside, rather than considering observations from within. She mentions the intimacy of the gaze into the private homes that back railway lines as an example, but the poet in the *Shields Daily Gazette* gives us an insight into this view too and the potential for emotional closeness that comes from the proximity of the crowded train.[71]

British short *Tunnel Visions* (2011) and Disney's short film *Paperman* (2012) join feature length films like *Falling in Love* (1984) and *While You Were Sleeping* (1995) in making the commute a site of speculative romance. *Paperman* is particularly interesting because the central character is a 'paper-pusher' who is literally pushed by the paper airplanes he has made from the forms he should have filed to find the girl he has glimpsed on the morning commute. Both shorts are outwardly and initially silent; in *Tunnel Visions*, speech is an inner monologue until the end, complete (as in *Reggie Perrin*), with a series of sexual fantasies. *Paperman* is silent but evocative not only of the burgeoning romance between two commuters but also of a mid-century office landscape and the endless and repetitive act of paper pushing.

While these examples conform to expectations about a soundless commute, they also offer a narrative about the complex and multifaceted emotional responses that take place behind the façade of the routine. In *Car Share*, the stance is slightly different again; encountering commuters who are also colleagues helps demystify aspects of the varied hierarchies between them. While John is an assistant manager, and Kayleigh a promotions rep, their relationship exists in a different form in the world of the car share. On several occasions, Kayleigh criticizes the management of the supermarket chain they both work for, and makes recommendations for improvement, in a manner which would not be acceptable within the hierarchy of their workplace. The car, unlike the train, becomes a space of both equality and familiarity that can shake up our cultural expectations about both professional hierarchies and assumptions of a boring commute. In doing so, *Car Share* reinforces, in many ways, the unique status of the commute as a site that can offer relief from the rigidity of both work and personal identities, a space that encourages, as the term itself implies, transformation.

Conclusion

Early critics like Masterman who depicted the suburban hordes as faceless commuters were drawing attention to zombie-like swarms of office workers who, they assumed, conducted most aspects of their lives in a blur of mediocrity. In a modern economy, people from multiple labour markets travel long distances to work but the cultural assumption remains that the commuter is a white-collar worker, and thus this indignity continues. Many of the depictions that remain in the cultural imagination further these impressions and contribute to the conflation of poor commuter as part of a herd that has little autonomy over their life paths. Perspectives of the commuter come often from outside; offered by those who watch the 'stream' but who are not part of it. This ranges from the disdain directed by Masterman and other critics, who were offended as much by the suburban-ness of the commuters as they were by the crowds rolling into the city as part of 'rush-hour', but it also includes young clerical hopefuls who find the coherence of the crowd intimidating as well as those who are excluded from it by gender or class (as in Woolf's *Night and Day*). Regardless of the circumstances that dictate their separation from the rush hour traffic, these depictions encourage a view of the commuting crowd as a surging mass that is indistinct and depersonalized. Those writing from within often make a point of discussing the varied and multiple emotional and psychological experiences of travelling as part of rush hour, drawing attention to the individuality of their commuters. In this sense, romance is a key marker of the deeply personalized moments that occur when those with a shared destination overcome the characteristic reticence of the public space and begin to interact with others around them.

Finally, this chapter has identified some of the long-running tropes associated with commuting – of silence, anonymity, depersonalization – but it is equally significant to consider these continued connotations as representative of something tangible about contemporary life more widely. Commuting symbolizes, perhaps more so than any other space, the quotidian in the twenty-first century. Just as it has been used a shorthand for the routine and the typical for over a decade, it continues to shape our everyday. In *Metroland*, Julian Barnes describes it best as 'relevant, fulfilling, sensibility-sharpening'. His discussion of his character's daily journey into London runs counter to the impressions that are widely associated with commuting, but he also encourages his reader to reconsider this quotidian site. Travelling to work is often depicted as deeply unsatisfying, but commuting is, in all its tedium, inherently real. While we often resent the commute for what it is not – faster, cheaper, more interesting, more meaningful – Barnes asks us to re-evaluate what it is. Like Carl, in *The 7.39* or Peter Kay's character in *Car Share*, Barnes reminds us not to miss the commute by wishing it away:

> I was not only interested in my journey, but proud of it. The termitary of Kilburn; the grimy, lost stations between Baker Street and Finchley Road; the steppe-like playing-fields at Northwick Park; the depot at Neasden, full of idle, aged rolling-stock; the frozen faces of passengers glimpsed in the windows of fast Marylebone trains. They were all, in some way, relevant, fulfilling, sensibility-sharpening. And what was life about if not that?[72]

This description counters the popular associations with the flood of suited workers flowing into the city each day, frustrated and worn down by late trains and traffic jams, but it also raises questions about the ways that we dismiss the commute as a site without substance. So many of those spaces historically associated with the lower middle class are undermined as being tedious or mundane, but as Barnes suggests, there is meaning to life in the outer suburbs of London, and in the mass of workers making their way into the city.

By focusing on the expressions of the everyday glimpsed from the railways, in a manner very similar to Richard Larch's observations made from a train in *A Man from the North*, Barnes also draws attention to the commuter as a key figure in the empathetic reading of the quotidian, a figure who both captures and sees everyday life in its quiet ordinary glory. Rather than disdain for the crowd, surging citywards to work, these depictions elucidate the inner monologues that see each commuter as distinct, empathetic and human.

4

The suburbs

Suburbia has had its fair share of analytical dissection over the course of the twentieth century; from scathing social commentaries to detached bemusement from scholars and the empathetic storytelling and gentle mockery of fiction and television, the suburban semi has provoked a wide range of responses. Sociologists, architects and social historians have explored suburbia's origins, aesthetics, socio-economic status and cultural meaning, with each new analysis bringing to the reader's attention the centrality of the suburb to the housing habits of the nation.[1] These studies have fallen into two camps – those which widely associate Britain's suburbanization with poor culture, homogeneity and offensive architecture and those which credit suburbia with the space and opportunities to enjoy a more comfortable life. The first of these generally represent wider assumptions about suburban life that make their mark in the media and many forms of popular culture. As Mark Clapson put it as recently as 2016, 'people who choose to live in a suburban home are still deemed to be contemptible for a self-consciously urbane commentariat who could never live somewhere so vacuous'.[2] Others, like Clapson himself, and including also Mark Swenarton and Peter Scott, have attempted to counter this negative narrative with their respective analyses of suburban culture, architectural history and working-class social mobility, but there remains very little change in wider attitudes towards suburbia.

Often these analyses have drawn comparison with that other heavily suburbanized nation – America – that saw the detached suburban property, with its neatly mowed lawn, as a crucial but nonetheless controversial part of the 'American Dream'. There are differences too in transatlantic suburbanization, as Robert Fishman and Clapson point out: while America quickly and comprehensively expanded its suburban growth in the twentieth century, Britain retained the essential structure of the earliest suburbs – the ring around the urban core.[3] As a result, while America is extensively 'suburban' as a nation,

Britain – or more specifically, in this case, England – can be better understood as '*the* suburban nation'.[4] Indeed, Clapson's statement of this fact was reinforced in the Smith Institution's 2016 executive summary by the author's reference to suburbia as the 'place where most people in the UK choose to live'.[5] Regardless of suburbia's positive qualities – many of which are based on the principals first outlined in the Tudor Walters Report of 1918, for 'healthier and better-designed homes' – we rarely celebrate being a suburban nation.[6] This too is despite the fact that, as Scott puts it, 'the "Tudorbethan" semi … remains, for many people, the ideal home'.[7] This is not a twenty-first-century bias, either; by the late nineteenth century, suburbia in Britain was already gaining a reputation for being culturally vapid and socially conservative – deemed an architecturally impoverished mode of living.

There are two parts of the narrative to suburbia – the first (the 'rise') is much shorter than the second (pitched, like Reginald Perrin's life, as a 'fall'). Initially, it was a step up from the crowded city, available only to those who could afford the green spaces on the capital's outskirts. Suburban histories like Nick Barrett's *Greater London: The Story of the Suburbs* (2012) chart the earliest expanse of London in the wider area beyond the river Thames and the middle-class industrialists and tradesmen who moved their families out of the smog and sewage of central London from the late seventeenth century onwards. Once this became more widely accessible to those on lower-middle-class incomes from the mid-nineteenth century onwards, with new suburbs developing to appeal to this market, suburbia became a more complex entity. Still popular amongst potential homeowners, there was an increasingly vocal section of society that repudiated suburbia as a cultural, architectural and ecological disaster zone. It was the clerks and their families who were blamed for this symbolic decline of late-Victorian suburbia. They were mocked for attempting to run fledgling suburban households with something approaching the respectability of the middle class, with young maids and pretentious decor. Those who continued to champion suburbia were equally vilified as having poor standards, little taste and limited funds.

For instance, despite the fact that his father escaped the centre of London to move out to the suburb of Herne Hill, John Ruskin wrote in *Fors Clavigera* (1873) about the 'pestilence of [houses] and unseemly plague of builders' work [that] has fallen on the suburbs of loathsome London'.[8] His response to the rapid rise of suburbia carried with it a particularly emotional dynamic in the perceived distortion and destruction of the London of his childhood – and particularly his home, which was, by most definitions, an early middle-class suburban villa.[9] In this, Ruskin's views were similar to the attitude of other writers such as H. G. Wells, who was equally verbose in his repudiation of mass suburbanization – none more so than in his description of Bromley in *The New Machiavelli* (1910) as: 'a dull, useless boiling-up of human activities, an immense clustering of futilities'.[10] Both authors object to the perceived architectural pollution of indiscriminate jerry building, the growing sprawl of the capital as it devoured land, destroying, as Dinah Birch puts it, the 'fragile co-existence of the rural and the urban' that categorized the earlier suburbs.[11] Arthur Conan Doyle too famously describes the 'long brick-feeler[s]' and 'monster tentacles', 'here and there, curving, extending, and coalescing' (or, as E. M. Forster calls it, 'creeping') into the countryside in his novel about the suburban idyll being shattered by the arrival of a new generation of aspirant villa-dwellers.[12] These new suburbans, white-collar workers and their families, were identified as those for whom builders were digging up the bucolic fields and woodlands around the homes of the middle classes.

The expansion of the lower middle class and anti-suburbanism are inherently connected, and the longevity of these negative views is particularly significant. Battlegrounds were soon drawn between hostile critics and impassioned supporters, who were aware of the alternative: urban slums or badly ventilated and poorly designed housing stock. Of note is that the process of suburbanizing the capital drew more ire than in any other location. The destruction of the quintessentially rural Home Counties as the capital's population moved further out – out of necessity, often, due to the sheer number of people who needed and continue to need to work in London – was the centre of a mid-nineteenth-century diatribe against suburbanization, which shaped the tone of much of the opposition. From the interwar period, as Clapson and Scott have shown, this included the migration of working-class families into suburban areas, with developers targeting campaigns at those with stable incomes and aspirations of better living.[13] This became particularly prevalent once the salaries of the poorer-paid white-collar workers were overtaken by the highest echelons of the working class.

The suburbs – and those who live in them – have polarized opinion throughout their history and they continue to do so, and this study argues that many views continue to be shaped by the snobbery and reactionism of the middle class towards the lower middle class in those early days of widespread suburbanism. More people live in the suburbs now than they have ever before – one mapping exercise that used the 2001–11 census data puts this at 59 per cent of the population – but attitudes towards the suburbs remain wedded to viewpoints that fundamentally take shape along the lines of cultural value rather than socio-economic perspectives.[14]

Suburbia, in its many guises, forms the basis for the following two chapters. To do it justice, it is divided into the wider cultural site of the suburbs and the family home (with its 'suburbanite' occupants). The first of these chapters examines the place of wider suburbia within the cultural history of the class, while the second moves on to discuss the relationship between the lower-middle-class family and their own suburban semi-detached; the values, hobbies and pastimes they formed within and the emotional connection with home that is deeply entrenched but not entirely unproblematic. This second chapter places at its core some of those (often neglected) cultural texts that follow what writer W. Pett Ridge called the 'romance in every house' narrative, chronicling the everyday lives of ordinary families.[15] In many ways, this structure gives two perspectives: the first offers the viewpoint of the many critics that have taken aim at this way of living, the second is an 'insider' view on the suburban lower-middle-class home.

While contemporary suburbia has become a much more diverse space, with many critics observing that the boundaries between the city and the suburbs have fragmented, involving a greater deal of movement across the two, this chapter and the one that follows it takes not the lived 'reality' of suburbia but the continuities that are still present in cultural representations. This mainly concerns the dominant narrative of the suburban home as a petit-bourgeois space that promotes 'vulgarity, insularity and conformity'.[16] Modern suburbs are fluid communities that often exist in close proximity to the cultural, political and economic centre (the city), but representations continue to define the two sites in opposition, forcing the distinctions between urban and suburban in unhelpful ways. The following chapter resituates the suburban home away from a discourse of insularity and counters assumptions about how we view suburbanites as homogenous and conformist, but first this chapter focuses on the ways this narrative was constructed over time.

'A country devoid of graciousness'

Attitudes to suburbia in popular culture were polemic even in the nineteenth century: from the admiration of Mr Aked, clerk and aspiring writer in Arnold Bennett's *A Man from the North* (1898), to the cynicism of commentators like T. W. H. Crosland, who blamed suburbia for every modicum of bad taste in his scathing *The Suburbans* (1905).[17] It is the latter view that remains dominant and continues to be reiterated in, as Clapson articulates, assumptions of 'impoverished' architectural and cultural landscapes of suburbia (and a resultant deficiency of the suburban occupant).[18] The opposing narratives of these two figures find their way into the introductions of nearly all academic writings about suburbia. Mr Aked's speech professing the value of suburbia opens Kate Flint's chapter 'Fictional Suburbia' (1986) and Roger Webster's introduction to *Expanding Suburbia* (2000), both of whom call it evidence of a 'plea' for study of the literary suburb.[19] Aked refers to the suburban landscape as deeply creatively stimulating:

> 'Child!' – his eyes were still closed, – 'the suburbs, even Walham Green and Fulham, are full of interest, for those who can see it. Walk along this very street on such a Sunday afternoon as to-day. The roofs form two horrible, converging straight lines, I know, but beneath there is character, individuality, enough to make the greatest book ever written.'[20]

Yet, while deference is duly paid to Aked's opinions, it is Crosland's counter-description from *The Suburbans* that remains more firmly in the memories of most critics:

> You have a big city, with the proper sections, commercial, residential, and fashionable, appertaining to a big city, and outside that – inexorably ringing it round – you have the eternal and entirely God-forsaken suburbs. Put together, they make the country which is the very saddest and most dreary and least delectable on all the maps. It is a country devoid of graciousness to a degree which appeals.[21]

While scholars of the suburb have made a call for more engagement with the cultural legacy of suburbia, Crosland's negativity is much more representative of nineteenth, twentieth and even twenty-first-century commentaries on the topic. His rantings about the suburbs – and more violently against the suburbanites themselves – are somehow more memorable than the gentle affection of someone like Bennett, or later writing of the interwar suburbs by authors such as R. F. Delderfield.

Most common was and is the attitude that for those who identify either with the city or the countryside, the suburb attempts to invoke each and consequently contaminates both. Indeed, as F. M. L. Thompson made clear and Todd Kuchta later interrogated, the widespread rhetoric of colonization used as the petite bourgeoisie spread across London suburbs like West Hampstead and Kilburn is highly revealing.[22] It highlights an 'othering' that is created within the suburban environment which later, as Robert Bueka has identified, becomes a parallel discourse rendering suburbia both a 'noplace' and a vision of Michel Foucault's 'hetereotopia' – an 'everyplace' that reflects wider culture.[23] In his defence of 'Dunroamin', Paul Oliver talks about the negativity of this 'Anywheresville/Nowheresville' dichotomy: uniformity means that the suburbs are simultaneously familiar and ambiguous.[24] Indeed, if one excuse for intellectual disdain is the growing social mobility that undermined suburbia as exclusively middle class, the other reason, as Webster suggests, for the strength of feeling towards the suburbs is exactly this type of otherness:

> [suburbia] occupies a space as much defined as what it is not as by what it is, constructed by difference and imitation rather than possessing innate and original features.[25]

Webster's description echoes the definition of lower-middle-class identity given earlier in this study – defined too 'as what it is not'. Suburban critics opt to focus on what they see as an indistinctive architecture that attempted to privilege function over form, with a secondary nod to the aesthetic. This is often lamented as problematic because exterior decorations took the form of a eulogy for a nostalgic representation of the British architectural past. Added to this was the necessity for certain features to cover the minor mistakes that came from the widespread use of unskilled labourers to keep up with demand, particularly for those houses aimed at the lower end of the market – pebble dash, for instance, could be used to hide poor rendering and subpar brickwork.[26] The mock Tudor styling of the 1930s, which offended architects with its inauthenticity, continues to shape expectations of new house building into the twenty-first century. Modern developments take as their inspiration local architectural trends, in a bid to 'blend in' – see, for instance, the distinctive style of early-twentieth-century housing estates around Norwich that copy the traits of rustic East Anglian barns. This recycling of forms that are familiar within the landscape return to that original tension between the familiar and the new, equally attempting to update the past and ingratiate the viewer within it.

In the mid-twentieth century, and as the ridiculing of suburbia reached a new peak, the block of flats, favoured by the modernists who criticized post-war suburbia, tried to provide the housing needed for so many. In many ways, this is highly ironic, given that the high rise is the ultimate manifestation of uniform housing, with symmetries of layout being crucial for maximizing the space. And yet, houses that, as Oliver et al. point out, were labelled 'jerry built' are still standing (having survived extensive bombing campaigns in the Second World

War), have risen in value, compete favourably with Victorian and newer housing developments in market terms and continue to provide suitable and flexible housing for modern families, while many of these architecturally stylized tower blocks were demolished as early as the 1970s and 1980s. There have been shifts – from the through-lounge to the kitchen-diner, for instance – but the simple layouts of 1930s semis are easily renegotiated. Yet, they seem unable to shake off the perception of being 'poor' value in cultural terms, forcing the occupant to endure 'soul-destroying anonymity'.[27] This is a complicated accusation, given that there is a much higher likeliness of being known in a cul-de-sac than a vast row of urban terraces in a bustling cityscape.

And yet, house-buying programmes like Channel 4's long-running *Location, Location, Location* (2000–) – which remains London-centric – refer to the commonplace assumption that couples starting a family 'have to' move further out to the suburbs. Young, sociable professionals give up their cosy neighbourhood bars and easy access to entertainment in order to negotiate a small garden or a third bedroom. While Scott comments on the marketing campaigns of the interwar period that 'sought to attach specific values to owner-occupation and living in modern, suburban estates', contemporary views of suburbia are instead framed as a compromise on urban living.[28] It is equally, however, seen as an inevitable part of the family lifecycle. When Thompson wrote in an early history of the suburbs, *The Rise of Suburbia* (1982), that it is an 'unlovely, sprawling artefact of which few are particularly fond',[29] he was, in many ways, ignoring the fact that, as Clapson points out much later, many millions of people continue to live in suburban semi-detached houses.[30] What Thompson was observing, just as Kirstie Allsopp and Phil Spencer reiterate on their series, is the implication that this is a necessity, not a pleasure.

Many accounts of suburbia, academic and otherwise, likewise begin with an admission that the author has at some point lived in a suburban semi. H. J. Dyos's *Victorian Suburb* (1961), one of the earliest histories of suburbia, begins with one such quietly made confession. In part, he acknowledges that he writes sentimentally, having lived in Camberwell for some time but he is also critical of many aspects of suburbia, reflecting his later middle-class values. As Tom Jeffery succinctly suggests people tend only to write about the suburbs when 'they have moved on to greater things'.[31] More positive identifications with suburban living can be found in the work of revisionists like Clapson, who declares in *Suburban Century* that he was brought up in a 'three-bedroomed semi-detached house in Reading', or Richard Harris and Peter Larkham's opening comment in their collection that 'we are both children of the English suburbs'.[32]

Of note is that this author grew up in a very typical 1930s semi-detached house, in a suburb that could stand as a model for suburbanization in the period: part of the suburban sprawl on the outskirts of a medium-sized town, which eventually connected with a historic village. The street comprised of several styles and a corresponding range of prices, from those which architectural critics would refer to as 'jerry built' to several 'architect-builder designed', including one which was slightly larger, intended (according to hearsay) for the builder's own family to live in. On the surrounding streets interwar council houses were built, each with their own driveways, gardens, municipal 'greens' and outhouses. The wide streets and extensive gardens of suburbia are noticeably absent where I live now, where rows of Victorian terraces remain the core of the housing stock, and yards and alleyways provide the only outdoor space for most residents. If anything, I have moved on to lesser things – I still miss the essential greenness of the tree-lined avenues and the liberality with which gardens were attached to even the smallest of houses. I envy my parents and the ease with which they can carry out simple DIY tasks that do not result in rubble-filled walls shifting in unpredictable (and generally costly) ways.

Growing up, I was vaguely aware of the condescension directed towards where I lived (more so once at university), but as an avid television viewer, suburbia felt incredibly every day. In the 1990s, in particular, there were very few television shows not set in suburban houses – from children's shows like *The Wild House* (1997–9), *My Parents Are Aliens* (1999–2006) and *Juliet Jekyll and Harriet Hyde* (1995–8) to family viewing like *Keeping Up Appearances* (1990–5), *One Foot in the Grave* (1990–2001), *2point4 Children* (1991–9) and repeats of such classics as *The Good Life* (1975–8). At its core, this is one of the complexities of the position of suburbia in cultural terms. It is a site of conflict between those who use it as a vehicle to represent the type of family-focused environment that is the stalwart of forms such as the situational comedy and those who have long argued that the inwards-facing prioritization of the nuclear family is one of the core problems in suburbanization (and society more widely). Amidst all of this is a hierarchical implication that the commentaries of 'experts' that condemn 'poor' architecture and negligible suburban planning are more sensible than those who celebrate the suburbs as a comfortable and enjoyable place to live. While critics continuously invite us to dismiss suburbia, popular culture across the nineteenth, twentieth and twenty-first centuries continues to demonstrate not only the affability of suburban life but its ongoing centrality to British life.

In many ways, of course, this only strengthens the argument of cynics that the suburbs are a place of lowbrow cultural pursuits. Television itself is subject to general snobbishness – often considered a poor cousin to film. Asserted as an unlikely source of creative integrity, suburbia has been tarnished with the brush of being, as Susan Brooks suggests, 'homogenous and conformist' – like the lower middle class themselves.[33] The suburbs were not a place where new forms could open up or creative dialogues would begin; instead, they were a platform for the bourgeois interests of the lower middle class, acted out often on the small screen. As Brooks suggests, this echoed an attitude that had been present in literature from the late nineteenth century and continued throughout the twentieth and into the twenty-first – the inner city is the site for charismatic, innovative, engaging fiction that could provide the thrust and energy that cultured readers need. Creativity that stems from suburbia, as is the case with singers like Freddie Mercury or David Bowie, is considered even more impressive because it goes against what is seen as the trend.

This ideological battleground is apparent in the scholarly work that examines the cultural legacy of suburbia. Those who study what Bennett called the 'psychology of the suburbs' are constantly faced with asserting the worth of the texts that are discussed.[34] See, for instance, the inevitable discussions around culturally loaded terms such as 'middlebrow' which are used when discussing fiction written by women in the early twentieth century and which are equally applied to the work of writers such as Bennett and Wells. John Lucas may talk about the 'chill authenticity' of Bennett's suburban fiction, but it is difficult for analysis to gain real traction when the overwhelming impression is of suburbia as a cultureless space.[35] This is despite the challenges to this one-dimensional viewpoint that authors such as D. J. Taylor and Ged Pope have made in recent years.[36] As Pope suggests, 'it is difficult to find serious and direct mention of the suburb in fiction; quite often they are usually glimpsed in writing that is primarily focused elsewhere'.[37] He attributes this, in part, to the fact that lower-middle-class lives are 'not the kind of experience that literature deals with'.[38]

While fiction has, to some extent, provided some insight into the suburban story, it is television that has made suburbia its mainstay. Telling the tales of the suburbs is at the centre of a generation of sitcoms from *The Good Life*, *Butterflies* (1978–83), *Ever Decreasing Circles* (1984–9), *Keeping up Appearances*, *One Foot in the Grave*, *2point4 Children*, *My Family* (2000–11), *Outnumbered* (2007–14), and through to *Gavin and Stacey* (2007–10), *Friday Night Dinner* (2011–18), and *Not Going Out* (2006–). Indeed, as Brett Mills has discussed, television very quickly 'placed itself within the routines of the home', making a marriage with everyday domesticity as its content a natural progression.[39] Just as middlebrow fiction in the first half of the twentieth century was dismissed by modernist critics because it did not challenge methods of drawing character and sequencing narrative, many of these sitcoms have faced criticism for being, as Mills puts it, 'traditional', with their laughter tracks and familiar narratives being used to justify equating 'popular' with 'poor quality'.[40] What these readings of sitcom suburbia achieve is the critical undermining of a genre that provides humour through relatable content in a form that is accessible to those same 'masses' that modernism was so resistant towards. By targeting suburbia as a site for the sitcom, these negative impressions combine antagonism to a wider conflation of the two. Instead of recognizing what Wells called the '[teeming] suggestions of indefinite, and sometimes outrageous possibility[ies], of hidden but magnificent meanings', critical discourse that places the sitcom in a 'low cultural position' equally looks down on the stories told of suburban lives.[41] This is exactly what the televisual suburbs represent – they deliberately counter impressions of suburbia as bland and uniform with their comical storylines and dramatic situations that both test and bring together the family unit. In fact, they often do so by foregrounding the seeming conformity of the family before allowing the viewer to see into their individuality.

This does not mean that the sitcom is without issue; for a long time, the form has been viewed as a platform for gently mocking suburban mores. More problematic is the methods through which sitcoms have reinforced certain hegemonic narratives that limited, for instance, the role of women to that of domestic drudge. Mills talks about the expectation within mid-century sitcoms that women fulfil the 'humble but noble calling in life [of] housewife and mother', facing ridicule where this ideal was not met.[42] Projects written by women, such as Carla Lane's *Butterflies*, attempted a revision to this orthodoxy, but, while it was groundbreaking in some aspects, it was equally limited by social restraints, as was *Ever Decreasing Circles*, in that ultimately, working within the confines of marriage remains crucial to the female characters. The sitcom has also rightfully been criticized for its focus on white suburban families, where British Asian or black British characters are part of a sitcom, as in the case of *Love Thy Neighbour* (1972–6), *Rising Damp* (1974–8) and *Terry and June* (1979–87) in the 1970s and 1980s, they often become a vehicle through which deeply problematic and racist stereotypes are displayed. Contemporary sitcoms continue to depict a version of London that ignores the ethnic diversity of many suburban areas. While American histories of suburbia have more recently focused on demographic shifts, the same attention has yet to be paid to the ethnic diversity of British suburbia.[43]

In part, the continued dialogue surrounding the London suburb reflects the ways that the capital is still at the centre of the British cultural imagination. In popular culture from Victorian novels onwards, the suburban setting is nearly within London's orbit. Despite the fact that suburbanization occurred all over the country, wherever there were towns that provided opportunities for growth, writers have focused on the suburbs round the capital as a natural *metier* for their narratives. In Victorian writing, this was often as a result of two things: the autobiographical nature of most suburban novels and a publishing market that encouraged authors (or would-be authors) to live in London. The trend shows little signs of abating. In contemporary television, there is a similar emphasis on suburban narratives that are inevitably set in the commuter-ville around the capital. From *The Fall and Rise of Reginald Perrin* to *Men Behaving Badly*, *The Good Life* to *Gavin and Stacey*, the quintessential suburban home is commutable to central London.

As Robert Fishman put it, in *Bourgeois Utopias*, suburbs exist because of 'two opposing forces, an attraction toward the opportunities of the great city and a simultaneous repulsion against urban life'.[44] Perhaps it is this diametrically based origin that is responsible for not only the generic response to suburbia but also its London focus. London is the antithesis of the rural environment in many ways, but both sites are also seen as 'authentic' because of what is seen as their clear and meaningful markers – rural equals green, natural, spacious; urban is cultured, heavily populated. Suburbia is much harder to define in concrete terms because it evolves and morphs into multiple types of space. In class terms, too, the suburbs are ill-defined, offering housing at multiple price levels that are often mixed, a feature that is, in part, responsible for the type of social self-consciousness for which it has become so well known. While this chapter would not argue that suburbia is monolithically lower middle class in composition, cultural attitudes remain fixated on the behaviours, values and characterizations associated with this group, in part because whilst suburbia destabilizes class boundaries, as a result it intensifies anxieties ascribed to the inhabitants who find this hardest: those who are most aware of their status as *lower* middle class.

It is the cultural amalgamation of suburbia and the lower middle class that this chapter takes as its focus. One thing is clear: the suburbs, as seen in the fiction of the late nineteenth century, the sitcoms of the mid twentieth and the wider cultural attitudes of the twenty first, remain central to the construction of class in British society. The vehement responses and opinions about suburbia are inextricably both shaped by and responsible for the assumptions made also about their occupants. When Thompson made his scathing comments about suburbia, he was, of course, directing his frustrations as much at the lower-middle-class suburbanites as he was the place itself:

> The suburbs appeared monotonous, featureless, without character, indistinguishable from one another, infinitely boring to behold, wastelands of housing as settings for dreary, petty, lives without social, cultural, or intellectual interests, settings which fostered a pretentious preoccupation with outward appearances, a fussy attention to the trifling details of genteel living, and absurd attempts to conjure rusticity out of miniature garden plots.[45]

Like others before him, Thompson was drawing attention to characteristics of the suburban that were already in circulation. They were the same criticisms directed at the pompous white-collar worker, lined up on the station platform with his cheap bowler hat and umbrella, ready to make his way to the city for the daily grind. The 'dreary, petty, lives' of the clerk and the typist were considered worthless by those who had little empathy or understanding of why the city worker might prize their quiet suburban home. Many historians and sociologists, whilst not as openly antagonistic as Masterman (whose greatest criticism is that suburbans are 'limited [in] outlook beyond a personal ambition'),[46] have nonetheless tended to keep their suburban lower-middle-class subjects safely at arm's length.[47]

The rejection of suburbia is based more on an innate snobbery about *who* was living there more than it was of the space itself. In many ways, suburbia was destined to be unpopular as soon as those who were not solidly and exclusively middle class began to be able to afford to move out of the city. What started as condescension towards the lower-middle-class clerk and his suburban wife has become widespread cynicism about suburbia as a mode of living. In this sense, and without underplaying the significance of other factors (such as the minimal planning involved in suburban spread, the architectural conservatism of builders, etc.), it is the significant role of the lower middle class in the near condemnation of suburbia that is examined here. Clapson draws attention to the origins of hostility when he refers to the role that characters like Charles Pooter and George Bowling played in early suburban culture:

> The suburbs were allegedly full of 'clerks', a pejorative catch-all term. This mockery stemmed from George and Weedon Grossmith's caricature Mr Pooter ... and continued to George Orwell's Stanley [sic] Bowling in the 1930s novel *Coming Up for Air* ... Clerks lived routine and uneventful lives dictated by the times of commuter trains and the monotony of office life. According to their literary critics, they were passive creatures, devoid of finer feelings and high culture. They tended their little gardens, were mesmerised by advertisements for material things, and obsessed by the petty symbols of respectability and status.[48]

Reiterated are references to these belittling traits – gardening, DIY, new furniture and sprucing up the place. The next chapter will challenge assumptions made about material objects and 'petty symbols', but there is a wider argument about suburbia and class that is prevalent in Kuchta's work. The clerks epitomize the lower middle class, and they are inherently suburban. Fast forward to a twenty-first-century television series like *Gavin and Stacey*, and this conflation of home and identity continues to ring true. Housing type continues to demark the personality within, and hobbies and interests map onto the interior of the home. Gwen, working class and Welsh, lives in a tiny terrace house in Barry, makes simple omelettes and goes to the Bingo hall for entertainment. Mick and Pam, in contrast, live in Billericay, a typical commuter town in Essex, in a 1970s dormer bungalow on a very typically suburban street (Figure 4.1). Mick is part of Thatcher's working class 'made good', a company director at a large engineering firm, while his wife Pam stays at home engaging in the type of suburban hobbies Margo Leadbetter and Hester Fields took part in – jujitsu and fencing. They are lower middle rather than middle class, however, not only because of regional intimations about Essex and class but also because of certain social anxieties. Pam's mock vegetarianism is a result of her desire to host successfully, as is her not-so-subtle disclosure that she and Mick have paid for the wedding rather than Pam. More importantly, Pam's loud and brash use of 'Mick – Michael' whenever she is in an argument, and her extensive gossiping about the other women in her social circle, place her socially within a conflated suburban-Essex lower-middle-class fusion.

Figure 4.1 Suburban Billericay in *Gavin and Stacey* (2007)
© BBC

Gavin and Stacey's success derives from its representation of 'ordinary' people; Pam and Mick combine factors that evoke the contemporary every day. Their house is nice but not too nice, large but would still benefit from the conservatory that Smithy is building for them and has features like a power shower that is considered (by Bryn) a boon. They follow a trajectory of lower-middle-class suburban homes on screen that are nice but not excessively showy (like the semi in *Terry and June*, Hyacinth Bucket's modern bungalow, and the functional but homespun interior of *The Good Life*). What these shows all draw our attention to is the way in which we can so easily read houses like we can character. Designers can depict, as they can in the office, the social status of any family in the emphasis on certain details and decorative choices. To return to *Gavin and Stacey*, Smithy's mum, Cath, lives in a small semi-detached house (that looks possibly like it may be former council housing stock), that instantly substantiates her place in the hierarchy above Gwen but below the Shipmans. These examples demonstrate the ways that we can still read class and social status in housing alone, before knowing very much else about a character. Suburban homes are layered with easily identifiable meanings, many of which are founded on stereotypes about class, and in the case of *Gavin and Stacey*, the intersection of region. The longevity of this type of association is also significant because it reiterates the type of crucial delineations and demarcations that have long persisted in suburban landscapes: the importance of identifying and consequently maintaining hierarchical boundaries.

Back to the city

One of the most poignant aspects of *Gavin and Stacey*, and the only issue that threatens to disrupt the romantic happiness, is their differing attitudes towards life in Billericay. The young married couple live with Pam and Mick, and Stacey finds this claustrophobic. Pam finds it difficult to understand Stacey's position, as does Gavin, who would rather live with his parents than waste money in renting. Their inability to afford their own home so close to London is a point of tension across the second series, resolved only by Gavin relocating to a Cardiff office at his firm so the pair can live with Stacey's mum, Gwen, in what is a much smaller house. Pam sees Stacey's behaviour as incomprehensible because suburban space in Billericay is, to her mind, far more generous, while the proximity of London underscores Pam's superior attitude at various points across the sitcom more widely. She sees the suburban luxury of their detached bungalow in a quiet cul-de-sac as the epitome of contemporary comfort, particularly because it has been hard won.

Pam's attitude is reflective of many in her generation: at the beginning of the twentieth century, a series of writers ended their narratives with aspirations of moving out to the suburbs – or further out to better suburbs – for the benefit of their children, but it did not follow that their offspring would be particularly grateful for this move. The first generation to be brought up in the suburbs in the 1950s, the 1960s and the 1970s often wrote about their desperation to return to the city that their parents had left. Like Julian Barnes, whose first novel *Metroland* (1980) charts his desperation to leave suburbia, many wanted to rebel against the decisions their parents had made, which is a natural part of what Paul Barker refers to as the inevitable 'adolescent rejection of suburbia' that derives from the fact that all teenagers 'reject the place they grew up in'.[49] They were a revolutionary generation that viewed the suburbs as a homogeneous space ruined by conservative values and restricting social emulation. Their views were in tune with the wider scepticism that had been levelled at suburbia for a few decades by this point, but their frustration was personal – they had experienced the suburbs first-hand and felt trapped by it. While their parents believed they were providing a suburban haven, the children experienced this as a cloistered space, charged with repression and frustration.

Sarah May expressed it well when she used the following dedication in the preface to *The Rise and Fall of the Queen of Suburbia* (2006): 'to all parents who dream of bringing their children up in a better world, out of harm's way ... and to all children who dream of escaping and getting in harm's way'.[50] May captures the tension between those parents who felt they were raising their children in safe space and the rebellion this inspired in those who did not want to be part of it. The suburbs were a battleground for children who wanted to break free, precipitated by social and cultural movements in the middle of the twentieth century and beyond. As Queenie, in the film *This Happy Breed* (1944), puts it: 'I hate living here. I hate living in a house that's exactly like hundreds of others ... I hate washing up and helping Mum darn Dad's socks'.[51] Queenie signposts the coming generations, which would go on to include the Angry Young Men of the 1970s, who saw the capital as the centre of a sexual and cultural revolution and felt trapped by domesticity and everyday mundanity in the suburbs. Washing up and darning socks foreshadows the ironing that triggers Jimmy's angry outbursts on stage in John Osbourne's *Look Back in Anger* (1956).

Hanif Kureishi's *The Buddha of Suburbia* is often discussed in light of this radical moment, where the stifling society of the suburb is challenged both by

Karim, in his desire for sexual adventure and creative development, and his father, who uses his Indian heritage to construct a spiritual orientalism that is both welcomed by the repressed suburban community and offers Haroon a way out. Nigel Williams similarly explored the eagerness with which the suburbanites of the 1980s and 1990s welcomed the spiritually adventurous, using the parallel interests in spiritualism and ufology to suggest that what seems like a moment of deep introspection is actually simply another manifestation of 'keeping up with the Joneses' in *They Came from SW19*.

One of the methods through which teenage rebellion is often articulated is in the (usually male) adolescent obsession with masturbation. In Williams's *They Came from SW19*, like Martin Knight's *Barry Desmond is a Wanker*, and *The Buddha of Suburbia*, masturbation is a symbolic transgression in the suburban bedroom, which feels like it goes against the social conservatism and sexual repression of the wider suburbs. This private sexual moment is on a basic level offered as something that disrupts the boredom of suburban life; as Simon puts it in *They Came from SW19*: 'the suburbs are hell. They go on and on like Sunday afternoons'.[52] This type of adolescent sexuality formed the basis of *The Inbetweeners* franchise, with its teenage boys and their awkward sexual encounters played out in suburban bedrooms. In *Gavin and Stacey* too, Stacey suggests that she enjoys sex more in Billericay because it feels more subversive in the suburban home than in her mother's cramped terrace. Suburban sexuality is 'dirtier', just as Hyacinth's sister Rose's hyper-sexuality is largely ignored in the working-class home of Daisy and Onslow but not tolerated in Hyacinth's bungalow.[53]

While Hyacinth is widely considered repressed (and repressive), the intimations about her son's life at university do hint at a more liberal sexual experience. Sheridan Bucket lives with Tarquin and shows no interest in girls, a fact his mother choses to interpret as a commitment to his degree in needlework. Perhaps, like Karim in *The Buddha of Suburbia*, Sheridan's sexuality is an image of suburban reaction. Karim talks about how growing up in the suburbs contributes to his restlessness, resulting in his desire for 'trouble, any kind of movement, action and sexual interest I could find'.[54] He refers to his family and upbringing as 'so gloomy, so slow and heavy', much of which focuses on his mother's inhibited lower-middle-class values (she permits herself one bite of Walnut Whip every fifteen minutes to prolong the joy, while defending her right to eat it at all). Rita Felski talks about the similarities that persist in the 'structures of feeling' between Orwell's fictional lower-middle-class suburbs and Kureishi's, but she also draws attention to Kureishi's repositioning of the suburbs as a space undergoing a revolution. This is, in one aspect, connected to Karim's Indian father, and the shifts in the ethnic composition of suburbia that Karim identifies with. But *Buddha* is also a narrative about the ways that codes of class are resistant to social change and how ethnicity is recoded until it slots into the hierarchies of social status as defined traditionally still by class.

While postcolonial critics like Berthold Schoene have focused on *Buddha* as a text of post-imperial ethno-English writing, and other writers have considered the counter-culture prevalent in the text as commentary on the 'deviant' 1970s, this reading of the novel considers suburbia in the context of sexuality. Karim's bisexuality opens debate about the ways that the petite bourgeoisie are often presented as sexually conformist. Indeed, in sitcoms, the middle-aged and nightgowned suburban shares a marital bed that is rendered nostalgically safe and comfortable. Hyacinth and Richard sleep in a fussily bedecked double, covered in frilly valances and excessive quantities of lace. They, like Victor Meldrew and his wife in *One Foot in the Grave*, wear full pyjamas and dressing gowns, in contrast to Onslow and Daisy, Hyacinth's brother-in-law and sister, who sleep in vests and badly fitting nighties. In *Men Behaving Badly*, Gary sees the quantity of clothing in bed as a marker of the slide into suburban middle age. He chastises girlfriend Dorothy for wearing more as they get older, remarking: 'at this rate, in a few years we'll be sitting up in bed in tweed jackets and sensible hats'.[55] Part of Gary's observation addresses their diminishing sex life, an aspect of lower-middle-class life that is commonly articulated.

The Buddha of Suburbia counters this with the exploratory sexuality of not only Karim but his father, who begins an affair in middle age. Despite being a poorly paid clerk for the civil service, shaped and moulded by routine, Karim's dad finds love and transcends his suburban-ness. Karim, too, looks to his sexuality to help him 'scour the suburban stigma' off his body, just as his new stepmother, Eva, does. He also recognizes what Eva does not, that this project is doomed, because there is 'nothing more suburban than suburbanites repudiating themselves'.[56] Kureishi himself, in an interview with the *Observer*, talks about how he may have got out of the suburbs but the suburbs is not yet out of him.[57] Karim's attempts to use sexuality to symbolize the wider rejection of suburbia is predicated on the perceived discomfort which the suburban subject has of their own body.

George Orwell refers to this in *Keep the Aspidistra Flying* much earlier in the twentieth century. Gordon Comstock conflates a series of associations with suburbia, the final of which directs anger at petit bourgeois sexual mores:

> To settle down, to Make Good, to sell your soul for a villa and an aspidistra! To turn into the typical little bowler-hatted sneak – Strube's 'little man' – the little docile cit who slips home by the six-fifteen to a supper of cottage pie and stewed tinned pears, half an hour's listening-in to the BBC Symphony Concert, and then perhaps a spot of licit sexual intercourse if his wife 'feels in the mood'.[58]

Comstock attacks suburbanism for facilitating subpar expectations of culinary, cultural and sexual lives. The three, as in *Buddha*, are connected, and they represent the reduced horizons that the suburban semi evokes. The suburbs are distinctly anti-masculine; domestic femininity undermines independence, sexuality and even taste. Orwell hints at the sexual dynamic that Victoria Wood would go on to so comically capture in her caricature of lower-middle-class marriage, 'The Ballad of Barry and Freda', with its sexually expansive and unrepressed wife and her subservient and anxiety-ridden middle-aged suburban husband, who would rather potter and do DIY than have sex.

In her representation of lower-middle-class marriage, Wood picked up on a strand of characterizations that date back, once more, to the days of Charles Pooter. A. James Hammerton has written two articles on marriage and the lower middle class, both of which focus on *Diary of a Nobody* and the satirizing of gender roles. He talks about the stereotypes surrounding both late-nineteenth-century marriage as an institution and the emphasis within representations of the lower middle class. Pooterism, as he suggests, has come to define the sort of 'despondent weakness and inflated social pretension of white collar workers' that is often played out within the work environment (think David Brent in *The Office*) but which, as Hammerton argues, was equally 'powerful' in the suburban villa.[59] As Melanie Tebbutt suggests, this was reinforced in the many lower-middle-class autobiographies presenting an effeminized domestic masculinity that became 'easy meat for satirists, who lampooned lower-middle-class husbands as dependent weaklings in thrall to their wives'.[60]

Like many of the stereotypes attached to the lower middle class, this domestic Pooterism has become fundamental in the conveyance of comedy in a variety of forms. The dichotomy of the ridiculous patriarch, attempting to substantiate a hierarchy within the home counter to the one that exists at the office, but who is thwarted at every turn by a long-suffering wife, began with Pooter but remained powerful throughout the twentieth century. It can be seen in, for instance, *Dad's Army*, in the relationship between Captain Mainwaring and his – oft-cited but never seen – wife Elizabeth. Glimpsed through mentions of Elizabeth's behaviour on stage, and manifest in several bruises on Mainwaring's face, their domestic turbulence is, as typical of the 1960s, writ large in comedic terms. Elizabeth's violence, coded through Mainwaring's injuries, further renders the bank manager as a weakly male specimen, hen pecked and subservient, while reinforcing another symbolic iteration of the lower-middle-class male in popular culture. Mainwaring is patently a victim of domestic abuse, but *Dad's Army* simply makes comic yet another environment in which he is incapable of asserting himself. The short tempers of lower-middle-class wives who allow their husbands a thinly veiled position as head of the family unit are widespread in British popular culture. Prunella Scales's Sybil Fawlty is fiercely efficient in the light of her husband's series of social blunders and organizational incompetence in *Fawlty Towers* (1975–9), just like Annette Crosbie's often-exasperated Margaret Meldrew in *One Foot in the Grave* (1990–2001).

Even Roy Clarke's classic 1990s sitcom *Keeping Up Appearances*, while inverting the principles, conforms to Pooterish displays. Hyacinth Bucket stands out because she is the fussy, hysterical, proud suburban rather than her husband, but Richard still manages to fulfil expectations as a browbeaten husband whose wife has the upper hand. As a female Pooter type, Hyacinth manages to heighten certain stereotypes about the lower middle class – her social emulation, cultural aspirations and keen sense of social hierarchy – while Richard also reinforces characteristics that have become associated with the class. His status as an office worker (a local council civil servant with a generic role) is characteristic of many of the features highlighted across the previous hundred years of fictional representation: he is, predictably, middle aged, cautious and reticent. Clarke somehow disrupts the lineage of sensible and respectable lower-middle-class wives (Mrs Darling, Elizabeth Perrin, Sybil Fawlty) whilst maintaining the stereotypical representation of lower-middle-class men as socially, and in gender terms, vulnerable.

In parodying the sex lives of these lower-middle-class figures, these texts substantiate petit bourgeois sexuality as part of their suburban repression. If we applied Arlene Young's argument that lower-middle-class culture holds a mirror up to the middle class, this notion of repression versus articulation is an interesting one. It implies that freely ridiculing the sexual antics of the suburban lower-middle-class bedroom is an attempt to redirect attention away from middle-class inadequacies. By owning their sensuality, lower-middle-class characters like Pam and Mick (who role-play as royals, Charles and Camilla) reassert their right to a distinct and individual sex life within their own suburban home, just as Karim's erotic adventures are part of his bid to establish a greater sense of his own individuality.

Sitcomland

Pooter began a dialogue about the petit-bourgeois suburban as the unwitting clown that has remained prominent, but which has found its natural home on the small rather than the big screen. Andy Medhurst talks about how 'representations of suburbia in British cinema occur with surprising infrequency', while Clapson mentions that documentary film-makers find little to say about suburbia that does not merely perpetuate stereotypes.[61] Medhurst also observes though, how from *29 Acacia Avenue* (1945) onwards, 'suburbia and comedy become indissolubly intertwined',[62] reminding readers that Masterman himself said that the suburbans, as he called them, 'only appear articulate in comedy'.[63] The suburban situational comedy is a culmination of this type of articulation that has evolved from early depictions like *Diary of a Nobody* via other forms such as the music hall tradition. Pooterish behaviours still hold a place in twentieth-century sitcoms, with the format beginning in the suburban home and largely staying there.

These lower-middle-class comic codes include slapstick physical comedy (the broken toilet falling on Terry's head in *Terry and June* or Hyacinth hanging on to the back of a lorry in *Keeping Up Appearances*), the awkward social scenario and the farcical performance of everyday rituals (getting the children out of the door in time for school in *Outnumbered*, for instance, or the birthday party in *Motherland*). These can all be traced back to details of Charles Pooter's life: the red bath, the Mayor's Ball or the late train to work. This type of quotidian comedy shares much of its material with other forms such as observational stand-up performances, but it is also what inspires writers like Simon Pegg to create hyper-parodies like *Shaun of the Dead* (zombies in suburbia) or *Hot Fuzz* (masonic social control in an idyllic village). It is, of course, for this reason that, as Stephen Wagg has put it, there has always been 'widespread derision for the banality, suburbanism and heavy-handedness perceived in the average British sitcom'.[64]

Not only are the performances grounded in earlier lower-middle-class culture, but the small screen has captured the symbols of suburbanization and made them into stalwart aspects of British comedy. Concerns that began in Victorian society – for example, domestic femininity that threatened to undermine the male patriarch – have become core features of the late-twentieth-century sitcom. The white-collar worker, who comes home worn out after a long day at work, continues to be met by an assertive wife who organizes his leisure time and highlights any slight incompetence. Elizabeth Perrin (*The Fall and Rise* of *Reginald Perrin*), Ann Bryce (*Ever Decreasing Circles*), Barbara Good (*The Good Life*) and Susan Harper (*My Family*) are wives that follow Carrie Pooter's lead in demonstrating, to various degrees, the organization and efficiency of the suburban matriarch. Of note is that few of these couples have children (due, in part, perhaps to the casting of child actors), but where they do – as in *My Family* – they provide, as for Pooter, an additional cause for consternation and concern for the male suburban, rather than the female.

Another trait less frequently considered is that the spouses of comic suburbans – Martin's wife, Ann, from *Ever Decreasing Circles*, for instance – deliberately offer a foil to the mad schemes and obsessive behaviours of their partners. Ann is intelligent, insightful and often depicted as frustrated by those around her, who conform only to expected behaviours. She acts as a reminder to the audience that stereotyping suburbia, and indeed stereotyping more generally, is problematic. In a similar way, David Nobb's Reginald Perrin books, and the later television series, make clear that there should not be assumptions about the way that the suburbanite should or can act. Perrin's relationship with his wife Elizabeth is dampened by the routine expectations of everyday life, but as their remarriage at the end of the first novel signifies, it is not their love that is two-dimensional or performed as a social expectation. Their early marriage after Reginald's supposed death flaunts their lack of conformity in this sense.

Perrin's faked suicide is an equally direct confrontation of the patterns of behaviour that are associated with an office-working, suburban, middle-aged man. The only way he can disconnect from the cultural assumptions that are made about a 'man like him' is to metaphorically 'kill' Reginald Iolanthe Perrin and start again. Interestingly, the most successful disguise he adopts is as a working-class gardener for whom, it is implied, these complex codes are more easily negotiable. These hints at the undercurrents of suburban stereotyping are too often ignored in light of the comic aspects of these sitcoms. As with *Diary of a Nobody*, the central comedic figure, who is often a dissection of assumptions of suburbia, overwhelms the more nuanced attitudes that can be represented within suburban comedy.

Regardless, there is a longevity of typing that threatens to reassert a simple narrative of pettiness and snobbery. Just as Simon Nye's sitcom *Men Behaving Badly* – set in a London suburb – was mistakenly criticized for celebrating the 'laddish' culture of the 1990s, because viewers did not always understand the ways that it actually mocked and undermined the male characters, comparing them unfavourably to the strong female leads, suburban sitcoms more generally are read in one-dimensional ways. In this light, they reassert what are seen as 'typical' behaviours, rendering them old-fashioned in terms of both comedy and content in the eyes of critics. At the same time, sitcoms are usually incredibly popular with audiences, who either want to enjoy watching television that deals with what is familiar to them (the immense ratings for *Gogglebox* (2013–) indicate that this is a more significant part of audience identity than has previously been considered) or, like the female fans of *Men Behaving Badly*, can understand the multiple levels on which the suburb can be understood on screen.

Keeping Up Appearances is a useful example. Clearly, the comedy rests on Hyacinth's obsession with status and her attempts to make her way into middle-class society. But her schemes are often floored by her very working-class family's appearance and her, usually failed, bids to hide her relationship with them. Snobbery is her most dominant characteristic, but Hyacinth remains strangely likeable as a character because she is redeemed by her duty towards her family – another supposedly suburban trait. This belief in familial obligation becomes her redeeming feature. Ignoring her family in favour of her social superiors might be an intention, but ultimately Hyacinth is there when they need her. Their closeness, despite her despair, demonstrates her humanity and often her humility. Richard, too, this time taking the role usually played by the suburban wife, is an effective foil, reminding the viewer that the suburban can be sensible, inclusive, warm-hearted and endlessly patient.

Keeping Up Appearances was part of a 1990s sitcom heyday that saw British sitcoms not only dominate on home screens but also do well in international sales. This heyday (which began in the 1960s) saw the suburb feature as a core setting in a format that generally revolved around a family unit. Shows such as *Butterflies*, *Ever Decreasing Circles* and later *Keeping Up Appearances*, *2point4 Children* and *One Foot in the Grave* had turned suburbia into sitcomville. Even an iconic programme like *Dad's Army* that was technically set in a seaside town, was, as Jeffrey Richards put it, 'indelibly suburban' with its cast of lower-middle-class and middle-aged bank clerks, vicars and shopkeepers.[65] Sitcom ascendency fell with the creation of more naturalist comedy such as *The Office* at the end of the twentieth century, amid too a growing appetite for American shows on British screens. The downturn of the sitcom – characterized in the highly critical reviews of sitcom-king Ben Elton's work at the beginning of the twenty-first century – almost saw semi-detached Britain slip from the screens.

New projects were urban in focus, featured an ensemble and were often taking the workplace as a natural location for airing contemporary British concerns (as we saw with *The Office*, alongside *Drop the Dead Donkey* (1990–8), *The Brittas Empire* (1991–7) and *The IT Crowd*). A decade or so into the twenty-first century saw another shift from the workplace back to the home, and the BBC's *Not Going Out* was one of the first to do this. Originally, it began as a twenty-somethings sitcom – one of the flat-sharing narratives speaking to millennials who could no longer afford to live alone in the city (seen first in the United States in *Friends* and later with *The Big Bang Theory* (2007–), *New Girl* (2011–18) and *2 Broke Girls* (2011–17)). More interestingly, *Not Going Out* radically changed its direction in series eight, with the eventual marriage, after many years of will-they-won't-they subtext, of main characters Lee and Lucy. Rather than continuing in their yuppie London pad, the couple make the move to suburbia, acquiring big-bang children and a presumably substantial mortgage.

Around this time, suburbia was getting a new treatment with writers subverting expectations of 'normality' or 'ordinariness' either through the playfulness of stylistic traits or the parody of setting. *Not Going Out*, however, with its deadpan delivery of almost relentless one-liners plays straight its old-fashioned sitcom credentials. It really is a return to the generically chaotic plot scenarios of *Ever Decreasing Circles* and *Keeping Up Appearances* – Lee attempts to do something the right way (be it a simple task like mowing the lawn for his in-laws), and a series of poor judgements and a dollop of bad luck lead to chaos. In some ways, Lee has become a sort of married-with-kids Mr Bean figure for whom life goes from bad to worse (attributed usually to the misfortune of having been from 'the North'). In a similar way, the recent popularity of the BBC sitcom *Two Doors Down* (2016–), set in Latimer Crescent in a fictional Glaswegian suburb, gives an insight into the continuing significance of the very traditional conflict between a pair of lower-middle-class and working-class neighbours. Like *Not Going Out*, it draws attention to a return towards nostalgia for suburban life, symbolic of an era when people could afford their own home and could, like the Pooters, be free to enjoy their hobbies, foibles and eccentricities.

Other more contemporary suburban sitcoms demonstrate respect for the form while reinventing creative aspects. Andy Hamilton and Guy Jenkin's *Outnumbered* stays mainly in the London suburban home; there are characters who are oft-described but never seen (just like Mrs Mainwaring in *Dad's Army*, Reginald Perrin's mother-in-law (the hippopotamus) and Sheridan Bucket, Hyacinth's son in *Keeping Up Appearances*), but its innovation lies in the improvised dialogue of the three child actors cast as the couple's young children. *The Inbetweeners* features the shifted perspective from adult suburban to teen and is, in some ways, related to Kureishi's *The Buddha of Suburbia*, another coming-of-age-in-the-suburbs narrative. *The Inbetweeners* works by making clear the frustrations of suburban living for young people whilst simultaneously demonstrating the benefits that come from supportive parents and the safe environment that the boys are completely blind to.[66] Simon Bird, who played a lead in *The Inbetweeners*, is now starring in another sitcom that once more focuses on the comedy of the seemingly 'ordinary' suburban family. *Friday Night Dinner* (2011–18) features all the stereotypical assumptions about suburbia and, in true sitcom style, injects both chaos and resolution into a weekly family meal.

Television comedy is renegotiating the suburban sitcom, perhaps as a result of the growing numbers of young people who find themselves back in their childhood bedroom in a London semi because of the pressure on the housing market in the capital. Sitcoms like *Gavin and Stacey*, *Friday Night Dinner*, *Cuckoo* (2012–) and *Together* (2016) draw comedy from the new dynamic of grown-up children living in a suburban semi with their parents, while shows like Channel 4's *Home* (2019) use the backdrop of stability and conformist suburbia to open up dialogues about community and belonging from the perspective of a refuge. Unlike the growing up and moving out emphasis of Kureishi's novel, or the implicit middle-agedness associated with characters like Howard and Hilda in *Ever Decreasing Circles*, new texts recognize that the suburbs have finally proven their worth in monetary terms, if little else, as house prices rocket in the city. Suburban life has become desirable for a new generation of writers who, like Arnold Bennett, want to live near the city but have the space to have their own families. The rows of villa-style houses, semi-detached and terraced that initially were synonymous with lower-middle-class pretension are newly worthy of attention, in part because it is only the middle class in London who can now afford to live in them. Financially, as London's housing market has grown at exceptional levels in the beginning of the twenty-first century, it is harder to mock homes that are, in a capital sense, worth so much in a contemporary economic market (a quick search online shows homes in Holloway that look remarkably similar to Pooter's 'The Laurels' are now worth nearly a million pounds). The sitcomland suburbanites who now face chaos at home and within the family are two-salaried middle-class professionals, struggling to balance high-powered parenting and the urban lifestyles they used to enjoy – see, for example, the BBC's *Motherland*.

Another reason for this return to the traditional suburban sitcom is perhaps nostalgia – just as remakes of comedy classics like *Porridge* (2017) and *Still Open All Hours* (2013–) seem to be popular at the moment, there is a deliberate return to older forms in shows like *Mrs Brown's Boys* or, in the United States, *The Goldbergs* (2013–). *The Goldbergs* is a reiteration of the family-focused, suburb-based American sitcom that has proved so instrumental to television from its inception, and it very openly plays with the nostalgic turn that has rendered 1980s culture appealing to contemporary audiences. Unlike the relentless parodying of suburbia in *Suburgatory* (2011–14), just a few years ago, *The Goldbergs*, like *Not Going Out*, marks the continuous shift of attitudes towards suburban sitcoms and the complex position that suburbia has held in popular culture since the 1890s.

Assumptions of what the suburbs should be make them so open to pervasive and continuous stereotyping. Expected patterns of behaviour that date back to the types of concerns raised in the early twentieth century continue to shape people's views. Ideas about sober conservativism and obsessive social performance equally render features that challenge these behaviours unorthodox. The case of the Soviet spies Peter and Helen Kroger in the 1950s, who lived in a suburban bungalow in Ruislip, and the suburban neighbours who helped Special Branch catch them, was viewed as extraordinary because it happened in a quiet London suburb. This incredible tale of Cold War espionage played out in a bungalow inspired a film – *The Ring of Spies* (1964), a BBC Play of the Month for television, *Act of Betrayal* (1971) and a stage production as *Pack of Lies* in 1983 (later also produced as a television movie in 1987). The television movie begins with the text 'London suburbs' and sets the scene with a quintessential dinner-party scene, featuring the sort of trifle Margo Leadbetter or Hyacinth Bucket would serve at one of their social soirees.

In the same way, much was made recently of the suburban location of a high-profile murder case from the 1990s in *Conviction: Murder in Suburbia* (2018), a real-life crime documentary about the murder of Linda Razzell. The presenters continually asserted, as the title too suggests, the argument that the murder was more shocking because it took place in a Swindon suburb rather than a major city. Clearly, as in the 1950s, there remains an assumption that subversive or immoral behaviours are outside of the imagination of those who live in suburbia – the parodying of which is at the heart of Nigel Williams's novels about Wimbledon.

What, then, is within the remit of what we expect from suburban culture? In many ways, it is the type of gentle, light-hearted comedy that has become enshrined in the British sitcom. In America, by contrast, the mood has turned darker. Alongside a similar appetite for the easy-viewing family sitcom set in a suburban home, American film and television has championed the dark suburb, full of powerful and dangerously subversive behaviours. It took what Bueka has described as the 'idealized image of middle-class life' and explored the 'very elements of society that threaten this image', producing complexly dark iterations that rock the stability of the bourgeois dream.[67] This ranges from the social and emotional isolation of films such as *All That Heaven Allows* (1955), *The Stepford Wives* (1975), the surrealism and violence of *Blue Velvet* (1986) and *Parents* (1989) and the glut disturbing depictions around the turn of the millennium, such as *Pleasantville* (1998), *The Truman Show* (1998) and *American Beauty* (1999). Since then, films like *Revolutionary Road* (2005), *The Joneses* (2009) and *Suburbicon* (2017) have been shown in tandem with television portrayals such as *Suburgatory* (2011–14), *Modern Family* (2009–) and *The Goldbergs*.

On British screens, the suburb has resurfaced, evidence of a new generation that are once more back in their parent's semi-detached homes. New situational comedies once more find humour in the same sort of social tensions that writers such as Bob Larbey and John Esmonde identified in the 1970s, the 1980s and the 1990s, but they add in new inter-generational factors that update the form, while retaining a focus on the lower middle class. It is the focus on the individual lives within that have facilitated this return to suburbia as a key cultural site – the comedy that can be found in the every day eccentricities and behaviours of the suburban remain instrumental to our concept of humour, while we continue to root for the familiar faces on our screens, those who we see as a reflection of ourselves.

5

The home

This chapter sets up the home as a space that, unlike the office, the commute or suburbia as a wider entity, is largely private. It also argues that the suburban semi was, in many ways, a cornerstone of a twentieth-century philosophy that advocated and normalized the nuclear family as the heart of the suburbanite's universe. Alongside this development – and connected to it – was the rising mechanization in the office that made the white-collar worker feel increasingly like a number at work and merely part of a mass on the daily commute. The home was a valuable space in which to be an individual, an environment where the white-collar worker could reassert aspects of humanity that were being lost within their professional environment. In turn, the safety of the semi-detached home protected and nurtured the suburban offspring, raising a generation who had known only those comforts that their parents had often faced years of hard work to achieve. Suburbia was, as Peter Scott has argued, the 'ideal environment for these new values' of the '"privatized" family- and home-centred lifestyles' that placed great emphasis on the experience of bringing up children in hygienic, well-designed and comfortable homes.[1] Mass-house building in the interwar period brought these opportunities to the expanding lower middle class, as well as increasingly to those on more stable working-class wages, making the 'suburban aspiration' – that which Simon Gunn describes as a 'desire to live in the suburbs, a desire based upon certain preferences and values which were, and still are, shared by a majority of people in England' – a reality.[2]

As the last chapter explored, few features of suburbia survive the cynicism of its critics, and even those that appear, on the face of it, to be positive rarely remain unspoiled. Generous green spaces are portrayed in comical terms (the erstwhile attempts of amateur gardeners); garages are hotbeds of unwanted clutter and half-finished DIY projects; the 'through-lounge' of the 1980s is looked down upon from the new 'kitchen-diner' of the twenty-first century. The cul-de-sac, planned for privacy and space, became, as Joe Moran puts it, 'a byword for

Figure 5.1 Margot Leadbetter (Penelope Keith) anxiously watches her neighbours in *The Good Life* (1975)
© BBC

curtain-twitching suburban respectability, self-interest and withdrawal from the social sphere'.[3] Even neighbours, a key part of the much-lauded romanticization of the working-class community, provided endless comedy in the lower-middle-class suburban home. They were ready and waiting to upstage their fellow suburbanites – capturing deviant behaviour with a video camera in Alan Plater's *Beiderbecke Connection* (1988), watching in bemusement over the garden wall in *The Good Life* (Figure 5.1) or hiding behind the living room curtains in *Keeping Up Appearances*.

There is, however, a narrative around the suburban home as a space of safety which began with the very earliest of suburban texts, where the Victorian villa was a marker of security at work and greater comfort at home. In Charles Dickens's *Great Expectations* (1861), Wemmick's home is a metaphorical castle, a drawbridged stronghold from which Wemmick can escape the office and establish a deep privacy that is almost impermeable. Wemmick, like the Goods in the 1970s, makes his own attempts at self-sufficiency, recalling the pastoralism of his forebears, those who E. M. Forster saw in *Howards End* in 1910 as the ploughboys of the eighteenth century who knew the land and their place in it. Critics tend to look on Wemmick as typical of lower-middle-class eccentricity, in his fierce protection of private space and his desperation to mark territory in what is a fraught and unyielding social-scape. What Wemmick manages to achieve, though, is a security that few clerks at that time could afford. His affection for home and family remains the core aspect of lower-middle-class suburban life long into the twenty-first century, reaching new heights in suburban sitcoms over 150 years later.

Suburban havens

When scholars use H. G. Wells's *War of the Worlds* (1898) as evidence of his sometimes-callous attitude towards the suburbs, they ignore the ways that his other novels often draw attention to what is really at risk when the aliens invade. His tales of characters desperate to make their way from an urban flat or lodgings into a suburban villa show that, unlike many middle-class commentators, Wells knew also about the alternative to suburbia – the insecurity of tenancy and the impoverishment of city life on a lowly clerk's wages. Despite his own miserable childhood recollections of suburbia's sprawl, played out in the metaphorical revenge seen in *War of the Worlds*, Wells does show an awareness that, for most of the lower middle class, suburbia was preferable to the misery of housing in more central areas of London. In fact, looking more closely at *War*, we see that the narrator survives by hiding within the ruins of a suburban home in Sheen – in this case, the house acts as a literal haven – whilst the emotional reunion with his wife takes place symbolically in the dining-room of their Woking house.

Frequently seen in Wells's work are narratives where the lower-middle-class clerk works hard to relocate himself and his family from a suite of rooms to a small suburban property – a tale that is told across many middlebrow novels of the early twentieth century. Many characters (Richard Larch in *A Man from the North* (1898), for instance, or Shan Bullock's Robert Thorne (1907) and Galbraith in Swinnerton's *The Young Idea* (1910)) live with landladies or in small and uncomfortable lodgings whilst dreaming of what they see as suburban luxury. These characters, far from dismissing suburbia as soulless or anonymous, champion the suburbs as distinctly individual. There is little sense of ownership or independence in lodgings that are pre-furnished, often by a fierce middle-aged spinster, who polices not only the interior decoration but the moral and social behaviour of her lodgers. The suburban villa, on the other hand, with its neat garden, freedom to add decorative touches and social autonomy is immeasurably unique.[4] Charles Pooter's interest in DIY (more on which later) features in critical commentaries as evidence of his fundamental Pooterishness, but the few parties he hosts are an often-overlooked signifier of freedom. They are, of course, ripe with the Grossmiths' quiet satire on Victorian social etiquette, but minor events like these also demonstrate that the Pooters are free to entertain when and whom they like. Their perceptions of class and position can shape what they think they ought to do, but there is no omniscient figure insisting that they keep the noise down or adding a curfew to proceedings.

Bennett's *A Man from the North* gives an example of the influence of the landlady on the immediate environment of the young clerk. Initially, Larch lives right in the centre of London, in Raphael Street, Knightsbridge, but only as a lodger in a small dwelling. His room is described as

> a long, rather low room, its length cut by the two windows which were Mrs Rowbotham's particular pride; between the windows a table with a faded green cloth, and a small bed opposite; behind the door an artfully concealed washstand; the mantelpiece, painted mustard yellow, bore divers squat earthenware figures, and was surmounted by an oblong mirror framed in rosewood; over the mirror an illuminated text, 'Trust in Jesus', and over the text an oleography, in collision with the ceiling, entitled 'After the Battle of Culloden'.[5]

Bennett makes clear that these are decorative touches added at minimal cost by an austere landlady who wants to influence her lower-middle-class bachelor tenant; the religious text reminds the occupant of high moral standards, the oleography draws attention to patriotism and the personal washstand encourages cleanliness. The furnishings are universal, the necessities for any urban clerk living in the home of an impoverished spinster, just like Bullock's Robert Thorne has merely a 'narrow bed and a strip of old carpet ... a rickety washstand and a cracked mirror ... [and] nails in the door' to hold his clothes.[6]

It was not just single clerks and secretaries living in the city for the first time that faced scrutiny as a tenant. For married clerks like Robert Thorne, a suburban home is an incredibly significant marker not just of status but also of security. Thorne, who has worked his way up from a dismal attic to a suite of rooms, pays seven shillings a week to live in a four-room upper flat in Dulwich, whilst he and his wife dream of further advancement into suburban life 'proper' – 'it was a goodly way, we knew, from an attic in Kensington to a villa in Surbiton'.[7] Thorne's senior colleague Mr Oliver lives in such a house, and from the moment that Thorne views this state of domestic happiness, Oliver is cast as the perfect role model, both professionally and privately. In Wells's *Love and Mr Lewisham*, a schoolmaster's assistant exists in a dismal domestic situation whilst trying to support his young wife and begin his career. Marrying before he has finished his degree, Lewisham places himself under dire financial strain while simultaneously trying to impress his new bride with an idyll of domesticity. Their home just south of Brompton Road is simply 'a minute bedroom and a small sitting-room, separated by folding-doors on the ground floor'.⁸

As Richard Church, the poet, wrote in his memoirs, 'to a boy coming out of Battersea, [Dulwich] was half-way to paradise'.⁹ Church's *Over the Bridge* (1955) recounts an upbringing that shares much in common with the novels of Wells and Bennett; his father worked for the Post Office and the family travelled further out of the city with each respective move until his mother died when he was in his teens. Church himself left school to be a clerk and worked in the Civil Service into his forties until he made enough money from writing to support himself. Church's autobiography is a rare voice preaching fondness for suburbia, and a central part of the narrative of his own creative life is the relative stability and comfort of the suburban home and the space to read widely. The move out to suburbia also fostered a love for the countryside around his Kent home (fed by the long bicycle rides that he took with his father, a very keen cyclist). Cycling, like rambling, became a key suburban pastime – as is evident in Wells's novels *The Wheels of Chance* (1896) and *The History of Mr Polly* (1910), where it symbolizes freedom in the outdoors and a counter to the sedentary nature of white-collar work.¹⁰

Whilst Charles Pooter is a suburban caricature, pottering about in his garden with his paintbrush and his fine red enamel paint, the Grossmiths equally use these hobbies to evoke an authentic fondness for his suburban home. Pooter captured the new focus on the domestic sphere as a site of self-improvement through interior design, small DIY projects and gardening. Following in Pooter's footsteps, small household jobs have continued to perplex the lower-middle-class suburban in popular cultural representations. Martin botches fixing the bed in the early hours of the morning in 1980s sitcom *Ever Decreasing Circles*, and Lee destroys his father-in-law's artificial lawn (by cutting it with a lawn mower) in the recent young-singles-comedy-turned-suburban-family sitcom *Not Going Out*.

Pooter's attention was not limited to interior design; he adds various observations to his diary about gardening plans – noting useful places for growing radishes and mustard-and-cress and commenting on his pleasure at finding a cheap guide to gardening at a bookstall. His seeds never quite take, and there is very little harvested from the garden at 'The Laurels', but his green-fingered enthusiasm is an established trope of the suburban occupant. While Richard Dennis suggests that the name The Laurels 'neatly summarises London suburbia of the 1890s [and] the desire to be close to nature, to have a garden', this is by no means limited to the earliest suburban development.[11] As Scott makes clear, interwar suburban development created four million new gardens, most of which were surrounding houses occupied by lower-middle and working-class families.[12] Consequently, gardening became (and continues to be) one of Britain's most popular hobbies, following 'interwar working and lower-middle-class garden pioneers' who were proud of their sense of ownership 'over their own little patch of British soil'.[13] In R. F. Delderfield's novel *The Dreaming Suburb* (1958), a novel that indulges playfully in various stereotypes of the suburban class, Edgar Frith symbolizes the 'typical' suburban husband who spends all of his evenings in his greenhouse. Like many other fictional henpecked lower-middle-class husbands, Edgar is attempting to escape his wife Esther, who belittles or ignores him almost from the moment of their marriage.

Much more harmoniously, Tom and Barbara Good take their suburban gardening very seriously in 1970s sitcom *The Good Life*. Their horticultural dedication, however, does not prevent their escapades in the suburban garden from being inherently comic, ending often in disaster. The Goods' use of the garden as a site of practical sustainability evokes a much earlier impression of the suburban garden as a place in which to grow produce (for instance in the Second World War), and runs counter to their neighbours' contemporary designation of the patio as a performative platform from which to display horticulture in a social sense (admiring the flowers over evening cocktails). This tension between the functional and the aesthetic is at the core of the conflict between the two couples, and the comedy derived from this evokes the essential difficulties in the conception of the suburban home as a private space which is 'family-orientated rather than community-orientated [in] outlook' and the contradiction of the 'semi-detached' home, which in its very title gives an indication of this oxymoron.[14]

By the end of the twentieth century, Richard Bucket is another of Edgar Frith's gardening descendants, another submissive husband who attempts to evade his wife's scrutiny by hiding in the garden. Unlike the Goods, who represent the light-hearted battleground between suburban privacy and community, Richard reverts to an earlier template which sets the ideology of family-orientation within a less harmonious framework. Like Edgar Frith, Richard makes use of the front garden space because he gains a wider sense of freedom than within his suburban bungalow. His domineering wife, Hyacinth, still carefully retains surveillance of the garden, monitoring and advising on aspects of Richard's gardening attire, performance and behaviour, but there are also opportunities for limited external interactions – with their neighbours Elizabeth and Emmet.

In his 1990 satire of suburbia, *The Wimbledon Poisoner*, Nigel Williams talks about 'the dull wounded little man whose horizons were blunted by the daily journey to the office, the suburban garden and the suburban slug'.¹⁵ These are Richard's boundaries too – the only other settings he finds himself in are fraught by the type of social indelicacies that are so often associated with the lower middle class.

Gardening as a distinctly suburban pastime is, by this point, explicitly socially coded. Hyacinth insists that Richard wear a tie to garden because 'we have a social position to maintain' (Figure 5.2); his horticultural pursuits are channelled into marking out the Bucket's social superiority (in contrast, Hyacinth's working-class sister's house has a wild front yard filled with a rusting car and a feral dog).¹⁶ Hyacinth insists that their roses should be bigger than those next door because it is these markers of class that define her attitude even to her neighbours. The plants that Richard cultivates, like those that Pooter attempts to grow, are symbolically aesthetic only providing no sustenance and therefore little purpose. In contrast, Tom and Barbara eschew suburban values the minute they dig up their front lawn to plant vegetables, making an overt statement about the social façade that their neighbours are merely projecting.

There is an equally gendered relationship in the popular representation of gardening. Barbara Good stands out because unlike her neighbour, Margot,

Figure 5.2 Richard (Clive Swift) attempts to tend the garden in *Keeping Up Appearances* (1995)
© BBC

who delicately selects flowers for display at her social events, she and Tom are engaging in agriculture for subsistence, albeit on a very small scale. Generally, popular culture depicts the male suburban in the garden for specific reasons. Gail Cunningham identifies the 'escape' to the garden in *fin-de-siècle* texts as a symbolic resort to a 'male space' in response to the feminized domesticity of the suburban home.[17] In recent Channel 4 sitcom *Friday Night Dinner*, this trend continues, with suburban father Martin rigging out his garden shed with a comfy chair and a television so that he can hide himself (and a banned collection of old National Geographic magazines) from his wife. In a similar manner, the shed remains an iconic marker of male freedom (as indicated in the published parody, *Fifty Sheds of Grey: Erotica for the not-too-modern male* (2012)).

The status of the 'man cave' in contemporary interior design (and the many signs advertising this space that are available for sale) lends gravity to a long-standing association between the male suburban and the garden. While this is a particularly gendered interpretation of the domestic outdoors that continues to reassert assumptions about domesticity and femininity too, there is a wider dialogue about gardening in the twenty-first century which taps into discourse that has been significant at various points in the past 150 years. As for Pooter, who makes pioneering forays into suburban gardening, or Leonard Bast, who feels the pain of being excluded from the type of deeply evocative pastoral space in *Howards End*, there is a contemporary discussion about the distance between home and access to greenery that laments the loss of front driveways to make room for car parking, recognizing it as part of a complex renegotiation of our relationship with the outdoors and the rural. While middle-class Londoners, whose small-terraced homes have quadrupled in value in the last ten years, enlist the help of television shows like *Escape to the Country* to find their forever home in a perceived rural idyll, suburban gardens are a more realistic goal for many families who are keen to reap the benefits a garden brings to mental and physical well-being.

More than simply poking fun at the suburbans, what the Grossmiths began was a trend for stories that wrote against the grain of literary opinion; they give a voice to suburbanites who think that their life stories are as worthy of telling as those of the other classes. As Williams would later put it in his 1990s trilogy about Wimbledon: 'the stories of the suburbs, the tales that gave number 24, 69, 30 or 47 their right to the homes, these were, in their way, as substantial as the creation myths of the Eskimos'.[18] In this, Williams followed in the footsteps of writers like Keble Howard, who published *The Smiths of Surbiton* in 1906. His cheery and well-matched couple came to symbolize the story less often told of the contented suburbanites. Significantly where they live defines them (just as it does, in *The Good Life* – also Surbiton), in evidence from the title alone. The name of their 'cheery little villa' ('The Pleasance') equally sums up the tone of the entire novel. Howard, who was later referred to as the 'Laureate of Suburbia', wrote the story first as a series for *The World and His Wife*, having been asked to pitch something about a couple who had an income of six hundred pounds a year, which was to be 'absolutely realistic, entirely free from exaggeration and fictitious excitements'.[19]

Introductions to novels based in suburban houses have long had to negotiate what their authors perceive as a ready and waiting bias; Howard pre-empted his tale with a warning that 'Superior Persons' will not appreciate a story about a 'humdrum' family, who 'read the books they like, visit the theatres they like, and whistle the music they like'.[20] Likewise, in 1958, Delderfield confronted any potentially hostile readers when, in the beginning of *The Dreaming Suburb*, he commented that ' "suburban" is never said without a sneer or a hint of patronage'.[21] In writing *The Smiths of Surbiton*, Howard, like Delderfield, challenged the type of middle-class critic who assumes that a novel about contented suburban living will contain references to 'low' literature, middlebrow tastes and typically tedious anecdotes about a mundane existence. Indeed, this was certainly the perspective of one *Spectator* reviewer who revisited the novel for a second time as a result of 'praise in the Press'. The widespread popularity of the book certainly did little to appease this reviewer, who used high sales as a justification for lamenting the intelligence of the wider population:

> They want the glamour of romance thrown over their everyday life, 'for', will argue Mrs. Jones of Dulwich, 'if Mrs. Smith of Surbiton is worth writing a story about, is not my life, which I have sometimes thought dull, an equally fit theme for fiction?' Perhaps it is no small achievement to have succeeded in pointing this out to many hundreds of perfectly commonplace, everyday people. It is, at any rate, the only achievement with which a critic who deems literary distinction essential in a novel will feel free to credit Mr. Keble Howard's study in suburban romance.[22]

Another, this time in *The Saturday Review*, was even more scathing about the readers of such suburban fiction:

> There are probably several thousands of families in the suburbs precisely like 'The Smiths of Surbiton', ordinary, worthy, dull people, contented with small incomes, small interests, small talk and a generally humdrum existence.[23]

By the time a new edition was published in 1925, the novel had already enjoyed, as Howard himself declares, 'twenty years; many editions; many languages; [and] many friends', as well as, inevitably, 'a few sneers'. Moreover, it 'sold with astonishing rapidity', was published in many countries, did particularly well in America and led to two sequels – *The Smiths of Valley View* (1909) and *The Smiths in War Time* (1917) – and a play. Clearly, aspiring to successful suburban living was a popular topic for reading regardless of how it was being portrayed more broadly.

Middlebrow texts from the nineteenth century onwards were often keen to substantiate the place of the suburban home as a space that inspired its occupants, nurtured them, encouraged and protected them. Early writings in support of suburbia firstly established the home as a site of shelter and then tried to use this assertion as protection from the sort of condescension already in play. They then directed their energies at relaying the type of lives that unfolded behind the front doors of suburbia's new houses in a new wave of lower-middle-class life writing. Arnold Bennett's Mr Aked has become a sort of figurehead for the positive revision of suburban culture, and the speech he gives to Richard Larch inspires his young muse to put pen to paper to capture the diversity of life within the houses that surround him:

> How many houses are there in Carteret Street? Say eighty? Eighty theatres of love, hate, greed, tyranny, endeavour; eighty separate dramas always unfolding, intertwining, ending, beginning, – and every drama a tragedy. No comedies, and especially no farces! Why, child, there is more character within a hundred yards of this chair than a hundred Balzacs could analyse in a hundred years.[24]

Aked offers a useful voice in favour of capturing the suburban life in popular culture – which is why this speech is so often cited in suburban histories. Many other novelists joined Bennett, trying to counter the assumption that a mass-produced exterior undermines the individuality of those who live within. Bullock, for instance, sets up one of the homes in his novel *Robert Thorne* in this way:

> It was a semi-detached villa of red brick; a grass patch between iron railing and bow window in front, a longer patch bordered with flower beds behind; cork-faced plant boxes on the sills; flat brass bands adorning the bedroom windows; right and left a hundred other residences exactly like it.[25]

The scene is a familiar one – it is an 'everyplace' – and what Bullock does with it is interesting. Rather than projecting the similarity of the surrounding houses as an immediate indicator of the type of two-dimensional suburban homes that authors such as T. W. H. Crosland were sneering at, he suggests that Mr Hope's house – and by implication his story – is almost universal. As Bennett would put it, behind those hundred other doors are more than a hundred other stories.

Within the novel, Bullock does not gloss over the difficulties of suburban life, and what he wants by the end of the narrative is not a glorified suburbia, but he does make very clear that there are individual desires and ambitions connected to improving the quality of life, regardless of status. His suburban inhabitants are fiercely resistant to the typing that comes with the suburban home, but they also eulogize a rural over an urban life. Mrs Hope, the wife of Robert's colleague, sees London as the eternal 'other' to the Devonshire home she was brought up in, but she lives in suburbia because it presents the only viable alternative while her husband works at the Tax Office. The Thornes holiday with Mr Hope and his family once he retires, and it gives them an insight into country life that they find hard to reconcile with their lives in London. Whilst the Thornes reject their suburban home, in favour of an attempt at farming in New Zealand, they symbolize the variety of attitudes, feelings and desires that drive people who live in suburbia. Bullock attempts to give his characters freedom from the assumptions already in circulation: that of the endlessly emulative suburban desperate to merely 'keep up with the Joneses'.

In his second novel, Bullock comes back to address the criticisms of suburban living. *Mr Ruby Jumps the Traces* (1917) is almost a sequel to *Robert Thorne*; rather than the young clerk in the city of the first novel, the protagonist this time is a figure who has much in common with David Nobbs's Reginald Perrin of the 1970s or Carl Matthews of television drama *The 7.39* in 2014. Middle-aged Ruby is bored of his life. On his commute into London, he watches the dock workers unload exotic goods off the ships and imagines running away. Bullock writes of the tedium of the daily grind and the routine that sees Ruby constantly having to account for his whereabouts – either in the office or to his wife at home in the suburbs. The novel does not, though, criticize suburbia in the way that might be expected. While Ruby's daughter is cynical about her parents' quiet and unadventurous lives, Bullock is clear that suburbia is not to blame for Ruby's discontent. In *The 7.39*, the daily details of Carl's suburban routine are equally monotonous (each morning he cuts himself feeding the cat and complains about inadequately rinsed dishwashing), but, as for Ruby, these elements only grate when he is negotiating a mid-life crisis moment. Knocking on his old front door once his affair with Sally has finished is an allegoric homecoming that leads ultimately to the final scenes of domestic happiness at the dining-room table two years down the line.

If we return to Bullock's novel, Mr and Mrs Ruby live in Camberwell on a 'pleasant enough, wide, straight, open, quiet, respectable road'.[26] It is a very similar landscape to the one that surrounds Carl in the twenty-first century, which has become synonymous with the acres of wide streets so typical of London suburbs. While the Rubys' house could be symbolic of what Crosland dismisses as the 'miles and miles of villas with bay-windows and little-black yards', Bullock focuses on the human element, arguing that 'behind the long dreariness of glass and brickwork were humans with aspirations as individual as their diverse selves'.[27] Like Bennett and Church, Bullock is concerned not with the aesthetics of suburbia, nor the repetition of architectural features, but the suburban subjects themselves. Ruby's problems, Bullock suggests, are in danger of being ignored by assuming that the people within each suburban villa are bland and without individuality. In many ways, the novel precedes Nobb's books in suggesting that the outward codes of performance – the bowler hat, the suit, the briefcase, leaving the suburban semi and the 'avenue', for the 7.57 – are in danger of masking the frustrations of the individual.

This refusal to accept that there might be personality within the suburban environment is, in part, what cultivated a determination for outwardly visible symbols of individual flair. One manifestation of this, mocked endlessly by critics, was the naming of suburban villas. Many of these names were subtle indications of the same sort of rebellion that Ruby's trip to sea captures. They are inventive signals to a wider world, often evoking the type of natural features that were becoming harder to find in the capital, as in Agatha Christie's *The Big Four* (1927):

> A few moments more saw us ascending the steps of The Laurels, as Mr Ingles' residence was called. Personally, I did not notice a laurel bush of any kind, so deduced that it had been named according to the usual obscure nomenclature of the suburbs.[28]

It is easy for Captain Hastings to sneer; his status is more easily assured, having travelled widely both in the military and with famous Belgian detective Hercule Poirot. But for office workers who face the tedium of the desk each day, a hint at the wide, green world outside was surely welcome. While they might not be strictly representative of the features of the house, or its surroundings, suburban names cover would-be holidays in exotic places or nostalgically reference trips to beauty spots in Britain – in the rugged Celtic edges of Cornwall and Wales.

W. Pett Ridge talks about the free ranging creativity of suburbans who began to think beyond the features that their homes replaced: 'the early numbers went on conventional lines, and called themselves for no reason The Firs, The Oaks, The Elms, The Beeches'. He continues, 'these being exhausted, there came turmoil of the mind and the summoning up of daring conceit. Thus you have Plas-Newydelln ... La Maisonette ... Beau Rivage; Ben Nevis, Beethoven Villa, St. Moritz'.[29] They are aspirational and outward facing, referencing a wider world of cultural significance.

George Orwell was famously critical of this practice in *Coming Up for Air* (1936) when he writes of 'the inner-outer suburbs ... as much alike as council houses and generally uglier ... The Laurels, the Myrtles, the Hawthorns, Mon Abri, Mon Repos, Belle Vue'.[30] He mocks what he sees as the pretension of the lower middle class that is absent in their working-class neighbours. Lower-middle-class authors like Bullock risk ire by suggesting that the naming of suburban villas (Mr Ruby's house is called *Caseta* – 'a name in which the Rubys had pride') is actually in recognition of the 'diverse selves' that dwell within.[31] While critics like Orwell were damning about what they perceived as the ignorance behind these evocative names, they are symbolic because they challenge ideas of the lower middle class as inward looking. The narrative of social aspiration and endless emulation dominates any discussion of the naming of the suburban home as a recognition of the relationship between the home and the world, the family and society. Or even, of the pride of ownership as anything other than boastful or gloating. This type of criticism comes historically, of course, from the middle class, for whom home ownership was an unquestioned right.

In J. M. Barrie's *Peter Pan and Wendy*, the Darlings' home (the nondescriptly named 'No. 14') simultaneously conforms to certain traits associated with the lower middle class whilst disrupting a narrative of dull suburbia with the great emotional trauma that occurs when the children disappear. Mr Darling is a very typical white-collar figure, with little imagination and some limited knowledge of stocks and shares. His penny-pinching ways run counter to his desire to appear socially respectable, which leads, of course, to his hiring a St. Bernard dog as a nanny. Their home, though, is a sanctuary – the nursery, with its soft night-lights and cherubic occupants, is a product of the emotional and psychological centre of the suburban mother. From within this suburban environment, the children are whisked off on an adventure to Neverland, a place which their mother too remembers from her own childhood. The lives of these suburbanites are not limited or unimaginative, rather this development comes as an inevitable process of growing up. It is being an adult that is without wonder, rather than being trapped in a suburban home itself.

A similar thread runs through recent film adaptations of Edwardian children's classics such as *Hook* (1991) – itself a reimagining of *Peter Pan* – *Paddington* (2014) and *Christopher Robin* (2018). In each of these films, the adult in the suburban home must remember their childhood capacity for wonder and break free of their white-collar lives to embrace their inner child. *Hook* rests on the grown Peter Pan's need to recall his lost abilities in order to rescue his kidnapped children, which ironically sees Peter return to Neverland in a much more active capacity than George Darling in the original, who simply waits for his children to return. George is a bank clerk, and thus represented as being incapable of any response that would involve him leaving his comfort zone in either suburbia or the office to enter a mythical land of mermaids and pirates. In the suburban nursery, it is Mrs Darling's love that will draw the children home. In *Paddington*, Mr Brown must overcome his suburban sensibilities and learn to accept the eccentricities of his new houseguest – in fact, Brown's suburban neighbours all grow to depend on the childlike exuberance and emotional grounding that Paddington brings.

Julian Barnes showed a similar attitude in his first novel *Metroland* (1980). His character is not overly enamoured with suburbia, but he does recognize the place that it holds on a personal level for those who live there. Like No. 14, the soft glow of the night-light in his baby daughter's room provides the symbol of suburban comfort and safety. Late in the twentieth century, this sense of familial nurturing is at the heart of the suburban sitcom. The resolution of whatever chaotic events have shaped the narrative is symbolized in the family returning to the home – often to the figurative centre (in *Men Behaving Badly* this is the sofa, in *Fresh Fields* (1984–6) and *My Family* (2000–11) it is the kitchen table, for instance). In *Keeping Up Appearances*, Hyacinth Bucket's utterance 'Take me home, Richard' marks her usual resignation about whatever madcap scheme she has become embroiled in. At home, she is in control, capable of arranging the interior to match her self-perception in terms of status and class.

Hyacinth is not the most positive example of the ways that the suburban house can nurture and give confidence to its occupants (although her unseen son Sheridan is happily away at university studying Advanced Needlework), but the ways that home is a space in which her world makes sense is a crucial part of the suburban narrative that is often overlooked. The suburban home is both a metaphorical and a literal haven, and where critics have sneered at the proud lower-middle-class homeowner, it reflects the challenge to the established middle class that more widespread home ownership represents. In response to this, middlebrow fiction of the late nineteenth and early twentieth centuries, followed by suburban sitcoms of the 1960s onwards, all focus on the home as a place of individuality, where characters display their charming eccentricities and have full expression of their values, politics and opinions. In many of these examples, the suburban semi (or bungalow) is shown in opposition to the white-collar workplace – an environment in which characters are required to submit to rules and behaviours that are not necessarily their own. Richard, perhaps, is the exception here; part of the pathos of his character is that there is no escape – at home he has even less freedom than in the office, and his tastes and interests are constantly sidelined for those in which Hyacinth thinks he *ought* to participate (see, for instance, the episode where Hyacinth buys Richard skis for his birthday – just so that he can drive around with them on the roof of the car).[32]

What is also of note are the generational changes that have increasingly seen the suburban, keen and proud, as part of an older demographic. If, as the last chapter suggests, the latter half of the twentieth century saw the adolescent and young adult suburbanite eager to fledge the suburb and make a bid for the chaos and culture of the city, there is a now a renewed sense of nostalgia for the semi-detached homes of youth. As home ownership stretches out of reach of young couples and families until later in life, the space, greenery and comfort of the suburban home has become synonymous with an older generation, those who are the parents and grandparents in both lower-middle and middle-class families. The comedic suburbanite is, like the Buckets, elderly and chaotic in a manner that does not befit their age and (what should be) wisdom. In *Friday Night Dinner*, the parents – those who should be beacons of respectability and conservatism as representatives of suburban conformity – are often immature and irrational, leaving their two sons to act sensibly. This inversion of the child–parent dichotomy is, of course, a stalwart aspect of British comedy, manifesting in various guises in *The Office* (between Brent and those he supposedly manages) as well as in the marriage of Richard and Hyacinth (the former often acts as the exasperated parent in the face of Hyacinth's childishly simplistic schemes) and the relationship between Gary and Dorothy in *Men Behaving Badly*.[33]

Keeping up appearances

There is a common assumption that consumerism is key to demonstrating superiority over neighbours from the working class and to attempt to keep up with the middle class. Consequently, a desire to impress has been used as another rod with which to beat the lower middle class, but rarely is the association between the suburbanite and their ownership of meaningful objects harnessed in argument of a suburban culture that this is not merely performance or status symbolism. Instead of viewing aspiration as entirely bound up with material gains, I argue that lower-middle-class texts and media try to emphasize a more holistic message about the value of cultural and educational development. This message can be easily lost amidst the comedic value of status and outward social mobility, but it helps to counter the cynicism that is so often levelled at the lower middle class – and by extension, anyone who lives in suburbia.

Keeping Up Appearances is perhaps one of the most visible and prevailing symbols of the suburban home, finding itself an unlikely export that has been sold worldwide. The Laurels, the humble villa at the heart of Charles Pooter's narrative in *Diary of a Nobody* is more frequently discussed by academic analyses, but it is perhaps useful to consider *Keeping Up Appearances* alongside it as a powerful reminder of the longevity of certain views that surround the suburban home. In many ways, and as Scott Banville highlights when he compares another pair of lower-middle-class texts (in his case, the British department store comedy, *Are You Being Served?* and American suburban sitcom *Everybody Loves Raymond*), this is an act of 'remediation' for a contemporary audience. This is true of the relationship between Hyacinth and Charles, but it also speaks more widely to the intertextualities prevalent across many of the texts under discussion in this study. There are identifiable threads of intertextuality – responses and rewritings that are directed at earlier subjects in the lower-middle-class canon – but there is also a general pool of tropes and characteristics that are appropriated to flesh out and substantiate generic impression of the lower middle class in popular culture.

Both Hyacinth Bucket and Charles Pooter value their suburban homes; they each take delight in adding personal touches, updating décor and pruning their respective gardens. They characterize influential moods that have spanned the nineteenth, twentieth and even twenty-first centuries: cyclical fads and phases in which home improvement (or DIY), gardening and social etiquette have each had more than a few days in the sun. Ben Highmore argues that the British home is 'a place where you are meant to express your taste, your cultural loyalties and your aspirations'.[34] In fact, as the owners of the unassuming bungalow that was used to film the exterior shots of *Keeping Up Appearances* noted, their home became integral to the iconography of tastes, cultural loyalties and aspirations of the nation, with visitors continuing to visit from around the world long after filming finished.[35] The same was true of the 1930s semi-detached house in

Northwood, North London, that became Tom and Barbara Good's unorthodox fictional small-holding in *The Good Life* in the 1970s and the terrace house used for filming *Gavin and Stacey* in Barry. Part of this fascination comes from the crucial association between the suburban home and the late-twentieth-century sitcom. This is evidence of what Robert Bueka has drawn attention to in the early development of the American sitcom, the relationship between 'the fledgling medium of television' and suburbia that has resounded long into the twenty-first century.[36]

Hyacinth and Richards's home is a 1970s bungalow in Binley Woods on the outskirts of Birmingham, in a neighbourhood that Hyacinth approves of (although there is an 'element' that does not meet her exacting social standards). The bungalow is neat and tidy with a meticulously pruned garden, maintained by a faithful Richard with Hyacinth's assistance when it suits (usually at a moment when she is keen to observe the behaviour of a neighbour). Inside much is made of the hallway as the space into which guests are graciously received and tradesmen are excluded. Hyacinth's propitious use of the two doorways – the symbolically significant 'front' and 'back' doors – becomes a comedic device for negotiating the type of embarrassing situations that require people of a different status not to meet within this precious hall space. For Pooter too, the hallway symbolizes the 'coming and going' (of 'Cummings and Gowings') that causes social anxiety, particularly when the formal front door is out of commission and his side door (which should be for tradesmen and deliveries) is deemed an unsuitable replacement.

Like Pooter, who in his diary details his cherished moose antlers and his red-painted enamel bath, Hyacinth is at pains to demonstrate the value of the objects within her home. In one episode, when Richard forgets their wedding anniversary, instead buying Hyacinth a security system, the salesperson faces a long list of the assets on display in their suburban bungalow. The telephone ('a private, slim-line, white telephone with no connection whatever to business or trade')[37] becomes a key part of the comedy of possession that makes up so much of the tone of the show, as does Hyacinth's 'Royal Doulton [tea-set] with hand-painted periwinkles'. Hyacinth uses the phone – with its beautifully and comically articulated specification – to simultaneously exude social niceties while excluding the unworthy.[38]

Unlike the front door itself, the doorstep of which – as in *Diary of a Nobody* – encourages arguments about status and eligibility, the phone can be used to screen people with fewer social consequences. The telephone, as Highmore argues, is a complicated mix of the intimate and the public, placed in the 'quasi-public'

Figure 5.3 On the slim-line phone in *Keeping Up Appearances* (1995)
© BBC

space of the hallway but essentially connecting people in direct and one-on-one conversation.³⁹ Hyacinth uses it as a method of consulting in hushed tones with her working-class family while keeping this interaction private, particularly from her neighbour Elizabeth, who is often within hearing distance (Figure 5.3). She can also make use of the phone as a tool of public promotion – shouting out suitably impressive updates about her sister Violet to a listening Elizabeth or going out into the street to draw attention to passers-by that Richard is on the phone to the Chinese Embassy. And, of course, it is a key method through which she can communicate to the Major and her other upper-middle-class acquaintances that she is hosting one of her infamous candlelight suppers. The phone becomes a contemporary symbol of the lost servant, where in *Diary of a Nobody* it is the etiquette of the maid that communicates social status; in the 1990s sitcom the housewife is more directly responsible.

The telephone is also a symbol of Hyacinth's social anxiety; her need to remind every caller of its quality is a manifestation of snobbery that comes not from her self-confidence but insecurity. In part, this rests on what Simon Gunn has recognized as an inherently gendered aspect of social status; he suggests that 'middle-class women were not the makers of class, they were cast as the pre-eminent bearers of class'.⁴⁰ In this sense, Hyacinth is rendered passive in the generation of income (thus affecting where and how she can live), but she carries the weight of how that is *communicated* – an area in which the telephone becomes a significant marker. On one level, Hyacinth's use of the phone is evidence of a longstanding narrative about the lower middle class as endlessly desirous of the types of possessions that they believe the middle class hold dear. On another, it hints at a deeper underpinning hierarchy – as *Young Hyacinth* (2016) drew out, Hyacinth's desperation to separate herself from 'trade' may well indicate her experiences as part of a family who were later reimagined as dependent on a father whose work as a canal lock-keeper failed to adequately provide for his family. While multiple sources from 1850 onwards imply that the lower middle class were unusually preoccupied with material goods, individual accounts present something more nuanced than emulation purely for the sake of social status. In many ways, these texts raise questions about how we view emulation, but also how we draw the relationship between having and not having, needing and desiring and consumerism in contemporary society. Attitudes have long been shaped by the view that the middle class have items because they desire them, but that there is a morally transgressive quality to the working and lower middle class when they also desire these items.

Shan Bullock's Robert Thorne, for instance, initially sees social progression in a symbolic series of household items: 'a house somewhere, with steps to the door and mahogany furniture in the rooms and gilt mirrors standing behind ormolu clocks'.[41] These objects mark out the 'man made good'; they are valuable status pieces, solid and lasting. His desire for them is not just about the ownership of tangible objects that project a certain lifestyle; instead they represent the safety and security of an income that can support and give comfort to his family. They indicate the freedom to make decorating choices that comes from long-term rent or home ownership. In addition to this, they symbolize a legacy for the children of the future that ensures a more economically stable upbringing. Robert's dream, indicated through the steps and the clock, is not narrow in focus – based on possessions and social trappings – but shows an aspiration for the life that these items suggest. While Bullock validates coveting these markers of stability, Robert's story becomes a rejection of this dream. By the end of the novel, Robert trades slow progress at work for a chance to rethink his ambitions, refocusing on quality of experience (rural life in New Zealand) rather than quality of possession.

Condescension, levelled at the lower middle class because of a perceived desire for better material comforts, ignores the difficult circumstances many within the class faced. It also underplays the aspirations that make education a recurrent trope within representations of the suburban home, just as it was in the office. Many of Wells's lower-middle-class characters, for example, attempt a series of instructive activities in their free hours – as John Batchelor puts it, 'Wells's objectives [are] to make a good plan, get a good education, and live'[42] – and Bennett's Larch similarly forms a strict timetable of reading, writing and other scholarly pursuits to undertake before he goes to work. Edwin Pugh's *The Broken Honeymoon* (1908) also sees the main character rising at 6 am to practice his writing skills. Much of this is predicated on the clerk wanting to become an author, deconstructing his status as a clerical machine and attempting to become a creator rather than a copier of text. For these authors, culture provides what Rita Felski calls 'an empty but potent signifier, a talisman that offers the promise, however opaque, of entry into a higher world', making it a promising method of escaping a dreary clerical life.[43]

By the mid-twentieth century, there is a new emphasis on learning and a new audience. This includes sitcom characters like Mildred, in *George and Mildred* (1976–79), who learns to drive to give herself an increased sense of freedom in her suburban life. Likewise, Tom, Barbara and Margo take up Thursday evening classes in weaving and pottery at the Evening Institute in *The Good Life*, and Ann in *Ever Decreasing Circles* begins an Open University degree. Hester Fields (of *Fresh Fields* (1984–6)) takes up endless new hobbies and learns new skills to counter her empty-nest syndrome, and Deborah, of *Men Behaving Badly*, goes back to university after being made redundant to turn her professional life around. Each of these lower-middle-class women turns to education to expand their horizons outside the suburban home or to widen their employment opportunities.

In *The Office*, receptionist Dawn represents a contemporary rendition of this desire for more. Her ambition to become an illustrator is offered as a justification for her lack of interest in the role of receptionist and the time she wastes with Tim (who also sees office work as a dead end). In an interview with the fictional camera team in the show, she is candid about this:

> DAWN: for years I was an illustrator who did some reception work. … And, you know, then you're knackered after work and it's hard to fit in time for the illustrating. So now when people say, 'What do you do?', I say, 'I'm a receptionist.'[44]

The transition from illustrator (receptionist) to receptionist demonstrates the sense of futility felt by many in the office environment. Tim's belief in Dawn's ability to make a difference, however, is the signifier that marks the beginning of their romantic relationship. When he presents Dawn with a symbolic set of artist pens, he validates her ambitions where figures like David Brent dismiss them. In this, Tim follows a lineage of suburban men who have supported their wives in following their ambitions – unlike many of these early figures, however, who have often alternative motives for encouraging these activities (partly representative of the slow-shifting assumptions about women's position in the home in the 1970s and 1980s), Dawn is a working woman who wants to deploy her artistic skills rather than a suburban housewife seeking employment or further education for the first time.

The wider aspiration that Dawn embodies forms a distinct part of lower-middle-class popular culture, with education and cultural enrichment continuing to feature as a trope that is under-evaluated when exploring the values of the class. As Ben Walters points out, all of the characters in *The Office* have aspirations – David Brent's desire to be an entertainer is an obvious example, but he also wants to improve his lot when stuck as a travelling sales representative in series two.[45] Middle-class critics make much of aspiration as a capitalist impulse seeing the context as a material one, but, as Jeffery suggests, there is a more nuanced philosophy at the heart of this understanding of mobility: 'if there was aspiration, it was aspiration to learn, to take their limited education further'.[46] The new Class Calculator featured on the BBC still placed great emphasis on factors like engaging with concerts and theatre productions as gateways to the former middle class, but interestingly it makes no mention of education, which is arguably a driver for aspirational values as well as a stimulant for social mobility. There have been some subtle shifts, from the young men who were desperate to 'get on' in late Victorian and Edwardian fiction to middle-aged suburban women who want to start again, but the continued emphasis on the value of education is frequently overlooked.

Suburban culture

In the earlier twentieth century, two of George Orwell's characters were similarly assessing and dismantling assumptions about consumerism and suburbia. Gordon Comstock and George Bowling wrestle with the 'Money Code', a shorthand that usefully captures the complexity of pandering to a structure that essentially encourages individuals – and, at this time this usually meant suburban men – to sell their soul in return for the freedom to own more symbols of respectability. Later, it is this same renegotiation of capitalism that leads Reginald Perrin to establish 'Grot' in *The Return of Reginald Perrin* (1977), the shop that only sells items that are inherently useless or unattractive (which, in line with capitalist principles of demand becomes an outrageous postmodern success).

In Orwell's novels, the characters find their way out of their ideological dilemma, and back into a begrudging acceptance of suburbia, through the recognition that there is an essential difference between *cultural* aspiration and commodity aspiration. *Keep the Aspidistra Flying* references the strand of cultural development so often associated with lower-middle-class clerical types: creative writing. So many writers began their working lives in offices – they still do – and suburban fiction and television often represent the ways that this environment shapes their creative ideas. Early novelists, those trapped in the poky flats described earlier in this chapter, found urban life overwhelming and desperately sought the quiet solitude of suburbia. Much later, and once almost universal suburbanization moved many families out of the city, London became the antithesis to what was now viewed as the cloistered and claustrophobic suburban home. This stance has become the most widely referenced, and it often gets swept into a discourse about how intellectually or creatively 'vapid' the suburbs are. There are many texts written against this grain that are often ignored because they counter the widely held view that suburbia has no cultural value.

In Orwell's *Keeping the Aspidistra Flying*, for instance, Gordon Comstock is outwardly dedicated to his writing and hates the cheap novels in the windows of the bookshop where he works just as he despises the advertising image of 'spectacled rat-faced clerk' Roland Butta with his mug of Bovex.[47] Both mock Gordon's deep desire to make something of himself through his authorial pursuits. The novel is a retelling of Orwell's time as a part-time assistant in a second-hand bookshop and, more specifically, of how he almost gave up on his literary ambitions because of the dismal nature of 'living in bed-sits, making a pint in a pub last a whole evening, fearing rent day, and knowing that the post brought only rejection slips'.[48] This frustration resonates with many generations of London workers – those who flock to the capital to follow creative careers and instead face a struggle to afford to live while having to work intensive hours in administrative or service jobs that are time-intensive and poorly paid. The result, as Gordon Comstock says, is that 'you're always too washed out to write'.[49] This failure to become an author is attributed to a host of factors: Comstock is too tired and poor to write, Wells's Mr Lewisham has to share a small Clapham house with his wife, mother-in-law and lodgers, and Bennett's Richard Larch struggles with the 'lack of harmonious surroundings'.[50] These characters live in rented rooms, or lodging houses, often occupying at best a 'set of rooms' rather than their own home.

This type of fiction is often referred to as 'suburban' even though these are technically tales of the city, where they reflect suburban culture is in their narrative about urban life and how that is positioned in relation to an aspirational positivity that is projected onto the suburbs. This type of middlebrow 'prig' novels, as Batchelor calls them, also override the traditional portrayal of the target market for suburbia as being emulative of material positions and desperate for a suburban lifestyle because of its associated commodities.[51] Instead, they posit education as the key acquisition for the lower middle class; cultural development is more important that consumerism. Several of these novels also fit what David Lodge describes as 'the autobiographical-novel-about-a-boy-who-will-grow-up-to-be-a-writer tradition' – usually associated with modernist works such as Joyce's *A Portrait of the Artist as a Young Man* (1917) and Lawrence's *Sons and Lovers* (1913), but also a feature of works by Wells, Bennett and conceived of by writers as early as George Gissing.[52] This raises questions around how we label texts, particularly when 'suburban' novels are usually considered culturally conservative when compared with their modernist counterparts.

As manifestoes for authorial ambitions, they are also quite complicated. Whilst in many cases these are autobiographical novels, written by boys who *do* grow up to be writers, their fictional protagonists often fail to achieve this, or, as Lucas writes, they endure the 'downward curve from would-be-writer to ex-non-writer'.[53] Rather than finishing with promising prospects and freedom from the office, they end with a new commitment to clerical work and a desire to do well, supporting a move to the suburbs (think of Tim, and the stage direction from chapter two: '*back in the office, still trapped behind his desk*').[54] The final – and more hopeful – message is this: if the would-be-writer can have children in the suburbs, those children will have the money, space and independence to be truly creative.

In concluding their novels in this way, Edwardian writers attempted to complicate the negative narrative that was already encircling suburbia. They recognized not only the potential for what Cunningham has referred to as the 'imaginatively stimulating "multitudinousness"' of suburbia but also the ways that the suburbs could shape ordinary lives.[55] This is what Malcolm Bradbury identifies as a key part in Wells's success:

> [*Love and Mr Lewisham*] was the first of a row of novels Wells produced rapidly over the Edwardian period, all with somewhat similar themes, all about the excitement of life in a time of change and promise. Wells was above all readable; he was the novelist of ordinariness and familiarity, which he made excitingly unordinary and unfamiliar. His stories were mostly based on autobiographical materials, born out of lower-middle-class London suburban world from which he came, tales of aspiring, opportunity-seeking young men and women who

were taking on the adventure of social, educational, commercial and sexual self-transformation.[56]

Wells could take nondescript figures who, like his readers, were part of the lower middle class and turn their stories into adventures. There is evidence of soul-searching and heartache, but there is equally something optimistic in Edwardian literary culture that successfully represented the suburban experience for a wide readership that were in a similar position.

These hints of positivity about suburbia, however, do not mean that middlebrow fiction at this time was entirely uncritical about suburban life. Richard Larch is fully aware that he will not become a writer once he leaves the city:

> it would be impossible to write in the suburban doll's-house which was to be theirs. No! In future he would be simply the suburban husband – dutiful towards his employers, upon whose grace he would be doubly dependent; keeping his house in repair; pottering in the garden.[57]

Despite his earlier belief in the Zola-esque masterpiece, which could be teased out of the 'latent poetry of the suburbs', Richard's vision of a life in a suburban villa is clearly the opposite of the dream that so many clerks cherished.[58] He is committed to the propriety of taking his wife into the suburbs, seeing it as the right place for a 'lower-middle-class matron' and yet for him to settle into that life is, as for Gordon Comstock, to relinquish his creative ambitions.[59] After desiring suburban space, Richard slips into believing the stereotypes – that suburban life is not 'real' life but a toy-land in which he will perform a Pooterish role.

Just as in *Keep the Aspidistra Flying*, there is a choice presented between solitary authorship and companionate domesticity. Richard is mentally 'asphyxiated' early in the novel by the sight of a peasant woman glimpsed from a train. The implication of a 'hypothetical husband and children', despite their 'narrow' and 'dormant' intellectual capacities, provokes a surge of companionate desire.[60] Richard believes in the assumptions made about those who do not live in the city, that to have a family in comfort, he must renounce intellectualism. In contrast, the women he meets in the city are depicted in a similar way to those that J. Alfred Prufrock encounters in Eliot's poem. Richard even has his own Prufrockian moment, in which he worries that working endlessly at his writing will place him for ever out of the reach of women: 'he dreamt that he was in a drawing-room full of young men and women, and that all were chattering vivaciously and cleverly'.[61] The city saps his energy, and the suburbs, he fears, will extinguish it completely. Ultimately, though, his pursuit of his future wife Laura stems from an unarticulated episode with a prostitute that sparks a need for the type of physical intimacy that his writing cannot fulfil. Suburban companionship wins out over urban experiences.

The tensions between what Richard expects of certain environments and his experiences of them draw out the associations connecting landscape and culture. In the provinces, Richard is drawn to London as a centre of art, literature, politics, commerce, but the pace of life as a young clerk and relative poverty means that he, like Leonard Bast, can only be acquainted with the 'outside' of this world. Culture, for these young clerks, is not within reach despite its geographical proximity. In the suburbs, there is potential inspiration, but the powerful impressions of cloistered domesticity that are already in play at this time dash Richard's artistic hopes; he gives up before he has even moved, pinning his prospects not on himself but on his children.

The references to the 'suburban doll's-house' clearly echo Ibsen's *Doll's House* (1879). Rather than offering, like Ibsen, an exploration of the repressive patriarchy of suburban life, Bennett implies that suburbia is a claustrophobically feminine space – a narrative that has continued long into the twentieth century. Norman Collins, another novelist who writes generally sympathetically about lower-middle-class suburbia, uses the metaphor of the doll's house to betray the artificialness of suburban life:

> Dolls' houses appear to be the right dwelling places for these thousands, these tens of thousands, these hundreds of thousands, these half-urban hoards. Stand on the bridge at Liverpool Street Station at a quarter-to-nine in the morning and you see the model trains drawing in beneath you one after another, and swarms of toy-passengers emptying themselves on to the platform to go stumping up to the barrier – toy-directors, toy-clerks, toy-typists, all jerking along to spend the day in toy-town, earning paper-money to keep their dolls'-houses going.[62]

This description and the reduction of suburban lives into a toy-town is similar to Malvina Reynold's song 'Little Boxes' (1962), which explores the suburban hillside in America as a strange place without reality. In *Coming Up for Air*, Orwell echoes this sense of artifice or delusion when critiquing the suburban obsession with house-ownership:

> We're all bought, and what's more we're bought with our own money. Every one of those poor down-trodden bastards, sweating his guts out to pay twice the proper price for a brick dolls' house that's called Belle Vue because there's no view and the bell doesn't ring.[63]

These complex accounts show competing desires for suburbia and deep cynicism about the origins of that desire. The doll's house is an interesting metaphor. It is, of course, a problematic image for adult life, but in a symbolic sense, the doll's house is associated with the reassuring simplicity of childhood. Most crucial is the way that this imagery is used at the moment in which these writer-characters are consoling themselves about their professional failures. For example, Richard talks about the doll's house of suburbia when he realizes that he will not become a great writer. Instead, he transfers his ambition to 'a child of his [that] might give sign of literary ability. If so – and surely these instincts descended, were not lost – how he would foster and encourage it!'[64] The doll's house life will be a haven to inspire literary confidence; these suburban children, nurtured in an idyllic setting by attentive parents, will be successful, unlike poor orphaned Richard, who had no such stability. As Wells's Lewisham cries: 'The future is the child.'[65]

In a strikingly similar scene, Gordon Comstock disposes of his great and unfinished work *London Pleasures* in an act of great selflessness for his unborn child, giving over his soul to the 'money-code' to 'get married, settle down, prosper moderately, push a pram, have a villa and a radio and an aspidistra'.[66] Moving into the suburbs is intellectually positioned as a negative outcome, and yet, even though Gordon must renounce his principles, the novels ends with a hopeful image: Gordon kneeling against the 'softness of [his new wife's] belly' listening to the stirrings of new life.[67] By the end of the novel, and in a very similar narrative arch to that of Wells and Bullock, Comstock repeats the generational pattern, wanting to place his family within that same secure environment:

> The lower-middle-class people in there, behind their lace curtains, with their children and their scraps of furniture and their aspidistras – they lived by the money-code, sure enough, and yet they contrived to keep their decency. The money-code as they interpreted it was not merely cynical and hoggish. They had their standards, their inviolable points of honour. They 'kept themselves respectable' – kept the aspidistra flying. Besides, they were *alive*.[68]

Comstock thus arrives at the same conclusions that Richard Larch and Robert Thorne do, that the suburbs are the only place for lower-middle-class culture to be defended, nurtured and promoted and that on an individual basis the retreat to suburbia is the preservation of lower-middle-class identity. Like the earlier authors, Orwell was, as Bernard Crick points out, 'not simply writing *about* the lower middle class, he was also writing *for* a readership of men like George Bowling'.[69]

Richard Church's autobiography *Over the Bridge* demonstrates the fulfilment of these suburban dreams. Nurtured by what Church refers to variously as the 'pocket of civilisation utterly quiet and self-sufficient', the 'jungle of aspidistras' and the 'close intimacy of a lower-middle-class home', he develops from avid reader to published poet.[70] Church was the son of a post office worker, whose passion for the Civil Service led to his insistence on Church's own entrance into the clerical world. By 1933, Church gave up life as a clerk to turn to writing as a full-time occupation, becoming a well-known poet and writer (*Over the Bridge* won the *Sunday Times* Prize for Literature). The suburban literary dream personified, Church offers what Lewisham, Comstock and Larch seek for their own offspring – although, notably, it was not the future that Church's own father envisioned, being, as he reminisces, as loyal to the Civil Service as 'a soldier to the regiment'.[71]

Finally, I want to turn to Julian Barnes's *Metroland* (1980) to consider the ways that these early-twentieth-century novels gave voice to a story that would outlive their Victorian and Edwardian origins. Like *A Man from the North* and *Keep the Aspidistra Flying*, *Metroland* gives a narrative of the journey from office worker to would-be author to suburban. Protagonist Chris's attitude to suburbia reflects the conflict between wanting to dismiss it (expected by both his close friend Toni and wider society) and finding it a positive place to live:

> Everyone in this suburb of a couple of thousand people seemed to have come in from elsewhere. They would have been attracted by the solidly built houses, the reliable railway service, and the good gardening soil. I found the cosy, controlled rootlessness of the place reassuring; though I did tend to complain to Toni that I'd prefer something '... more elemental'.[72]

Chris articulates the unpopular truth about suburbia – that it is practical, sensible, spacious and comfortable – but he also mediates his response for Toni, hiding behind the vague language of the 'elemental' to convey the impurity of the suburban experience.

Metroland contrasts with the 'limitless sexual, social, and political freedom' of Chris's liberating experiences in central Paris. Ultimately, though, it is to suburbia that Chris returns because 'it's an efficient place to live'.[73] Not only is Chris now a bone-fide suburban, he is, like Gordon Comstock, a copywriter – a deliberate nod to the literary would-be authors of the previous century: 'There were poets and novelists in advertising, they said; though I could never quite remember their names when asked'.[74] Barnes's 'coming of age book' sees the two childhood friends standing in a suburban garden discussing the realities of adulthood – Toni as a failed poet, Chris defending charges of being a 'budding fat cat'. As for Richard Larch and Gordon Comstock, Chris's contentment lies 'in having a child'.[75] 'So this is it?' asks Chris, as his daughter wakes him with her 'grizzl[ing]'.[76] The glow of the suburban streetlight, which doubles as a night light for baby Amy, gives a final lingering impression of the protagonist's happiness.

Barnes's novel is a modern retelling of that semi-autobiographical lower-middle-class narrative written like so many earlier novels of this type while Barnes was a journalist rather than a full-time novelist. As in those earlier novels, he writes of the first pretensions of early maturity, virginal forays into the romantic, the grey reality of office work and, in the end, youthful ambitions replaced with the suburban dream. The universalization of the suburban novel rests, then, not only in the lower-middle-class protagonist but also in the manner of telling the universal (suburban) narrative. Like the ending of *The 7.39*, where Carl sits at the table, helping his son practice lines for a play, the children centre the suburban family. In Carl's case, after the disruption of his affair, his children symbolize a bridge across the emotional distance between him and his wife, allowing his reintegration into suburbia.

These narratives imply the extent to which the widespread views of suburbia as a constricting space permeate popular culture. Whilst attempting to review the position of suburbia, and developing a distinct suburban culture, these texts do not always counter the impression of suburban mundanity. Instead, they posit suburbia as a blank canvas from which the new generation can fulfil the dreams of their parents. As Carey comments about Bennett's novel, having children is 'mysteriously elevating'; it certainly counters the frustration that should accompany the repeated rejections these characters receive when it comes to their attempts to be writers.[77] In part, this references the distinct style of these suburban narratives; they are an evocation of the everyday, and the endings capture this essential ordinariness. As Merritt Moseley puts it, there is an emphasis on the 'maturing process [that] involves a shrinking of horizons and an acceptance of the ordinary'.[78] He is writing about *Metroland*, and he adds that this is an important part of the realism in the novel, but this idea is equally applicable to *A Man from the North*, *Keep the Aspidistra Flying*, *The 7.39* and other texts such as Wells's *Love and Mr Lewisham*. Simon James talks about this as an inversion of the emphasis of the *bildungsroman*: 'Instead of the hero's wayward desires being corrected by a more morally clear-sighted world, the insufficient world is instead blamed for not fulfilling the more laudable of those desires'.[79] Suburbia is a retreat into which the protagonist can escape from the frustrations of the city, which was incapable of recognizing the originality of the would-be writer.

The endings of these novels also complicate Kate Flint's suggestions in 'Fictional Suburbia' that

> While Gissing, Henry James and others were experimenting with inconclusive endings, with themes of unfulfilment, of wrong choices made, of the sadness of middle-aged protagonists forcing a future of nothing certain but its tedium, [suburban fiction] maintained the convention of events leading to a happy ending.[80]

These novels do not offer straightforwardly 'happy' endings, instead they build to a series of failures and a growing self-awareness about the limitations of urban life. The suburbs are not a perfect solution, but they do offer a potential for sacrifice. Moving to a suburban home will mean a life of white-collar work (to pay the mortgage) and middle-aged discontentment, but it equally offers aspirations for the next generation to avoid that same clerkly future.[81] Whether or not that generation would be grateful for these opportunities, as we saw in the previous chapter, was less predictable.

Conclusion

The place of the suburban home in the status of the nation is much in evidence; the patterns of housing, the continued reliance on the 'semi-detached' dwelling – so little found elsewhere in Europe or North America – and the neat, if somewhat reduced in terms of size, square of front and back garden demonstrate the architectural significance of interwar modes of housing. Tudor-bethan frontages still grace even these new builds, with bay windows and wooden facias remaining a key aspect of our national suburban aesthetic. There are changes – those which were recognized by the most forwards-thinking of planners and builders even in the 1930s – road access remains the core functional aspect of suburban planning, where the railways provided much of the advertising impetus at earlier stages. Inside these new builds, ubiquitous kitchen-diners have replaced through-lounges, and en-suites have proliferated, but many of the values by which we construct our private dwelling remain embedded in our planning and design culture – fenced gardens, restrictions around overlooking outdoor spaces and the placement of windows. Those key values of privacy, family and ownership remain core to the ways that we conceive of ourselves as a nation of suburbanites.

In this, the suburban home offers an answer of sorts to the growing mechanization of the office. For those struggling in the city for space, with the cost of living, or with the relentless pace, the suburbs are a beacon that boast semi-detached life with a neat garden, good schools and easy access to the city. In the suburban home, the lower-middle-class office worker is, once more, an individual – a status reinforced never more intensely than the moment that one becomes a parent. Suburbia envelopes the nuclear family in a protective stability that gives confidence to those who grow up within it, despite critics' suspicion of the suburban home as 'too family-centred and materialistic'.[82] For those who have not benefitted from this type of upbringing, it is an aspirational place that offers everything that they did not have – as evidenced by orphaned writers like Bennett, who focus on the constancy and permanence of suburbia. And while many, as Clapson argues, write off suburbia as tedious, 'unlovely' and uninspiring, the popular move from the city to the suburbs once family life is underway begs the question: why do so many people choose to live in suburbia? As Clapson points out, very few histories or social commentaries on suburbia ask this of the suburbanites themselves, preferring to attribute vigorous feelings that are largely predicated on stereotypes and attitudes that linger from the nineteenth century.[83]

Many of these assumptions focus on the comparison drawn between growing consumerism and the commodity aspiration often linked with the lower middle class. And yet, as this chapter explores, there is a strand of representations that support the association between social mobility, aspiration and education that is overlooked. The interest in hobbies from cookery (*Fresh Fields*) to self-sufficiency and the smallholding (*The Good Life*) to sport and community building (*Ever Decreasing Circles*) are a continuation of the aspirations seen in the work of Bennett, Orwell and Wells. Most importantly, there remained a focus on education in the representation of suburbia that demonstrated an understanding that its occupants were not only interested in material symbols but in personal development. *Ever Decreasing Circles* is a good example here too – while the comedy comes from Martin's closed-minded attitudes towards respectability and social standards in the close-knit suburban community, Ann starts a degree in Twentieth Century Studies with the Open University, challenging his ideas about hierarchies of social value.

While this chapter has explored aspects of suburban life that counter wider narratives about suburban monotony and blandness, it must finish by highlighting areas of further research that are required to further break down the stereotypes surrounding suburban lives. Most significant is the continued assumption that suburbia is 'full of dull *white* conformists', a crucial admission identified by Clapson in 2000 which has, thus far, continued to receive only limited critical attention. Clapson's own study examines briefly the position of black, Jewish and Asian communities within suburbia, but his dual focus on American and English history limits the space to discuss British contexts in detail. Studies such as Orly Clergé's very recent *The New Noir: Race, Identity and Diaspora in Black Suburbia* (2019), which takes America as its focus, offers a useful model for considering race, identity and British suburbanization in more detail. While the emphasis in this chapter equally falls foul of criticisms that historians of suburbia tend to focus on homogeneity in class structures rather than race, within the wider context of this study, which is explicitly exploring the continuities of lower-middle-class representations, this is arguably justified.[84] However, this does not excuse the omission but rather invokes a call to place more emphasis on research into those cultural texts which offer a counter reading to suburbia as a deeply white space.

What this chapter does suggest is that there is a clear narrative trajectory from the Grossmiths' Charles Pooter to Orwell's George Bowling to Roy Clarke's Hyacinth Bucket that stands as evidence of the significance of suburban culture in the twentieth century. These 'dreary, petty lives without social, cultural, or intellectual interests' proved capable of producing a body of writing which was, at times, self-critical but which offered their lower-middle-class reader/viewership a vision of a suburban future.[85] Repeatedly in middlebrow fiction, as Cunningham remarks, 'suburbia, culturally categorized as home to the commonplace and mundane, is conceptualized with great imaginative vigor'.[86] In sparking the imagination, the suburbs thus act as 'cultural provocation' to a generation of writers (and readers/viewers) for whom it was their home. There is something crucial, and underappreciated, in the skill required to turn the everyday into a setting that can surprise and entertain. It is the ability of those writing novels and sitcoms to capture this environment – which is at once 'typical' and 'commonplace' – and make it meaningful, full of emotion, nuance, understanding, pathos and comedy, which makes the suburban home so crucial to everyday life.

Conclusion

By tracing the persistent use of certain representational tropes, and by teasing out threads of discursive continuity, this book has made a series of suggestions about the lower middle class in Britain, from the nineteenth to the early twenty-first century. It is in many ways an examination of the petite bourgeoisie in popular culture that stems as much from the contemporary observations of the author as it does from the historical study of the lower middle class in Victorian society. It began, as so many monographs do, as a thesis that sought to examine the longevity of perceptions of the Pooterish figure, inspired by A. James Hammerton's articles on domesticity and *Diary of Nobody*. And while the first iteration explored Victorian and Edwardian masculinity and class, there was always more to be said about the ways that contemporary life is still defined by the issues that so shaped Charles Pooter's world: social anxiety, professional self-doubt, ridicule in the very act of finding sanctuary in your own home.

By drawing upon examples from popular culture across the previous one hundred and fifty years, this study has attempted to disentangle a series of tropes and characteristics that have been historically associated with the white-collar clerk while becoming more widely intertwined with popular stereotypes of the lower middle class. The power of these physical, emotional and intellectual markers is impressively long lasting and across multiple cultural forms. They have also evolved to meet contemporary contexts, shaped by changes in the white-collar workforce, the suburban landscape and the shifting ideologies ascribed to the lower middle class. Many of the broader stereotypes that were originally associated with the male Victorian clerk have opened up, enveloping women and including a wider range of administrators, office workers and suburban dwellers.

There are, though, ways in which the legacy of the male clerk lingers; middle age is still associated with a crisis of masculinity in ways that are not always translated into the depictions of a female workforce. In a similar way, played out across multiple cultural forms is a type of physical humour that correlates features such as balding and diminutive height and the lower-middle-class man. What is also of interest, as the two chapters on suburbia have shown, is that the long-lasting trend for ridiculing the male suburban, which developed at the end of the nineteenth century, led to a radical portrayal of their wives, and thus lower-middle-class women more generally. Because of the comedy that was so intrinsically centred on the pomposity, social awkwardness, physical littleness and other Pooterish behaviours, representations of the women who had to deal with these idiotic early clerks were invariably strong, sensible and practical. While the lower-middle-class man was run down and belittled, the corresponding strength and will of his wife only added to the comedy of his dented masculinity. As representations developed, the intelligence and determination of the early-twentieth-century lower-middle-class matriarch met feminism in the 1960s and started to carve a space for herself as a figure who could reprimand men for inequalities that persisted. In *The Squirrels*, a typically chauvinistic office sitcom of the 1970s, it is often the wives of the office workers who come together to enact real change, challenging and rebuking their husbands for their patriarchal failings.

At the same time, as much earlier texts such as *Robert Thorne* show, there was a narrative that tried to demonstrate the less comic aspects of lower-middle-class life that attempted to draw out empathy and understanding for the clerk 'breaking [his] back on a high stool'.[1] While these stories feature less frequently as the twentieth century goes on, they entwine with the comic features that the Grossmiths ascribed to their clerk, forming the sort of sympathetic humour of the suburban situational comedy or the gentle self-deprecating of diarists like Adrian Mole. They can also become dark narratives and have done more so in American films that depict the black comedy of suburbia or the office environment and the swirling undertones of frustration and resentment that fuel dangerous desires. In British literature, these stories crop up occasionally, often in writing by those who have experienced, at first hand, the infuriation and dissatisfaction of the daily grind – in P. D. James's short story about a sadistic sexual predator who is mocked in the office or B. S. Johnson's *Christie Malry*.

This does not mean that there are no differences between the Victorian clerk and the contemporary office worker. Changes are already occurring in the white-collar sector, and they will intensify as artificial intelligence alters the economic and social landscape of our daily working lives. In this, narratives about earlier technologies and their expansion into the white-collar workplace are, perhaps, reassuring in the ways that the clerical workforce adapted. Suburban development, new housing and social housing present a multifaceted array of new hierarchies in architecture and sociology, and the notion of a stable and homogenous suburbia is in flux, as it has been since the late nineteenth century, but the home remains a haven, a space in which individuals can freely assert their own values and aspirations. What this study suggests is that many of these changes, whilst visible and recognizable in modern society, are not always at the forefront, though, of how we conceptualize contemporary culture. Television writers, authors and media commentators return endlessly to images, stereotypes and a shorthand that reiterates, repeats and reinterprets features that were already a core part of lower-middle-class identity a hundred years ago.

The spaces covered by this study – the office, the commute, the suburbs – are not exclusive to the petite bourgeoisie; they are, of course, part of a diverse culture that makes up various socio-economic groups of a variety of class, ethnic and gender identities. But the clerks who first inhabited them, and more importantly, in many ways, the middle-class critics who helped to draw attention to this lower-middle-class figure – through spite, anger, fear or simply for comedy – created a synergy between these spaces and this class that is long-standing. They shared a conjured image of mundanity, and the banal that has been characterized as lower middle class for over a century, and while many of us know these spaces as our ordinary and every day, they are tainted by the triviality that has encircled them since the Victorian period. Class structures have shifted and will change further, but we still rely on a deeply ingrained series of associations between personal behaviour, possessions, homes, occupations and a sense of hierarchy. While this persists, and whilst the notion of an aspiration to be middle class lasts, there will always be a place for the lower middle class – as a method of labelling those who are not quite part of that exclusive group.

These case studies also demonstrate the ways in which place starts to hold considerable meaning in the construction of lower-middle-class stereotypes. The office is where ideas about the clerk began; early representations make clear that stooping over a high desk from a rigid stool was a key part of the ways that clerks would go on to be portrayed as hunched, pale and weak. Once this clerk started to move out into suburbia, this new commuter class – so easily identified with their cheap suits and inky fingers – became just as obvious a target. The suburban villa, already an object of scorn for the middle class who were worried about their new lower-middle-class neighbours, led to an emergent discourse that undermined and belittled the suburban clerk where possible. In status-conscious Britain, this developing rivalry between the middle and lower middle class became the perfect focus for new comic forms. Displaying the sort of reticent humour that has become identifiably British, making comedy out of class tensions allowed the middle class to both poke fun at their nearest adversary while acknowledging that they were really laughing at themselves.

Equally, the tensions between subsections of the middle class show little sign of abating. While the middle class were equally important in the formation of these spaces, this study reasserts the notion of a distinct lower-middle-class culture that grew alongside the office, the suburbs and on the commute. Typical impressions of 'the office', for instance, are much more likely to take the form of the 'underling's' office than that of the boss, from a call centre not a boardroom. Rather than asserting the widespread nature of the middle class in contemporary society – or even, as many have done, in Victorian society – grouping together those whose lives are on some levels similar makes it much harder to position the tensions that simmer between them. The middle class is considerable enough to warrant at least this subsection. These low-level, and ultimately respectable and restrained, set of frictions continue to provide comedy on screen and in fiction, and to understand and analyse this specific feature of British humour, we need to understand the historical relationship between the middle and the lower middle class.

The nostalgic return to older forms makes this a clear priority for contemporary television studies. In transatlantic situational comedy, there is a turn once more towards the family home, in a deliberate retreat to the safety and security of suburbia. In Britain, this characterises an essentially sentimental impulse that addresses concerns and anxieties about the twenty-first century and Britain's position within a global context.[2] The immense popularity of a show like *Mrs Brown's Boys* incorporates just this kind of return to a much older style of comedy, as does *Two Doors Down*, the sitcom set in Latimer Crescent, a 'typical' suburb in Glasgow. Entering its fourth series in 2019, the show rests on the conflict between a lower-middle-class couple and their socially inferior neighbours. It is the *Terry and June* of the twenty-first century and its popularity shows how little has changed.

By positing that Britain is, at heart, a lower-middle-class nation, I am not denying the radical shifts in social composition that have taken place since the Victorian period and over the last ten years especially. While this study has argued for an approach that separates the *petite* from the *bourgeoisie*, this is not just about trends, stereotypes and other depictions in popular culture. There is an economic justification for this too. Many of the sites under discussion are synonymous with contemporary lifestyles, predicating the suggestion that we live in a middle-class nation, yet since the recession, and particularly over very recent years, the social and fiscal implications of a lost job or a period of bad fortune are more likely to result in near Victorian outcomes. Those divides between the 'haves' and 'have nots' are becoming more relevant than they have been perhaps for a generation, just like Victorian assessments of poverty (deserving and undeserving) are creeping back into discourse about the British welfare system – a key indicator of our class structures. Redundancy is increasingly a part of everyday dialogue, across all sectors of the economy, including the white-collar world, just as it was in the late nineteenth century and again in the 1980s and 1990s. There may well have been a time between 1850 and the present day when Britain might arguably have been closer to being a middle-class nation, but it is not now. Just as television has returned to discussing the tiny social differences that cause tension in the suburban sitcom, society is facing a new era of economic uncertainty that will reinforce the structures that separate us from our neighbours.

What is clear, though, is that Britain is as fractured as it has ever been, and while there are multiple political and ideological explanations for this, the class divide remains as crucial as ever. In arguing that we are, in fact, a lower-middle-class nation, this study reminds us of things we have in common. The democratization of quotidian spaces can bring us together, and as Joe Moran asserts, we need to view the everyday as 'the real space in which we lead our actual lives' in order to bring about real social change from within.[3] This study has attempted to offer a reading of lower-middle-class culture that is not reductive or, as Arlene Young put it, 'disparaging',[4] but which draws attention to the universality with which we view certain aspects of our everyday lives. In this respect, the suburbs have certainly been ignored, as we continue to project images of our nation from within the urban/rural dichotomy that has long been established.[5] Arcadian landscapes continue to form a significant part of our national self-identity, as witnessed in everything from *Countryfile* to the floral patterns of Cath Kidston.

Finally, as Brexit negotiations have unfolded during the last stages of writing this book, it is perhaps worth considering Britain's relationship with social class as a metaphor for our position on a global platform. While we may not want to see ourselves as a lower-middle-class nation, perhaps preferring to think of ourselves as firmly middle class, we are the Hyacinth Bucket of the international stage. Just as *Keeping up Appearances* is our biggest national television export, so too Britain is increasingly positioning itself as an endlessly emulative, perhaps unrealistically aspirational nation, desperate to keep up with the Joneses overseas. In this sense, a clearer reading of our own understanding of lower-middle-class culture is needed now more than ever before, if we are to appreciate the way the rest of the world will see us.

Notes

Introduction

1. Gregory Anderson, *Victorian Clerks* (Manchester: Manchester University Press, 1976), 2.
2. F. M. L. Thompson, *The Rise of Respectable Society: A Social History of Victorian Britain 1830–1900* (London: Fontana Press, 1988), 68; Michael Heller, *London Clerical Workers 1880–1914: Development of the Labour Market* (London: Pickering & Chatto, 2011), 1.
3. Norman Collins, *London Belongs to Me* (London: Collins, 1947), 9.
4. Geoffrey Crossick (ed.), *The Lower Middle Class in Britain, 1870–1914* (London: Croom Helm, 1977).
5. Arlene Young, 'Virtue Domesticated: Dickens and the Lower Middle Class', *Victorian Studies* 39, no. 4 (1996): 485.
6. John Carey, *The Intellectuals and the Masses* (London: Faber and Faber, 1992), 58; Richard Higgins, 'Feeling Like a Clerk in H. G. Wells', *Victorian Studies* 50, no. 3 (Spring 2008): 461.
7. See Todd Kuchta's *Semi-detached Empire: Suburbia and the Colonization of Britain, 1880 to the Present Day* (Charlottesville: University of Virginia Press, 2010).
8. Richard Price, 'Society, Status and Jingoism: The Social Roots of Lower-Middle-Class Patriotism, 1870–1914', in *Lower Middle Class*, ed. Geoffrey Crossick (London: Croom Helm, 1977), 97.
9. Price, 'Society, Status and Jingoism', 97.
10. Mark Clapson, *Invincible Green Suburbs: Brave New Worlds, Social Change and Urban Dispersal in Post-war England* (Manchester: Manchester University Press, 1998), 6.
11. Ross McKibbin, *Classes and Cultures: England 1918–1951* (Oxford: Oxford University Press, 1998), 45.
12. According to the Official Labour Market Statistics, provided by the Office for National Statistics at www.nomisweb.co.uk (accessed 4 May 2018).
13. Arno Mayer, 'The Lower Middle Class as Historical Problem', *Journal of Modern History* 47, no. 3 (September 1975): 409–36.
14. Stephen Mihm, 'Clerks, Classes, and Conflicts: A Response to Michael Zakim's "The Business Clerk as Social Revolutionary"', *Journal of the Early Republic* 26 (Winter 2006): 608.

15 One of the earliest of these accounts was *The Condition of Clerical Labour* (1935), a Marxist critique of the social, economic and political situation of the clerk by F. D. Klingender. Klingender argued that the clerk had become proletarianized by the 1930s, thus contributing to the shrinking of the *bourgeoisie* that Marx had predicted. David Lockwood, in *The Blackcoated Worker* (1958), first countered this argument with the suggestion that clerical workers retained many of the privileges that continued to define them as being apart from the working class. This argument was supported by Ross McKibbin in 1998, who suggested that in terms of education, dress, salary and social aspiration, the clerk was middle class. By the 1970s, Anderson's discussion of areas such as pay, lifestyle and unionization contributed to the growing debate by supporting Klingender's original analysis – findings which Heller has very recently countered in *London Clerical Workers* as falling simply into a 'declinist' narrative. Crucially, Klingender and Lockwood began a debate about the position of the clerk, which would shape critical literature to the present day. See also Arthur McIvor's *A History of Work in Britain* for a succinct explanation of the various positions within this debate, and particularly the positions of the first two historians to set out the parameters – Klingender and Lockwood. Arthur McIvor, *A History of Work in Britain* (London: Red Globe Press, 2000), 61.

16 Anderson also goes into detail on many aspects of office work including recruitment, conditions, status, salaries, and clerk-employee relations in *Victorian Clerks*. Michel Crozier, *The World of the Office Worker* (London: Chicago University of Chicago Press, 1971); David Lockwood, *The Blackcoated Worker: A Study in Class Consciousness* (Oxford: Oxford University Press, 1989); F. D. Klingender, *The Conditions of Clerical Labour in Britain* (London: Lawrence, 1935); Graham Lowe, 'Class, Job and Gender in the Canadian Office', *Labour/Le Travailleur* 10 (Autumn 1982): 11–37.

17 Graham Lowe, *Women in the Administrative Revolution* (Oxford: Basil Blackwell, 1987), 142–3.

18 Meta Zimmeck, 'Jobs for the Girls: The Expansion of Clerical Work for Women, 1850–1914', in *Unequal Opportunities: Women's Employment in England, 1800–1918*, ed. Angela John (Oxford: Blackwell, 1986): 155.

19 Simon Gunn, 'Translating Bourdieu: Cultural Capital and the English Middle Class in Historical Perspective', *British Journal of Sociology* 56, no. 1 (2005): 53.

20 Inka Mülder-Bach, 'Cinematic Ethnology: Siegfried Kracauer's the White Collar Masses', *New Left Review* 226 (1997): 45.

21 Rita Felski, 'Nothing to Declare: Identity, Shame, and the Lower Middle Class', *PMLA* 115, no. 1 (January 2001): 34. Felski is referring to John Carey's conclusions in *The Intellectuals and the Masses*.

22 Ibid.

23 Michael Zakim highlights the pivotal role of the American clerk as the crux of 'all the new markets in the new market society' – following in the footsteps of Benjamin Franklin, who 'retroactively became America's first clerk'. Michael Zakim, 'Business Clerk as Social Revolutionary; or, a Labor History of the Nonproducing Classes', *Journal of the Early Republic* 26 (Winter 2006): 567, 603, 571.

24 Peter Bailey, 'White Collars, Gray Lives? The Lower Middle Class Revisited', *Journal of British Studies* 38 (July 1999): 276.

25 Geoffrey Crossick, 'The Emergence of the Lower Middle Class in Britain: A Discussion', in *The Lower Middle Class in Britain, 1870–1914*, ed. Geoffrey Crossick (London: Croom Helm, 1977): 11.

26 Jonathan Wild, *The Rise of the Office Clerk in Literary Culture 1880–1939* (Basingstoke: Palgrave Macmillan, 2006), 8.

27 Peter Scott, 'Marketing Mass Home Ownership and the Creation of the Modern Working-Class Consumer in Inter-War Britain', *Business History* 50, no. 1 (2008): 13–14; Mark Clapson, 'The Suburban Aspiration in England since 1919', *Contemporary British History* 14, no. 1 (2000): 152.

28 Mike Savage, *Social Class in the 21st Century* (London: Penguin, 2015), 369. The five questions are based on income, home ownership and savings, professional status of those 'known socially' and cultural activities. The new classes identified are: elite, established middle class, technical middle class, new affluent workers, traditional working class, emergent service workers and precariat.

29 Brigitte Le Roux et al., 'Class and Cultural Division in the UK', *Sociology* 42, no. 6 (2008): 1052.

30 Scott Banville, '"A Book-Keeper, Not an Accountant": Representing the Lower Middle Class from Victorian Novels and Music-Hall Songs to Television Sitcoms', *Journal of Popular Culture* 44, no. 1 (2011): 17.

31 Le Roux et al., 'Class and Cultural Division in the UK', 1052.

32 Simon Gunn, 'Class, Identity and the Urban: The Middle Class in England, c. 1790–1950', *Urban History* 31, no. 1 (2004): 30.

33 Ibid., 32.

34 Mike Savage, 'Changing Social Class Identities in Post-War Britain: Perspectives from Mass Observation', *Sociological Research Online* 12, no. 3 (2006): n.p.

35 Ibid., Section 3.2.

36 Mike Savage, Gaynor Bagnall and Brian Longhurst, 'Ordinary, Ambivalent and Defensive: Class Identities in the Northwest of England', *Sociology* 35, no. 4 (2001): 875–92.

37 Ibid., 887.

38 Charles Dickens is a good example here. Arlene Young talks about how he 'often represents them as inherently comic'. 'Virtue Domesticated', 494.

39 Carl Rhodes and Robert Westwood, *Representations of Work and Organisation in Popular Culture* (Oxon: Routledge, 2008), 95.
40 Helen Davies and Sarah Ilott (eds), *Comedy and the Politics of Representation: Mocking the Weak* (London: Palgrave Macmillan, 2018), 7.
41 Young, 'Virtue Domesticated', 494.
42 Ibid.
43 Davies and Ilott (eds), *Comedy and the Politics of Representation*, 1.
44 Young, 'Virtue Domesticated', 498, 507, 498.
45 Dickens, *Sketches by Boz* (London: Penguin, 1995), 7.
46 Jon Wilde, 'I Hope *Diary of a Nobody* Is in Safe Hands', *Guardian*, 23 April 2007. Available online: https://www.theguardian.com/culture/tvandradioblog/2007/apr/23/ihopediaryofanobodyisin (accessed 24 May 2017).
47 Kevan Davis, 'Diary of a Nobody'. Available at https://www.diaryofanobody.net/ (accessed 13 June 2017). The weblog runs as a daily feed, restarting on 3 April each year; text is taken from Project Gutenberg.
48 Roger Silverstone, 'Introduction', in *Visions of Suburbia*, ed. Roger Silverstone (London: Routledge, 1997): 9–10.
49 Andy Medhurst, *A National Joke: Popular Comedy and English Cultural Identities* (London: Routledge, 2007), 1.
50 Stephen Wagg, '"At Ease, Corporal": Social Class and the Situational Comedy in British Television, from the 1950s to the 1990s', in *Because I Tell a Joke or Two: Comedy, Politics and Social Difference*, ed. Stephen Wagg (1998): 2.
51 Brett Mills, *Television Sitcom* (London: British Film Institute, 2005), 64.
52 Wagg, '"At Ease, Corporal"', 2.
53 Jeffrey Richards, *Films and British National Identity: From Dickens to Dad's Army* (Manchester: Manchester University Press, 1997), 355; Mills, *Television Sitcom*, 42.
54 J. B. Priestley, *English Humour* (London: Longmans, Green, 1930), 18.
55 Richards, *Films and British National Identity*, 355.
56 Martina Kessel, 'Introduction: Landscapes of Humour: The History and Politics of the Comical in the Twentieth Century', in *The Politics of Humour: Laughter, Inclusion and Exclusion in the Twentieth Century*, ed. Martina Kessel and Patrick Merziger (London: Toronto University Press, 2012): 4.
57 Michael Hogan, 'Colin's Sandwich Boxset Review – Mel Smith's Wannabe Horror Writer Is a Timeless Sitcom Hero', *Guardian*, 11 September 2014. Available online: https://www.theguardian.com/tv-and-radio/2014/sep/11/colins-sandwich-box-set-review-mel-smith (accessed 13 June 2018).
58 Davies and Ilott (eds), *Comedy and the Politics of Representation*, 1.
59 Medhurst, *A National Joke*, 19.
60 Davies and Ilott (eds), *Comedy and the Politics of Representation*, 8.
61 Ibid., 1.

62 Glyn White and John Mundy, *Laughing Matters: Understanding Film, Television and Radio Comedy* (Manchester: Manchester University Press, 2012), 9.
63 Brett Mills, *The Sitcom* (Edinburgh: Edinburgh University Press, 2009), 87.
64 Ibid., 79, 87.
65 Julian Dutton, *Keeping Quiet: Visual Comedy in the Age of Sound* (Gosport: Chaplin Press, 2015), 3.
66 Inger-Lise Kalviknes Bore, *Screen Comedy and Online Audience* (London: Routledge, 2017), 2.
67 Andy Medhurst, 'Negotiating the Gnome Zone: Versions of Suburbia in British Popular Culture', in *Visions of Suburbia*, ed. Roger Silverstone (London: Routledge, 1997): 248.
68 Bailey, 'White Collars, Grey Lives', 272.
69 Shan Bullock, *Mr Ruby Jumps the Traces* (London: Chapman and Hall, 1917), 7.
70 H. G. Wells, *The History of Mr Polly* (London: Collins, 1969), 20; Victor Canning, *Mr Finchley Discovers His England* (London: Pan Books, 1970), 7.
71 R. F. Delderfield, *The Dreaming Suburb* (London: Hodder and Stoughton, 1964), 98–9.
72 Ibid., 15.
73 *The ABC Murders* (2018), [TV programme] 'Episode 1', BBC, 26 December.
74 Delderfield, *Dreaming Suburb*, 87.
75 Mark Lawson, 'Dad's Army at 50: The Secret History of 'Comedy's Finest Half Hour', *Guardian*, 24 July 2018. Available online: https://www.theguardian.com/tv-and-radio/2018/jul/24/dads-army-50-bbc-tv-comedy-home-guard-secret history (accessed 3 September 2018).
76 George and Weedon Grossmith, *The Diary of a Nobody* (Hertfordshire: Wordsworth Editions, 2006), 117.
77 *Mary Poppins* (1964), [Film] Dir. Robert Stephenson, U.S.A: Walt Disney Productions.
78 It is interesting to note that both actors – David Tomlinson and Arthur Lowe – were in the forces in the Second World War. Tomlinson was also, for a short period, a clerk, as was Lowe's father.
79 Alexia Panayiotou, '"Macho" Managers and Organizational Heroes: Competing Masculinities in Popular Films', *Organization* 17 no. 6 (2010): 674.
80 *The Office* (2002), [TV programme] 'Motivation', BBC, 21 October.
81 *The Office* (2002), [TV programme] 'Charity', BBC, 28 October.
82 See, for instance, the longevity of assumptions about suburbia as 'in opposition to ethnic minorities', identified by Clapson in 'The Suburban Aspiration in England since 1919': 152.
83 David Howell, 'The Property-Owning Democracy: Prospects and Policies', *Policy Studies* 4, no. 3 (1984): 14.

84 Tom Jeffery, 'A Place in the Nation: The Lower Middle Class in England', in *Splintered Classes: Politics and the Lower Middle Class in Interwar Europe*, ed. Rudy Koshar (London: Holmes and Meier, 1990): 71.
85 Ibid., 72.
86 Tom Jeffery, 'Politics and Class in Lewisham', in *Metropolis, London: Histories and Representations since 1800*, ed. David Feldman and Gareth Stedman Jones (London: Routledge, 1989): 191.
87 Jeffery, 'A Place in the Nation': 70–96; Susan Pennybacker, 'Changing Convictions: London County Council Blackcoated Activism between the Wars', in *Splintered Classes*, ed. Rudy Koshar (London: Holmes and Meier, 1990): 97–120.
88 Crossick, for example, argues that the relationship between the petite bourgeoisie and inter-war fascism has remained unduly prominent for too long. His own collection aims to 'undermine the inevitability of that link, by stressing not only the real national variations in the character of the petit-bourgeois political engagement, but also the ideological ambiguities of that move to the right'. For discussions on imperialism amongst the clerical class, see Richard Price's chapter on jingoism in the late nineteenth century and John Tosh's comments on New Imperialism and clerks' behaviour during the Mafeking celebrations. Crossick and Heinz-Gerhard Haupt, *The Petite Bourgeoisie in Europe 1870–1914: Enterprise, Family and Independence* (London: Routledge, 1995), 224; Price, 'Society, Status and Jingoism', 89–112; John Tosh, *Manliness and Masculinities in Nineteenth-Century Britain* (Harlow: Pearson Longman, 2005), 46.
89 Geoffrey Crossick, 'The Petite Bourgeoisie in Nineteenth-century Britain: The Urban and Liberal Case', in *Shopkeepers and Master Artisans in Nineteenth-century Europe*, ed. Geoffrey Crossick and Heinz-Gerhard Haupt (London: Methuen, 1984): 71–2.
90 Jeffery, 'A Place in the Nation', 72.
91 Ibid., 70.
92 Medhurst, *A National Joke*, 27.
93 Gunn, 'Class, Identity and the Urban', 37; Mike Savage, 'Urban History and Social Class: Two Paradigms', *Urban History* 20, no. 1 (1993): 70.
94 Ingrid Jeacle and Lee Parker, 'The "Problem" of the Office: Scientific Management, Governmentality and the Strategy of Efficiency', *Business History* 55, no. 7 (2013): 1074.
95 'Two Hour Daily Commute 'on Rise among UK Workers', *BBC News*, 18 November 2016. Available online: http://www.bbc.co.uk/news/uk-38026625 (accessed 21 November 2018); 'Annual Commuting Is Up 18 Hours Compared to a Decade Ago', 2017. Available online: https://www.tuc.org.uk/news/annual-commuting-time-18-hours-compared-decade-ago-finds-tuc (accessed 21 November 2018).
96 Dawn Foster, 'Commuting Is Now a Fact of Life: We Just Need to Make It Less Awful', *Guardian*, 28 April 2016. Available online: https://www.theguardian.com/

public-leaders-network/2016/apr/28/commuting-british-life-transport-links-housing (accessed 1 December 2018).
97 Robert Fishman, *Bourgeois Utopias: The Rise and Fall of Suburbia* (New York: Basic Books, 1987), 74.
98 See Joe Moran's conclusion in *Reading the Everyday* for a discussion of recent terror attacks and quotidian spaces like the commute. Joe Moran, *Reading the Everyday* (London: Routledge, 2005), 163–9.
99 Medhurst, 'Negotiating the Gnome Zone', 252.
100 Jacob Stolworthy, 'BBC's Most Popular Show Overseas Is … *Keeping Up Appearances*', *Independent*, 18 February 2016. Available online: http://www.independent.co.uk/arts-entertainment/tv/news/bbcs-most-popular-show-overseas-is-keeping-up-appearances-a6880806.html (accessed 13 June 2017).
101 John Betjeman, 'Slough', *John Betjeman's Collected Poems* (London: John Murray, 1962): 22.

1 The office

1 Christopher Baldry, 'The Social Construction of Office Space', *International Labour Review* 136 (1997): 365.
2 Francis Duffy, 'Office Buildings and Organisational Change', in *Buildings and Society*, ed. Anthony D. King (London: Routledge and Keagan Paul, 1980): 257.
3 Michael Zakim, 'Business Clerk as Social Revolutionary; or, a Labor History of the Nonproducing Classes', *Journal of the Early Republic* 26 (Winter 2006): 571.
4 See Martin Danahay's discussion of Thomas Carlyle and his almost religious worship of manual labour. Martin A. Danahay, *Gender at Work in Victorian Culture: Literature, Art and Masculinity* (Oxon: Routledge, 2016), 33.
5 'Education and Wages', *Spectator*, 2 October 1886. Available online: http://archive.spectator.co.uk/article/2nd-october-1886/11/education-and-wages (accessed 3 November 2018).
6 Agatha Christie uses this device a few times in her novels – see *Death in the Clouds* (1935) and *After the Funeral* (1953), for instance.
7 In Alan Plater's *The Beiderbecke Connection* (1992), for instance, the cyber-criminal Ivan is accepted into the suburban home of Jill, Trevor and baby First-Born because while he has served time in prison, he is not considered any real kind of threat. Ivan's disruption of the entire global banking system is, in fact, something Jill can reconcile with her own left-wing ideology.
8 Carl Rhodes and Robert Westwood, *Critical Representations of Work and Organization in Popular Culture* (Oxon: Routledge, 2008), 2.

9   Alexia Panayiotou, '"Macho" Managers and Organizational Heroes: Competing Masculinities in Popular Films', *Organization* 17, no. 6 (2010): 661.
10 Ibid.
11 The ONS UK Labour Market survey (2017) has the number of women in the Administrative and Secretarial category, for instance, three times the number of men. Likewise, the 2018 census showed that of the 3,360,000 workers classed in group four (Administrative and Secretarial Occupations), an overwhelming 2,543,000 were women – a trajectory that has remained constant since at least 2001. See Andrew Powell, 'Briefing Paper CBP06838', *Women and the Economy* (8 March 2019), 7. Available online: https://www.ons.gov.uk/employmentandlabourmarket/peopleinwork/employmentandemployeetypes/datasets/employmentbyoccupationemp04 (accessed 3 January 2020).
12 Ingrid Jeacle, ' "Beyond the Boring Grey": The Construction of the Colourful Accountant', *Critical Perspectives on Accounting* 19, no. 8 (2008): 1298.
13 Gideon Haigh, *The Office: A Hardworking History* (Melbourne: Melbourne University Publishing, 2012).
14 Gregory Anderson, *Victorian Clerks* (Manchester: Manchester University Press, 1976), 19.
15 Lousie Rhind-Tutt, 'The Manchester Building That's Been a Refuge since the 1890s', *I Love Manchester*, 13 September 2017. Available online: https://ilovemanchester.com/city-centre-building-thats-manchester-refuge-since-1890s/ (accessed 5 January 2019).
16 Timothy Alborn, 'Quill-driving: British Life Insurance Clerks and Occupational Mobility, 1800–1914', *Business History Review* 82, no. 1 (Spring 2008): 40.
17 Jeremy Lewis, ed., *Chatto Book of Office Life* (London: Chatto and Windus, 1992), 3.
18 John Lanchester, 'When Fiction Breaks Down', *Telegraph*, 29 January 2009. Available online: https://www.telegraph.co.uk/culture/books/7093699/When-fiction-breaks-down.html (accessed 23 January 2017).
19 Lee Ellis, 'Then We Came to the Next Office Novel', *New Yorker*, 2 February 2010. Available online: https://www.newyorker.com/books/page-turner/then-we-came-to-the-next-office-novel (accessed 23 January 2017).
20 Graham Thompson, ' "Dead Letters! ... Dead Men?": The Rhetoric of the Office in Melville's "Bartleby, the Scrivener" ', *Journal of American Studies* 34, no. 3 (2000): 399.
21 Lewis, *Chatto Book of Office Life*, 58.
22 Shan Bullock, *Robert Thorne: The Story of a London Clerk* (London: T. Werner Laurie, 1907), 37.
23 Ibid., 34–6.
24 Ibid., 36.
25 Shan F. Bullock, *Mr Ruby Jumps the Traces* (London: Chapman and Hall, 1917), 8.

26 Frank Swinnerton, *The Young Idea: A Comedy of Environment* (London: Hutchinson, 1910), 233; and Edwin Pugh, *The Broken Honeymoon* (London: John Milne, 1908), 119.
27 David Kynaston, *City of London: Illusions of Gold 1914–1945* (London: Random House, 2000), 271–4.
28 P. D. James, 'A Very Commonplace Murder', in *The Mistletoe Murder and Other Stories* (London: Faber and Faber, 2016): 67.
29 Lynne Reid Banks, *The L-Shaped Room* (London: Vintage, 2004), 34.
30 Gail Honeyman, *Elinor Oliphant Is Completely Fine* (London: HarperCollins, 2017), 3.
31 David Nobbs, *The Fall and Rise of Reginald Perrin* (London: Mandarin, 1990), 7.
32 *Ever Decreasing Circles* (1987), [TV programme] BBC, 6 December.
33 Lewis, *Chatto Book of Office Life*, 88; Nigel Williams, *The Wimbledon Poisoner* (London: Faber and Faber, 1990), 5.
34 John Lanchester, *Mr Phillips* (London: Faber and Faber, 2000), 52.
35 Lewis, *Chatto Book of Office Life*, 80.
36 Christopher Baldry, 'The Social Construction of Office Space', *International Labour Review* 136 (1997): 367.
37 Ben Walters, *The Office: A Critical Reading of the Series* (London: BFI, 2005).
38 'Episode Summary for Series 1, Episode 1'. Available online: https://www.bbc.co.uk/programmes/b03yvf3r (accessed 17 April 2020).
39 Sabina Siebert, '"A Deeply Troubled Organization": Satire in the BBC's W1A Comedy Series', *Scandinavian Journal of Management* 35 (2019): 59.
40 Duffy, 'Office Buildings and Organisational Change', 256.
41 *Reggie Perrin* (2009), [TV Programme] BBC, 8 May.
42 *Blackadder Goes Forth* (1989), [TV programme] 'Captain Cook', BBC, 28 September.
43 Note obvious parallels with J. M. Barrie's clerk, Mr Darling, of *Peter Pan and Wendy* (1911); both are weak-minded office workers who embrace a life of safety at the expense of adventure.
44 George Orwell, *Keep the Aspidistra Flying* (London: Penguin Classics, 2000), 48.
45 Bullock, *Robert Thorne*, 176.
46 Aldous Huxley, cited in Russell Kirk, *Eliot and His Age: T. S. Eliot's Moral Imagination in the Twentieth Century* (Wilmington, DE: ISI Books, 2014), n.p.
47 Stephen Mihm, 'Clerks, Classes, and Conflicts: A Response to Michael Zakim's "The Business Clerk as Social Revolutionary"', *Journal of the Early Republic* 26 (Winter 2006): 610.
48 *dinnerladies* (1999), [TV programme] 'Gamble', BBC, 23 December.
49 Arnold Bennett, *A Man from the North* (New York: George H. Doran, 1911), 27.
50 C. F. G. Masterman, *The Condition of England* (London: Methuen, 1909), 57.

51 *Notting Hill* (1999), [Film] Dir. Roger Michell, UK: Polygram Filmed Entertainment/Working Title Films.
52 B. S. Johnson, *Christie Malry's Own Double-Entry* (London: Picador, 2001), 13.
53 Ali Haggett, *A History of Male Psychological Disorders, 1945–1980* (London: Palgrave Macmillan, 2015), 7.
54 Bennett continues: 'The ceiling, which bulged downwards, was as black as the floor, which sank away in the middle till it was hollow like a saucer. The revolution of an engine somewhere below shook everything with a periodic muffled thud. A greyish light came through one small window'. Arnold Bennett, *Anna of the Five Towns* (London: Methuen, 1919) [Kindle Edition], n.p., location 503.
55 Bullock, *Robert Thorne*, 140.
56 The changes to office conditions came much later, Mary Sundstrom suggests, in the 1930s and 1940s. Mary Graehl Sundstrom, *Work Places: The Psychology of the Physical Environment in Offices and Factories* (Cambridge: Cambridge University Press, 1986), 31.
57 'The City Clerk's Diet', *The Times*, 30 October 1912: 6.
58 Anderson, *Victorian Clerks*, 19.
59 George Gissing, *A Freak of Nature, or, Mr Brogden, City Clerk* (Edinburgh: Tragara Press, [1899] 1990), 23.
60 P. G. Wodehouse, 'A Sea of Troubles', in *The Man with Two Left Feet* (Library of Alexandria, 27 December 2012) [Kindle Edition], 128–9.
61 D. H. Lawrence, *Sons and Lovers* (London: Penguin, 1995), 94, 101, 103.
62 In 2015, the *Guardian* reported that manual and lower-paid households had been a minority since 2000, with a steady decline continuing – by 2015, 54.2 per cent of households were categorised by ABC1 in the IPSOS MORI National Readership Survey. George Arnett (2016), 'UK Became More Middle Class than Working Class in 2000, Data Shows', *Guardian*, 26 February. Available online: https://www.theguardian.com/news/datablog/2016/feb/26/uk-more-middle-class-than-working-class-2000-data.
63 Zakim, *Business Clerk*, 574.
64 Mihm, 'Clerks, Classes, and Conflicts', 612.
65 Ibid.
66 See Geoffrey Spurr's article on 'The London YMCA: A Haven of Masculine Self-improvement and Socialization for the Late-Victorian and Edwardian Clerk', *Canadian Journal of History* 37, no. 2 (August 2002): 275–301.
67 Masterman, *Condition of England*, 94.
68 Anderson, *Victorian Clerks*, 17.
69 'Too Strenuous Exercise', *Daily Mail*, 8 August 1922. Available online via *Daily Mail Historical Archive*: http://tinyurl.galegroup.com/tinyurl/8j7yg6 (accessed 3 December 2018).

70 Dave Lyddon, 'Britain at Work: 1945–1995', Available online: http://www.unionhistory.info/britainatwork/narrativedisplay.php?type=healthandsafety (accessed 24 November 2018).
71 'Multiple Display Advertising Items', *Daily Mail*, 20 August 1953. Available online via *Daily Mail Historical Archive, 1896–2004*: http://tinyurl.galegroup.com/tinyurl/8j8Q87 (accessed 9 December 2018).
72 'A. Thomas & Co', *Daily Mail*, 11 September 1967. Available online via *Daily Mail Historical Archive, 1896–2004*: http://tinyurl.galegroup.com/tinyurl/8j8cy3 (accessed 9 December 2019).
73 See the full-page consumer test by Stephanie Zinser in the *Daily Mail* on 'chairs that stop you getting a bad back'. Zinser (1999), 'Chairs That Stop You Getting a Bad Back', *Daily Mail*, 15 June. Available online via *Daily Mail Historical Archive, 1896–2004*: http://tinyurl.galegroup.com/tinyurl/8j8kZ7 (accessed 9 January 2019).
74 Louise Atkinson, 'Losing Weight in the Office', *Daily Mail*, 25 February 1992. Available online via *Daily Mail Historical Archive, 1896–2004*: http://tinyurl.galegroup.com/tinyurl/8j8vi4 (accessed 9 January 2019).
75 James Gallagher, 'Office Workers "Too Sedentary"', *BBC News*, 27 March 2015. Available online: http://www.bbc.co.uk/news/health-32069698 (accessed 3 March 2017).
76 Nicholas Lazard, 'Hidden Virtues?', *Guardian*, 6 January 2001. Available online: https://www.theguardian.com/books/2001/jan/06/fiction.reviews4 (accessed 13 June 2018).
77 Lanchester, *Mr Phillips*, 203.
78 Tessa Strain et al., 'Differences by Age and Sex in the Sedentary Time in Adults in Scotland', *Journal of Sports Sciences* 36, no. 7 (2018): 732–41.
79 Bullock, *Robert Thorne*, 276.
80 He cites a scheme run by the YMCA in which Manitoban farmers could find workers from the UK: 13,000 clerks applied from Manchester alone. John Tosh, *Manliness and Masculinities in Nineteenth-Century Britain* (Harlow: Pearson Longman, 2005), 204.
81 *The Parole Officer* (2001), [Film] Dir. John Duigan, UK: DNA Films.
82 John Carey, *Intellectuals and the Masses* (London: Faber and Faber, 1992).

2 The desk

1 Stephen Mihm, 'Clerks, Classes, and Conflicts: A Response to Michael Zakim's "The Business Clerk as Social Revolutionary"', *Journal of the Early Republic* 26 (Winter 2006): 608.

2   Gregory Anderson, *The White-Blouse Revolution: Female Office Workers Since 1870* (Manchester: Manchester University Press, 1988).
3   Lee Parker and Ingrid Jeacle, 'The Construction of the Efficient Office: Scientific Management, Accountability and the Neo-Liberal State', *Contemporary Accounting Research* (2019): 7.
4   Ibid., 22.
5   Ibid., 12.
6   Ibid.
7   Arnold Bennett, *A Man from the North* (New York: George H. Doran, 1911): 27.
8   Shan Bullock, *Robert Thorne: The Story of a London Clerk* (London: T. Werner Laurie, 1907), 73.
9   T. S. Eliot, 'The Waste Land', *Collected Poems* (London: Faber and Faber, 1969): 62, 68.
10 Julian Forest, *The Wooden Angel* (London: Hodder and Stoughton, 1938), 134.
11 Parker and Jeacle, 'Construction of the Efficient Office', 30.
12 Ibid., 29.
13 Alexandra Lange, 'White Collar Corbusier: From the *Casier* to the *cités d'affairs*', *Grey Room* 9 (Fall 2002): 62.
14 David Lockwood, *The Blackcoated Worker: A Study in Class Consciousness* (Oxford: Oxford University Press, 1969): 90; 'Modern Machines Take Charge of the Office', *The Queenslander*, 16 February 1938. Available online: http://nla.gov.au/nla.news-article18902901 (accessed 15 December 2013).
15 'Modern Machines Take Charge', 13; Frank Swinnerton, *The Young Idea: A Comedy of Environment* (London: Hutchinson, 1910): 66.
16 'Modern Machines Take Charge', 13.
17 Anderson, *White-Blouse Revolution*, 3.
18 Parker and Jeacle, 'Construction of the Efficient Office', 14.
19 For further literature on women in the clerical workplace see Graham Lowe's book, *Women in the Administrative Revolution* (Oxford: Basil Blackwell, 1987); Anderson, *White-Blouse Revolution*; Meta Zimmeck, 'Jobs for the Girls: The Expansion of Clerical Work for Women, 1850–1914', in *Unequal Opportunities: Women's Employment in England 1800–1918*, ed. Angela Johns (Oxford: John Wiley, 1986); and Julie Berebitsky's *Sex and the Office: A History of Gender, Power and Desire* (New Haven, CT: Yale University Press, 2012). See also F. D. Klingender, *The Condition of Clerical Labour in Britain* (London: Lawrence, 1935) and Lockwood, *The Blackcoated Worker*, both of which discuss the 'status-decline' in clerical work once women become employed. Graham Lowe, 'Class, Job and Gender in the Canadian Office', *Labour/Le Travailleur* 10 (Autumn 1982): 18, 20.
20 Lowe, *Women in the Administrative Revolution*, preface.
21 Ibid., 1 and 17.

22 A. McKinlay and R. G. Wilson, '"Small Acts of Cunning": Bureaucracy, Inspection and the Career, c.1890–1914', *Critical Perspectives on Accounting* 17 (2006): 661.
23 Ibid., 658 – original emphasis.
24 Norman Collins, *London Belongs to Me* (London: Collins, 1947), 14, 632.
25 Ibid., 633.
26 *People Like Us* (1999), [TV programme] 'The Estate Agent', BBC, 27 September.
27 Andrew Scott, 'AI and White-Collar Jobs', *London Business School Review*, 21 May 2018. Available online: https://www.london.edu/faculty-and-research/lbsr/ai-and-white-collar-jobs (accessed 9 January 2019).
28 Bullock, *Robert Thorne*, 140.
29 Ibid., 38.
30 Georg Lukács, *History and Class Consciousness: Studies in Marxist Dialectics* (London: Merlin Press, 1968), 88.
31 P. G. Wodehouse, 'A Sea of Troubles', in *The Man with Two Left Feet* (Egypt: Library of Alexandria, 27 December 2012) [Kindle Edition]: 130.
32 *The Good Life* (1975), [TV programme] 'Plough Your Own Furrow', BBC, 4 April.
33 Paul Jordan, *The Author in the Office: Narrative Writing in Twentieth-Century Argentina and Uruguay* (Woodbridge: Boydell and Brewer, 2006), 1.
34 For a critical response to Rose's interpretation see Christopher Hilliard, 'Modernism and the Common Writer', *Historical Journal* 48, no. 3 (2005): 769–87. Hilliard argues that Rose is merely using the narrative of working-class versus modernism to fight his own battles in contemporary American academic culture. Hilliard's aim is thus to dispute the suggestion that working class readers were the only readers to oppose modernism. Jonathan Rose, *Intellectual Life of the Working Classes* (London: Yale University Press, 2001), 393.
35 Paul Attewell, 'The Clerk Deskilled: A Study in False Nostalgia', *Journal of Historical Sociology* 2, no. 4 (1989): 360.
36 *Colin's Sandwich* (1990), [TV programme] 'Night Thoughts', BBC, 2 February.
37 *Colin's Sandwich* (1988), [TV programme] 'Flaunt It', BBC, 18 October.
38 Michael Hogan, '*Colin's Sandwich* Boxset Review', *Guardian*, 11 September 2014. Available online: https://www.theguardian.com/tv-and-radio/2014/sep/11/colins-sandwich-box-set-review-mel-smith (accessed 13 June 2018).
39 Jonathan Wild, *The Rise of the Office Clerk in Literary Culture, 1880–1939* (Basingstoke: Palgrave Macmillan, 2006), 17.
40 Ibid., 17.
41 Parker and Jeacle, 'Construction of the Efficient Office', 13.
42 Lee Parker, 'From Scientific to Activity Based Office Management: A Mirage of Change', *Journal of Accounting and Organizational Change* 12, no. 2 (2016): 177.
43 *Brazil* (1985), [Film] Dir. Terry Gilliam, UK: Embassy International Pictures.
44 Geoff Plimmer and Emse Cleave, 'Modern Office Design: Friend of Foe – Reviewing the Research', Centre for Labour, Employment and Work, Victoria

University of Wellington, 2017. Available online: https://www.wgtn.ac.nz/som/clew/publications/modern_office_design.pdf (accessed 3 July 2019).
45. Joe Moran, *Queueing for Beginners: The Story of Daily Life from Breakfast to Bedtime* (London: Profile Books, 2007), 47.
46. Alistair McKay, 'The W1A Way', *Evening Standard*, 26 March 2014. Available online: https://www.standard.co.uk/lifestyle/london-life/the-w1a-way-why-the-bbcs-new-office-comedy-feels-awfully-familiar-9216556.html (accessed 22 January 2018).
47. McKinley and Wilson, '"Small Acts of Cunning"', 671.
48. Graham Thompson, '"Dead letters! … Dead Men?": The Rhetoric of the Office in Melville's "Bartleby the Scrivener"', *Journal of American Studies* 34, no. 3 (2000): 398.
49. Michael Zakim, 'Business Clerk as Social Revolutionary; or, a Labor History of the Nonproducing Classes', *Journal of the Early Republic* 26 (Winter 2006): 591.
50. Houlston's Industrial Library, No. 7: *The Clerk: A Sketch in Outline of His Duties and Discipline* (London: Houlston, 1878), 45.
51. Robert White, 'Wanted: A Rowton House for Clerks', *Nineteenth Century* 42 (October 1897): 594–601.
52. Ibid.
53. W. H. Crosland, *The Suburbans* (London: John Long, 1905), 38.
54. Scott Banville, '"A Book-Keeper, Not an Accountant": Representing the Lower Middle Class from Victorian Novels and Music-Hall Songs to Television Sitcoms', *Journal of Popular Culture* 44, no. 1 (2011): 20.
55. Ibid., 20.
56. 'Ye Banks and Brays!', *Punch*, 29 November 1884: 257; 'Our Great Banks: IV Colonial Banks', *Boy's Own Paper*, 29 September 1894: 823.
57. 'There Is a Time for Everything', *Pick-Me-Up*, 5 October 1889.
58. Bullock, *Robert Thorne*, 37.
59. Lowe, *Women in the Administrative Revolution*, 105.
60. Ingrid Jeacle, 'The Bank Clerk in Victorian Society: The Case of Hoare and Company', *Journal of Management History* 16, no. 3 (2010): 318–19.
61. *Reggie Perrin* (2009), [TV programme] BBC, 1 May.
62. *Keeping Up Appearances* (1990), [TV programme] 'Stately Home', BBC, 12 November.
63. *Reggie Perrin* (2009), [TV programme] BBC, 1 May.
64. Brett Mills, *Television Sitcom* (London: British Film Institute, 2005): 104.
65. P. G. Wodehouse, *Psmith in the City* (Rockville, MD: Arc Manor, 2008), 25.
66. Bullock, *Robert Thorne*, 140.
67. Richard Church, *Over the Bridge* (London: William Heinemann, 1956), 220.
68. *Girl from Rio* (2001), [Film] Dir. Christopher Monger, UK/Spain: Lolafilms, S. A. and Casanova Pictures Production.

69 The clerk's 'propensity for criminal malfeasance', which Mihm identifies in American examples, can easily be verified by searching 'clerk' in British nineteenth-century newspaper archives; most of the articles stored under this search term are of crime notices and court listings. Mihm, 'Clerks, Class, and Conflicts', 613.
70 This is particularly true of Golden Age crime fiction: see Nicola Bishop, 'Mundane and Menacing: "Nobodies" in the Detective Fiction of Agatha Christie', in 'Re-appropriating Agatha Christie', *Clues: A Journal of Detection* (Spring 2016): 82–95.
71 John Lanchester, *Mr Phillips* (London: Faber and Faber, 2000), 6.
72 Ibid., 67.
73 Bullock, *Robert Thorne*, 38.
74 McKinley and Wilson, '"Small Acts of Cunning"', 658; Bullock, *Robert Thorne*, 39.
75 Bullock, *Robert Thorne*, 38.
76 Church, *Over the Bridge*, 220.
77 Wodehouse, *Psmith in the City*, 25.
78 Geoffrey Crossick, 'The Emergence of the Lower Middle Class', in *The Lower Middle Class in Britain: 1870–1914*, ed. Geoffrey Crossick (London: Croom Helm, 1977): 24.
79 *Punch* (July–December 1845). Available online: http://www.victorianlondon.org/professions/clerks.htm (accessed 13 January 2019).
80 Laurie Dennett, *A Sense of Security: 150 Years of Prudential* (Cambridge: Granta, 1998), 85.
81 Ibid., 87. *Is It Legal?* (1995), [TV programme] 'Whodunnit', ITV, 19 September.
82 Jerome Bjelopera, as cited in Timothy Alborn, 'Quill-Driving: British Life Insurance Clerks and Occupational Mobility, 1800–1914', *Business History Review* 82, no. 1 (Spring 2008): 51.
83 Dennett, *A Sense of Security*.
84 Ibid., 156.
85 Ibid., 159.
86 Ingrid Jeacle, '"Beyond the Boring Grey": The Construction of the Colourful Accountant', *Critical Perspectives on Accounting* 19, no. 8 (2008): 1297.
87 Dennett, *A Sense of Security*, 85.
88 Linda Kirkham and Ann Loft, 'Gender and the Construction of the Professional Accountant', *Accounting, Organizations and Society* 18, no. 6 (1993): 545.
89 Guy Routh, *Occupation and Pay in Great Britain 1906–79* (London: Macmillan, 1980), 24.
90 Anderson, *White-Blouse Revolution*.
91 Stephen Walker, 'Identifying the Women behind the Railed-in Desk: The Proto-Feminisation of Bookkeeping in Britain', *Accounting, Auditing and Accountability Journal* 4, no. 4 (2003): 606–39.

92 Lowe, *Women in the Administrative Revolution*.
93 Dennett, *A Sense of Security*, 83.
94 Jeacle and Parker, 'Construction of the Efficient Office', 42–3.
95 Ibid., 43.
96 Ibid., 83.
97 Ibid., 203.
98 Anderson, *White-Blouse Revolution*, 5.
99 Patrick Jenkins and Harriet Agnew, 'London: Sexism and the City', *Financial Times*, 16 January 2015. Available online: https://www.ft.com/content/7c182ab8-9c33-11e4-b9f8-00144feabdc0 (accessed 3 November 2018).
100 Anderson, *White-Blouse Revolution*.
101 *The Squirrels* (1976), [TV programme] 'The Renaissance', ITV, 13 August.
102 David Langdon, 'It'll Take Some Little Time for Me to Re-adjust to Her as an Audit Clerk', *Punch Historical Archive*, 23 December 1981: 1132.
103 *Ever Decreasing Circles* (1987), [TV programme] BBC, 6 December.
104 *Ever Decreasing Circles* (1984), [TV programme] BBC, 2 December.
105 George Gissing, *A Freak of Nature or Mr Brogden, City Clerk, an Uncollected Short Story* (Edinburgh: Tragara Press, 1990).
106 *The Rebel* (1961), [Film] Dir. Robert Day, United Kingdom: Associated British Picture Corporation.
107 *Men Behaving Badly* (1996), [TV programme] 'Cardigan', BBC, 18 July.
108 Ricky Gervais and Stephen Merchant, *The Office: The Scripts: Series 1* (London: BBC, 2004): 267.
109 *Paddington 2* (2017), [Film] Dir. Paul King, United Kingdom: StudioCanal.
110 *Dad's Army* (1969), [TV programme] 'War Dance', BBC, 6 November.
111 *The Good Life* (1975), [TV programme] 'Plough Your Own Furrow', BBC, 4 April – emphasis added.
112 *The Office* (2001), [TV programme] 'Judgement', BBC, 20 August.
113 Ricky Gervais interview, *The Office: Special Edition Box Set* (BBC, 2011).
114 Carl Rhodes and Robert Westwood, *Critical Representations of Work and Organisation in Popular Culture* (Oxon: Routledge, 2008), 102.
115 Jeffrey Richards, *Films and British National Identity: From Dickens to Dad's Army* (Manchester: Manchester University Press, 1997), 363.
116 *Men Behaving Badly* (1995), [TV programme] 'Playing Away', BBC, 13 July.
117 P. D. James, 'A Very Commonplace Murder', in *The Mistletoe Murder and Other Stories* (London: Faber and Faber, 2016), 71.
118 B. S. Johnson, *Christie Malry's Own Double-Entry* (London: Picador, 2001), 151.
119 Nigel Williams, *The Wimbledon Poisoner* (London: Faber and Faber, 1990), 173.
120 Jeacle, 'Beyond the Boring Grey', 1296.
121 Michael Heller, *London Clerical Workers 1880–1914: Development of the Labour Market* (London: Pickering & Chatto, 2011), 53.

122 Gissing, *The Odd Woman* (London: Virago Press, 1987), 403.
123 *The Times*, 17 April 1959: 13.
124 *Colin's Sandwich* (1990), [TV programme] 'Frank', BBC, 9 February.
125 *Colin's Sandwich* (1990), [TV programme] 'Night Thoughts', BBC, 2 February.
126 Charles Dickens, *Sketches by Boz* (London: Penguin, 1995), 122.
127 Swinnerton, *The Young Idea*, 47.
128 *The Rebel* (1961), [Film] Dir. Robert Day, United Kingdom: Associated British Picture Corporation.
129 In *The Squirrels*, someone from head office comes to examine the office space and make recommendations about improving efficiency. One of these is to move the filing cabinets closer to the desks; a simple act that, as she suggests, would save 'sixty-nine standard minutes' a day. H. G. Wells, *'42 to '44: A Contemporary Memoir upon Human Behaviour during the Crisis of the World Revolution* (London: Secker and Warburg, 1944), 38.
130 Ricky Gervais, as quoted in Ben Thompson, *Sunshine on Putty: The Golden Age of British Comedy from Vic Reeves to The Office* (London: Harper Perennial, 2004): 401–2.
131 Ibid., 402.
132 Bullock, *Robert Thorne*, 268.
133 Ibid., 268.
134 Ibid., 141.
135 Collins, *London Belongs to Me*, 13.
136 Ibid., 20.
137 Ibid., 42.
138 Ibid., 628.
139 Ibid.
140 Ibid., 23.
141 J. B. Priestley, *Angel Pavement* (London: Manderin, 1993), 34.
142 *Ever Decreasing Circles* (1984), [TV programme] BBC, 2 December.
143 Priestley, *Angel Pavement*, 34.
144 Ibid., 33.
145 Ibid., 34.
146 *The Legacy of Reginald Perrin* (1996), [TV programme] BBC, 22 September.
147 Ibid.
148 *Keeping Up Appearances* (1992), [TV programme] BBC, 6 September.
149 *The Good Life* (1976), [TV programme] 'Mutiny', BBC, 9 January.
150 *Men Behaving Badly* (1992), [TV programme] 'My Brilliant Career', BBC, 24 March.
151 Joe Moran, *Reading the Everyday* (London: Routledge, 2005), 47.

3 The commute

1. Scott Le Vine, John Polak, Alun Humphrey, 'Commuting Trends in England, 1988-2016', 2016. Available online: https://assets.publishing.service.gov.uk/government/uploads/system/uploads/attachment_data/file/657839/commuting-in-england-1988-2015.pdf (accessed 21 August 2018).
2. Gail Cunningham, 'London Commuting: Suburb and City, the Quotidian Frontier', in *London Eyes: Reflections in Text and Image*, ed. Gail Cunningham and Stephen Barber (Oxford: Berghahn, 2007): 7–25.
3. Nick Barrett, *Greater London: The Story of the Suburbs* (London: Random House, 2012), 107, 185.
4. Ibid., 185.
5. Michael Freeman, *Railways and the Victorian Imagination* (London: Yale University Press, 1999), 133–4.
6. Jeffrey Richards and John Mackenzie, *The Railway Station: A Social History* (Oxford: Oxford University Press, 1986), 166 and 169.
7. Freeman, *Railways and the Victorian Imagination*, 139.
8. John Ruskin, in Richards and Mackenzie, *The Railway Station*, 33.
9. Stephen Kern, *The Culture of Time and Space, 1880–1918* (Cambridge, MA: Harvard University Press, 1983), 15.
10. Richards and Mackenzie, *The Railway Station*, 94.
11. *The Times*, as cited in *Young Folks Paper*, 12 October 1889, 227.
12. H. G. Wells, *The War of the Worlds* (London: Pan Books, 1975), 166.
13. As Moran outlines, these quickly made up a fifth of breakfast cereal sales. Joe Moran, *Queueing for Beginners: The Story of Daily Life from Breakfast to Bedtime* (London: Profile Books, 2007), 19.
14. David Nobbs, *The Fall and Rise of Reginald Perrin* (London: Mandarin, 1990).
15. Simon Webb, *Commuters: The History of a British Way of Life* (Barnsley: Pen and Sword, 2016), 27.
16. Shan Bullock, *Robert Thorne: The Story of a London Clerk* (London: T. Werner Laurie, 1907), 137.
17. Richards and Mackenzie, *The Railway Station*, 95.
18. Nobbs, *Fall and Rise*, 17.
19. Bullock, *Mr Ruby*, 41.
20. Cunningham, 'London Commuting', 11.
21. P. G. Wodehouse, *Psmith in the City* (Rockville, MD: Arc Manor, 2008), 20.
22. C. F. G. Masterman, *The Condition of England* (London: Methuen, 1909), 70.
23. Ibid., 95–6.
24. Cunningham, 'London Commuting', 11.
25. Bullock, *Robert Thorne*, 138.

26 Virginia Woolf, *Night and Day* (London: George H. Doran, 1920), 440 – emphasis added.
27 Chris Moss, 'Ten Ways to Improve the Dreaded Daily Commute', *Telegraph*, 19 November 2013. Available online: https://www.telegraph.co.uk/lifestyle/10452040/Ten-ways-to-improve-the-dreaded-daily-commute.html (accessed 13 June 2017).
28 George P. Landow, 'London Bridge', 2001. Available online: http://www.victorianweb.org/photos/postcards/08.html (accessed 3 February 2018); Mark Sanders, 'Urbis'. Available online: www.marksanders.co.uk (accessed 3 February 2018).
29 John Betjeman and John Gay, *London's Historic Railway Stations* (London: John Murray, 1972), 102.
30 John Lanchester, *Mr Phillips* (London: Faber and Faber, 2000), 48.
31 Julian Barnes, *Metroland* (London: Pan Books, 1990), 58.
32 Webb, *Commuters*, 67.
33 W. Pett Ridge, *Outside the Radius: Stories of a London Suburb* (London: Hodder and Stoughton, 1899), 8.
34 *Dad's Army* (1970), [TV programme] BBC, 20 November.
35 Nobbs, *Fall and Rise*, 6.
36 R. F. Delderfield, *The Dreaming Suburb* (London: Hodder and Stoughton, 1987), 446.
37 Moran, *Queueing for Beginners*, 25.
38 *The 7.39* (2014), [TV film] BBC, 9 January.
39 Tom O'Dell, 'My Soul for a Seat: Commuting and the Routines of Mobility', in *Time, Consumption and Everyday Life: Practice, Materiality, Culture*, ed. Elizabeth Shove, Frank Trentmann and Richard Wilk (Oxford: Berg, 2009): 90–2.
40 Aldous Huxley, *Along the Road: Notes and Essays of a Tourist* (London: Chatto & Windus, 1927), 28.
41 The author of *The Railway Traveller* remarked that it is 'most unnatural and unreasonable' that railway users 'perform the whole of the journey in silence', while in the *Daily Telegraph* a rail user compared the chatter of holiday trains with the 'silent' and 'grim' faces of commuters. Chris Moss, 'Ten Ways to Improve the Dreaded Daily Commute', *Telegraph*, 19 November 2013. Available online: https://www.telegraph.co.uk/lifestyle/10452040/Ten-ways-to-improve-the-dreaded-daily-commute.html (accessed 13 June 2017); *The Railway Traveller's Handy Book of Hints, Suggestions and Advice: Before the Journey, on the Journey and after the Journey*, ed. Jack Simmons (Bath: Adams and Dart, 1862): 62; Peter K. Moss, 'That Happy Holiday Feeling', *Daily Mail*, 16 August 1973. *Daily Mail Historical Archive*, 1896–2004. Available online: https://link-gale-com.ezproxy.mmu.ac.uk/apps/doc/EE1862290429/GDCS?u=mmucal5&sid=GDCS&xid=882b2f80 (accessed 21 August 2019).

42 Joe Moran, *Reading the Everyday* (London: Routledge, 2005), 50.
43 Jamie Grierson, '"Tube Chat" Campaign Provokes Horror among London Commuters', *Guardian*, 29 September 2016. Available online: https://www.theguardian.com/uk-news/2016/sep/29/tube-chat-campaign-provokes-horror-among-london-commuters (accessed 21 June 2018).
44 *Reggie Perrin* (2009), [TV programme] BBC, 24 April.
45 Ibid.
46 Sabrina Barr, 'UK Weather: The Unspoken Rules of Commuter Etiquette during a Heatwave', *Independent*, 25 June 2018. Available online: https://www.independent.co.uk/life-style/commuter-etiquette-heatwaves-unspoken-rules-heat-summer-deodorant-water-eye-contact-a8415821.html (accessed 25 June 2018).
47 Guy Kelly, 'The Tube Door Secret Has Been Blown – but Here's How You Can Still Gain an Advantage over Other Passengers', *Telegraph*, 14 September 2017. Available online: https://www.telegraph.co.uk/men/thinking-man/tube-door-secret-has-blown-can-still-gain-advantage-passengers/ (accessed 19 August 2018).
48 Martin Knight, *Barry Desmond Is a Wanker* (London: London Books, 2010), 144.
49 Lanchester, *Mr Phillips*, 143.
50 Ibid., 47.
51 Ibid.
52 O'Dell, 'My Soul for a Seat', 92.
53 Arnold Bennett, *Hilda Lessways* (London: E. P. Dutton, 1911), 178.
54 George Orwell, *Keep the Aspidistra Flying* (London: Penguin Classics, 2000), 70.
55 Lanchester, *Mr Phillips*, 41.
56 *W1A* (2015), [TV programme] BBC, 14 May.
57 Bullock, *Mr Ruby*, 31.
58 Ibid., 198.
59 Gail Cunningham, 'Houses in Between: Navigating Suburbia in Late Victorian Writing', *Victorian Literature and Culture* 32, no. 2 (2004): 426.
60 Labour Force Survey, 'The Commuting Gap: Men Account for 65% of Commutes Lasting More than an Hour', 7 November 2018. Available online: https://www.ons.gov.uk/employmentandlabourmarket/peopleinwork/employmentandemployeetypes/articles/thecommutinggapmenaccountfor65ofcommuteslastingmorethananhour/2018-11-07 (accessed 21 September 2018).
61 Ibid.
62 Hanif Kureishi, *Buddha of Suburbia* (London: Faber and Faber, 1990), 46.
63 This is one of the (many) reasons that Dawn and Pete argue in sitcom *Gavin and Stacey*; Dawn chastises Pete for getting home late from work, smelling 'like a brewery'. *Gavin and Stacey* (2007), [TV programme] BBC, 13 May.
64 Moran, *Queueing for Beginners*, 25; Department for Transport, 'Transport Statistics Great Britain 2017', 2017. Available online: https://assets.publishing.service.gov.

uk/government/uploads/system/uploads/attachment_data/file/661933/tsgb-2017-report-summaries.pdf (accessed 8 January 2019).
65 A Google image search for 'commuters UK' gives results which are nearly universally of the major London stations, tube doors opening or red London buses, for instance.
66 Cunningham, 'London Commuting', 19.
67 Marsha Dunstan, 'The Great British Commute', *BBC Genome Blog*, 30 January 2018. Available online: http://www.bbc.co.uk/blogs/genome/entries/d64a2859-b651-4767-a9f6-8e808880caac (accessed 4 October 2018).
68 *The 7.39* (2014), [TV film] BBC, 6 January.
69 'Sonnets of a Commuter', *Shields Daily Gazette*, 3 August 1903, Issue 14676: 3.
70 Cunningham, 'London Commuting', 21.
71 Ibid., 18.
72 Barnes, *Metroland*, 61.

4 The suburbs

1 See, for instance, Alan A. Jackson's *Semi-Detached London: Suburban Development, Life and Transport, 1900–1930* (1973) for a detailed history. Becky M. Nicolaides and Andrew Wiese's *The Suburb Reader* (2006) is a comprehensive collection of documents about American suburbanization, and Kenneth T. Jackson's *Crabgrass Frontier* (1985) does a good job laying out the history of suburban America (as well as the title making clear some of the largest divergences in cultural implication for American suburbans compared to those in Britain).
2 Mark Clapson, 'The New Suburban History, New Urbanism and the Spaces In-Between', *Urban History* 43, no. 2 (2016): 336.
3 Ibid., 5.
4 Ibid.
5 Clapson, 'The Suburban Aspiration in England since 1919' *Contemporary British History* 14, no. 1 (2000): 151–74; Paul Hunter, 'Towards a Suburban Renaissance: An Agenda for Our City Suburbs', 2016. Available online: https://www.barrowcadbury.org.uk/wp-content/uploads/2016/07/Smith-Insitute-Towards-a-suburban-renaissance-July-2016.pdf (accessed 11 September 2019).
6 Peter Scott, *Making of the Modern British Home: The Suburban Semi and British Life between the Wars* (Oxford: Oxford University Press, 2013), 5.
7 Ibid.
8 Ruskin, as cited in David Rubinstein, *Victorian Homes* (Newton Abbot: David & Charles, 1974), 22.

9. Dinah Birch, 'A Life in Writing: Ruskin and the Uses of Suburbia', in *Writing and Victorianism*, ed. J. B. Bullen (London: Longman, 1997), 243.
10. H. G. Wells, *The New Machiavelli* (London: Penguin, 2018), 26.
11. Birch, 'A Life in Writing', 243.
12. Arthur Conan Doyle, *Beyond the City: The Idyll of a Suburb* (Fairfield, IA: 1st World Library, 2004), 10; E. M. Forster, *Howards End* (Harmondsworth: Penguin, 1961), 316.
13. See Peter Scott, 'Marketing Mass Home Ownership and the Creation of the Modern Working-Class Consumer in Inter-War Britain', *Business History* 50, no. 1 (2008): 4–25; and Mark Clapson, 'Working-Class Women's Experiences of Moving to New Housing Estates in England since 1919', *Twentieth-Century British History* 10, no. 3 (1999): 345–65.
14. Paul Hunter, 'Poverty in Suburbia: A Smith Institute Study into the Growth of Poverty in the Suburbs of England and Wales', 2014. Available online: http://www.smith-institute.org.uk/book/poverty-in-suburbia-a-smith-institure-study-into-the-growth-of-poverty-in-the-suburbs-of-england-and-wles/ (accessed 13 June 2018).
15. Wiiliam Pett Ridge, *Outside the Radius* (London: Hodder and Stoughton, 1899), 20.
16. Joe Moran, *Reading the Everyday* (London: Routledge, 2005), 122.
17. The quotation in the heading is from T. W. H. Crosland, *The Surburbans* (London: John Long, 1905), 16.
18. Clapson, 'Suburban Aspiration', 151.
19. Kate Flint, 'Fictional Suburbia', in Peter Humm, Paul Stigent and Peter Widdowson (eds), *Popular Fictions: Essays in Literature and History* (London: Routledge, 2003); Roger Webster, *Expanding Suburbia: Reviewing Suburban Narratives* (New York: Berghahn Books, 2000), 5.
20. Bennett, *A Man from the North* (New York: George H. Doran, 1911), 100–1.
21. W. H. Crosland, *The Suburbans* (London: John Long, 1905), 15.
22. F. M. L. Thompson, *Hampstead: Building a Borough, 1650–1964* (London: Routledge, 1974), 375.
23. Robert Bueka, *SuburbiaNation: Reading Suburban Landscape in Twentieth-Century American Fiction and Film* (New York: Palgrave Macmillan, 2004), 4 and 7.
24. Paul Oliver, Ian Davis and Ian Bentley, *Dunroamin: The Suburban Semi and Its Enemies* (London: Pimlico, 1981), 10.
25. Webster, *Expanding Suburbia*, 2.
26. Peter Scott, 'Marketing Mass Home Ownership': 6.
27. Oliver et al., *Dunroamin*, 10.
28. Scott, 'Marketing Mass Home Ownership': 13.
29. F. M. L. Thompson, *The Rise of Suburbia* (Leicester: Leicester University Press, 1982), 2.
30. Clapson, *Suburban Century*, 8.

31 Tom Jeffery, 'Politics and Class in Lewisham', in *Metropolis, London: Histories and Representations since 1800*, ed. David Feldman and Gareth Stedman Jones (London: Routledge, 1989), 193.
32 Clapson, *Suburban Century*, 9; Richard Harris and Peter Larkham (eds), *Changing Suburbs: Foundation, Form and Function* (London: Spon, 1999), xiii.
33 Susan Brooks, 'Suburban Space in The Buddha of Suburbia', in *British Fiction of the 1990s*, ed. Nick Bentley (London: Routledge, 2005): 209.
34 Bennett, *A Man from the North*, 102.
35 Lynne Hapgood comments, for instance, on the 'kind of artlessness' prevalent within work that is loosely autobiographical in suburban fiction. John Lucas, *Arnold Bennett: A Study of His Fiction* (London: Methuen, 1974), 22; Lynne Hapgood, *Margins of Desire: The Suburbs in Fiction and Culture 1880–1925* (Manchester: Manchester University Press, 2005), 171.
36 See his chapter in Webster's *Expanding Suburbia* on pop music and the suburbs.
37 Ged Pope, *Reading London's Suburbs: From Charles Dickens to Zadie Smith* (London: Palgrave Macmillan, 2015), 9.
38 Ibid.
39 Brett Mills, *Television Sitcom* (London: British Film Institute, 2005), 17.
40 Ibid., 62–4.
41 H. G. Wells, *Tono-Bungay* (London: Odhams Press, [1908] n.d.), 84; Mills, *Television Sitcom*, 27.
42 Mills, *Television Sitcom*, 21.
43 In American suburban studies, see Orly Clergé's *New Noir: Race, Identity and Diaspora in Black Suburbia* (2019). See also Hugh Muir's BBC Radio 4 documentary, *Black Flight and the New Suburbia* (2016).
44 Robert Fishman, *Bourgeois Utopias: The Rise and Fall of Suburbia* (New York: Basic Books, 1987), 26.
45 Thompson, *Rise of Suburbia*, 3.
46 C. F. G. Masterman, *The Condition of England* (London: Methuen, 1909), 65.
47 David Thorns sets out *Suburbia* (1973) as a study in which he aims to demonstrate that disdain for the 'middle-brow, conformist, respectable, uninspiring members of society who are quite content to potter around in their own rather limited world' was in fact a view that was 'divorced from the realities of suburban life'. However, by citing those who call the suburb a 'nightmare, humanly speaking' and a 'proliferating nonentity', and to the suburbanite as 'doomed to remain imprisoned in his box home', the critic must always tread a fine line between interrogating attitudes and perpetuating stereotypes. David Thorns, *Suburbia* (St. Albans: Paladin, 1973), 149, 16, 15.
48 Clapson, *Invincible Green Suburbs, Brave New Worlds: Social Change and Urban Dispersal in Post-war England* (Manchester: Manchester University Press, 1998), 6.

49 Paul Barker, *The Freedoms of Suburbia* (London: Frances Lincoln, 2009), 55.
50 Sarah May, *The Rise and Fall of the Queen of Suburbia: A Black-Hearted Soap Opera* (London: HarperCollins, 2006).
51 *This Happy Breed* (1944), [Film] Dir. David Lean, UK: Two Cities Films.
52 Nigel Williams, *They Came from SW19* (London: Corsair, 2013), 126.
53 *Gavin and Stacey* (2009), [TV programme] BBC, 26 November.
54 Hanif Kureishi, *Buddha of Suburbia* (London: Faber and Faber, 1990), 3.
55 *Men Behaving Badly* (1994), [TV programme] BBC, 8 July.
56 Kureishi, *Buddha of Suburbia*, 134.
57 Hanif Kureishi, 'I Got Out of the Suburbs, but Did They Get Out of Me?', *Observer (1901–2003)*, 25 February 2001. Available online: https://search-proquest-com.ezproxy.mmu.ac.uk/docview/478188446?accountid=12507 (accessed 13 April 2018).
58 George Orwell, *Keep the Aspidistra Flying* (London: Penguin Classics, 2000), 51.
59 A. James Hammerton, 'Pooterism or Partnership? Marriage and Masculine Identity in the Lower Middle Class, 1870–1920', *Journal of British Studies* 38 (July 1999): 291–321; A. James Hammerton, 'The Perils of Mrs Pooter: Satire, Modernity and Motherhood in the Lower Middle Class in England, 1870–1920', *Women's History Review* 8, no. 2 (1999): 261–76.
60 Melanie Tebbutt, 'Rambling and Manly Identity in Derbyshire's Dark Peak, 1880s-1920s', *Historical Journal* 49, no. 4 (2006): 1125–53.
61 Andy Medhurst, 'Negotiating the Gnome Zone: Versions of Suburbia in British Popular Culture', in *Visions of Suburbia*, ed. Roger Silverstone (London: Routledge, 1997): 243.
62 Ibid., 247.
63 Masterman, *Condition of England*, 56.
64 Stephen Wagg, ' "At Ease, Corporal": Social Class and the Situational Comedy in British Television, from the 1950s to the 1990s', in *Because I Tell a Joke or Two: Comedy, Politics and Social Difference*, ed. Stephen Wagg (1998): 2.
65 Jeffrey Richards, *Film and British National Identity: From Dickens to Dad's Army* (Manchester: Manchester University Press, 1997), 356.
66 The boys are, for instance, clearly out of their comfort zone in the city when they drive to a club and struggle to find a place to park the car.
67 Bueka, *SuburbiaNation*, 7.

5 The home

1 Peter Scott, *The Making of the Modern British Home: The Suburban Semi and British Life between the Wars* (Oxford: Oxford University Press, 2013), 14.

2   Mark Clapson, 'The Suburban Aspiration in England since 1919', *Contemporary British History* 14, no. 1 (2000): 169.
3   Joe Moran, *Reading the Everyday* (London: Routledge, 2005), 145.
4   Judy Giles, *The Parlour and the Suburb: Domestic Identities, Class, Femininity* (Oxford: Berg, 2004), 46.
5   Arnold Bennett, *A Man from the North* (New York: George H. Doran, 1911), 4–5.
6   Shan Bullock, *Robert Thorne: The Story of a London Clerk* (London: T. Werner Laurie, 1907), 10.
7   Ibid., 36.
8   H. G. Wells, *Love and Mr Lewisham* (London: Odhams Press, 1900), 97–8.
9   Richard Church, *Over the Bridge* (London: William Heinemann, 1956), 181.
10 See also Nicola Bishop, 'Ruralism, Masculinity and National Identity: The Rambling Clerk in Fiction, 1900–1940', *Journal of British Studies* 54, no. 3 (2015): 654–78.
11 Richard Dennis, *Cities in Modernity: Representations and Productions of Metropolitan Space* (Cambridge: Cambridge University Press, 2008), 181.
12 Scott, *Making of the Modern British Home*, 175.
13 Ibid., 175, 178.
14 Ibid., 139.
15 Nigel Williams, *The Wimbledon Poisoner* (London: Faber and Faber, 1990), 7.
16 *Keeping Up Appearances* (1990), [TV Programme] BBC, 'Stately Home', 12 November.
17 Gail Cunningham, 'The Riddle of Suburbia: Sub fictions of the fin de siècle', in *Expanding Suburbia: Reviewing Suburban Narratives*, ed. Roger Webster (New York: Berghahn Books, 2000): 57.
18 Williams, *Wimbledon Poisoner*, 54.
19 Keble Howard, *Smiths of Surbiton: A Comedy without a Plot* (London: Fisher Unwin, 1925), 8.
20 Ibid., vii–viii.
21 R. F. Delderfield, *The Dreaming Suburb* (London: Hodder and Stoughton, 1964), 2.
22 'Review of *The Smiths of Surbiton*' (1906), *Spectator*, 10 February. Available online: http://archive.spectator.co.uk/article/10th-february-1906/26/the-smiths-of-surbiton-by-keble-howard-chapman-and (accessed 7 October 2018).
23 'The Smiths of Surbiton' (1906), *Saturday Review of Politics, Literature, Science and Art* 101, 17 February. Available online: https://search-proquest-com.ezproxy.mmu.ac.uk/docview/9161703?accountid=12507 (accessed 9 May 2017).
24 Bennett, *Man from the North*, 100–1.
25 Bullock, *Robert Thorne*, 144.
26 Shan Bullock, *Mr Ruby Jumps the Traces* (London: Chapman and Hall, 1907), 11.
27 W. H. Crosland, *The Suburbans* (London: John Long, 1905), 19; Bullock, *Mr Ruby*, 11.

28　Agatha Christie, *The Big Four* (London: Fontana, 1978), 19.
29　William Pett Ridge, *Outside the Radius* (London: Hodder and Stoughton, 1899), 6.
30　George Orwell, *Coming Up for Air* (London: Penguin, 1989), 9.
31　Bullock, *Mr Ruby*, 12.
32　*Keeping Up Appearances* (1995), [TV programme] BBC, 1 October.
33　Gary refers to this dynamic when he talks about how 'when two people go out, one of you has to be the policeman, and the other one has to be the silly one, otherwise there's anarchy'. *Men Behaving Badly* (1997), [TV programme] 4 December.
34　Ben Highmore, *The Great Indoors: At Home in the Modern British House* (London: Profile, 2014), 7.
35　'Hyacinth's Home Has Buckets of Style!' (2005), *Coventry Live*, 12 January. Available online: https://www.coventrytelegraph.net/news/coventry-news/hyacinths-home-buckets-style-3138216 (accessed 17 March 2017).
36　Robert Bueka, *SuburbiaNation: Reading Suburban Landscape in Twentieth-century American Fiction and Film* (New York: Palgrave Macmillan, 2004), 10.
37　*Keeping Up Appearances* (1990), [TV programme] BBC, 29 October.
38　*Keeping Up Appearances* (1990), [TV programme] BBC, 5 November.
39　Highmore, *Great Indoors*, 33.
40　Simon Gunn, 'Class, Identity and the Urban: The Middle Class in England, c. 1790–1950', *Urban History* 31, no. 1 (2004): 55.
41　Bullock, *Robert Thorne*, 30.
42　John Batchelor, *H. G. Wells* (Cambridge: Cambridge University Press, 1985), 101.
43　Rita Felski, 'Nothing to Declare: Identity, Shame, and the Lower Middle Class', *PMLA* 115, no. 1 (January 2001): 36.
44　*The Office* (2002), [TV programme] 'Appraisals', BBC, 7 October.
45　Ben Walters, *The Office: A Critical Reading of the Series* (London: British Film Institute, 2005), 147.
46　Tom Jeffery, 'Politics and Class in Lewisham', in *Metropolis, London: Histories and Representations Since 1800*, ed. David Feldman and Gareth Stedman Jones (London: Routledge, 1989): 201.
47　George Orwell, *Keep the Aspidistra Flying* (London: Penguin Classics, 2000), 4.
48　Bernard Crick, 'Blair, Eric Arthur (pseud. George Orwell)' (2004), *Oxford Dictionary of National Biography*, 23 September. Available online: https://doi-org.ezproxy.mmu.ac.uk/10.1093/ref:odnb/31915 (accessed 3 June 2011).
49　Orwell, *Keep the Aspidistra Flying*, 100.
50　Bennett, *A Man from the North*, 238.
51　Batchelor, *H. G. Wells*, 101.
52　David Lodge, *The Art of Fiction* (London: Vintage, 2011), 208.
53　Lucas is referring to Richard Larch, from Bennett's *A Man from the North*. Lucas, *Arnold Bennett*, 22.

54　Ricky Gervais and Stephen Merchant, *The Office Scripts* (London: BBC, 2004), 267.
55　Gail Cunningham, 'Houses in Between: Navigating Suburbia in Late Victorian Writing', *Victorian Literature and Culture* 32, no. 2 (2004): 422.
56　Malcolm Bradbury, 'The Opening World, 1900–1915', in *Edwardian and Georgian Fiction*, ed. Harold Bloom (Philadelphia: Chelsea House, 2005): 296.
57　Bennett, *Man from the North*, 263.
58　Ibid., 106.
59　Ibid., 262.
60　Ibid., 61.
61　Ibid., 228.
62　Norman Collins, *London Belongs to Me* (London: Collins, 1947), 9.
63　Orwell, *Coming Up for Air*, 13.
64　Bennett, *Man from the North*, 264.
65　Wells, *Love and Mr Lewisham*, 172.
66　Orwell, *Keep the Aspidistra Flying*, 266.
67　Ibid., 266, 277.
68　Ibid., 268 – original emphasis.
69　Bernard Crick, as cited in Giles, *The Parlour and the Suburb*, 40.
70　Church, *Over the Bridge*, 18, 60, 118.
71　Ibid., 135.
72　Julian Barnes, *Metroland* (London: Pan Books, 1990), 33.
73　Ibid., 135.
74　Ibid., 139.
75　Ibid., 147.
76　Ibid., 174–5.
77　John Carey, *The Intellectuals and the Masses* (London: Faber and Faber, 1992), 171.
78　Merritt Moseley, *Understanding Julian Barnes* (Columbia: University of South Carolina Press, 1997), 18.
79　Simon J. James, *Maps of Utopia: H. G. Wells, Modernity and the End of Culture* (Oxford: Oxford University Press, 2012), 78.
80　Kate Flint, 'Fictional Suburbia', in *Popular Fiction: Essays in Literature and History*, ed. Peter Humm, Paul Stigent and Peter Widdowson (New York: Berghahn Books, 2000), 119.
81　Hapgood, Lynne. *Margins of Desire: The Suburbs in Fiction and Culture 1880–1925* (Manchester: Manchester University Press, 2005), 72.
82　Mark Clapson, *Suburban Century: Social Change and Urban Growth in England and the USA* (London: Berg, 2003), 6.
83　Ibid., 8.
84　Kevin M. Kruse and Thomas J. Sugrue (eds), *The New Suburban History* (Chicago: University of Chicago Press, 2016), 4.

85 F. M. L. Thompson, *The Rise of Suburbia* (Leicester: Leicester University Press, 1892), 3.
86 Cunningham, 'Houses in Between', 422–3.

Conclusion

1 Shan Bullock, *Robert Thorne: The Story of a London Clerk* (London: T. Werner Laurie, 1907), 33.
2 Consider, too, the number of programmes that deliberately use a discourse of 'Great' Britishness in their titles or which contribute to the growing genre of 'docu-lite' series that take British landscape as their focus. See also, Nicola Bishop, 'Presenting the Past: New Directions in Television History', in *Histories on Screen: The Past and Present in Anglo-American Cinema and Television* ed. Sam Edwards, Michael Dolski and Faye Sayer (London: Bloomsbury, 2018): 277–92.
3 Joe Moran, *Reading the Everyday* (London: Routledge, 2005), 169.
4 Arlene Young, *Culture, Class and Gender in the Victorian Novel: Gentlemen, Gents and Working Women* (Basingstoke: Macmillan, 1999), chapter 2.
5 Roger Webster, *Expanding Suburbia: Reviewing Suburban Narratives* (New York: Berghahn Books, 2000), 4.

Filmography

2point4 Children (1991–9), [TV programme] BBC.
2 Broke Girls (2011–17), [TV programme] CBS.
The 7.39 (2014), [TV film] BBC.
The ABC Murders (2018), [TV programme] BBC.
Absolute Power (2003–5), [TV programme] BBC.
Act of Betrayal (1971), [TV programme] BBC.
Are You Being Served? (1972–85), [TV programme] BBC.
As Time Goes By (1992–2005), [TV programme] BBC.
The Big Bang Theory (2007–19), [TV programme] NBC.
A Bit of Fry and Laurie (1987–95), [TV programme] BBC.
Blackadder Goes Forth (1989), [TV programme] BBC.
Bodyguard (2018), [TV programme] BBC.
Brazil (1985), [Film] Dir. Terry Gilliam, UK: Embassy International Pictures.
Bridget Jones's Diary (2001), [Film] Dir. Sharon Maguire, UK: Miramax.
Brief Encounter (1945), [Film] Dir. David Lean, UK: Cineguild.
The Brittas Empire (1991–7), [TV programme] BBC.
Butterflies (1978–83), [TV programme] BBC.
Campus (2009–11), [TV programme] Channel 4.
Christopher Robin (2018), [Film] Dir. Mark Forster, USA: Walt Disney Pictures.
Colin's Sandwich (1988–90), [TV programme] BBC.
Conviction: Murder in Suburbia (2018), [TV programme] BBC.
Cuckoo (2012–19), [TV programme] BBC.
Dad's Army (1969–77), [TV programme] BBC.
Damned (2016–18), [TV programme] Channel 4.
Diary of a Nobody (2007), [TV programme] BBC.
dinnerladies (1998–2000), [TV programme] BBC.
Drop the Dead Donkey (1990–8), [TV programme] Channel 4.
Escape to the Country (2002–), [TV programme] BBC.
Ever Decreasing Circles (1984–9), [TV programme] BBC.
Everybody Loves Raymond (1996–2005), [TV Programme] CBS.
The Fall and Rise of Reginald Perrin (1976–9), [TV programme] BBC.
Falling in Love (1984), [Film] Dir. Ulu Grosbard, USA: Paramount Pictures.
Fawlty Towers (1975–9), [TV programme] BBC.
A Fine Romance (1981–4), [TV programme] Channel 4.
Fresh Fields (1984–6), [TV programme] ITV.

Friday Night Dinner (2011–18), [TV programme] Channel 4.
Friends (1994–2004), [TV programme] NBC.
The Full Monty (1997), [Film] Dir. Peter Catteneo, UK: Channel Four Films.
Gavin and Stacey (2007–10), [TV programme] BBC.
George and Mildred (1976–9), [TV programme] ITV.
Girl from Rio (2001), [Film] Dir. Christopher Monger, UK/Spain: Lolafilms, S.A. and Casanova Pictures Production.
Gogglebox (2013–), [TV programme] Channel 4.
The Goldbergs (2013–), [TV programme] ABC.
The Good Life (1975–8), [TV programme] BBC.
Happiness (2017), [Short] Dir. Steve Cutts, UK: Steve Cutts.
Henry 9 'til 5 (1970), [Film] Dir. Bob Godfrey, UK: Bob Godfrey Films.
Hook (1991), [Film] Dir. Steven Spielberg, USA: Amblin Entertainment.
Hot Fuzz (2007), [Film] Dir. Edgar Wright, UK: StudioCanal.
The Inbetweeners (2008–10), [TV programme] Channel 4.
The Incredibles (2004), [Film] Dir. Brad Bird, USA: Pixar Animation Studios.
Is It Legal? (1995–8), [TV programme] ITV.
The Island with Bear Grylls (2014–18), [TV programme] Channel 4.
The IT Crowd (2006–13), [TV programme] Channel 4.
Jonathan Creek (1998), [TV programme] BBC, 31 January.
Juliet Jekyll and Harriet Hyde (1995–8), [TV programme] BBC.
Keeping Up Appearances (1990–5), [TV programme] BBC.
Kiss Me Kate (1998–2001), [TV programme] BBC.
Last of the Summer Wine (1973–2010), [TV programme] BBC.
The Legacy of Reginald Perrin (1996), [TV programme] BBC.
Love Actually (2003), [Film] Dir. Richard Curtis, UK: Universal Pictures.
Mary Poppins (1964), [Film] Dir. Robert Stephenson, USA: Walt Disney Productions.
Men Behaving Badly (1993–9), [TV programme] BBC.
The Mindy Project (2012–17), [TV programme] Fox Network/Hulu.
Mrs Brown's Boys (2011–19), [TV programme] BBC.
Mutiny (2017), [TV programme] Channel 4.
My Family (2000–11), [TV programme] BBC.
My Parents Are Aliens (1999–2006), [TV programme] ITV.
Not Going Out (2006–18), [TV programme] BBC.
Notting Hill (1999), [Film] Dir. Roger Michell, UK: Polygram Filmed Entertainment/ Working Title Films.
The Office (2001–3), [TV programme] BBC.
Office Gossip (2001), [TV programme] BBC.
One Foot in the Grave (1990–2001), [TV programme] BBC.
Outnumbered (2007–16), [TV programme] BBC.
Paddington (2014), [Film] Dir. Paul King, United Kingdom: StudioCanal.
Paddington 2 (2017), [Film] Dir. Paul King, United Kingdom: StudioCanal.

Paperman (2012), [Short] Dir. John Kahrs, USA: Walt Disney Animation Studios.
The Parole Officer (2001), [Film] Dir. John Duigan, UK: DNA Films.
Peep Show (2003–15), [TV programme] Channel 4.
People Like Us (1996), [Radio programme] 'The Managing Director', BBC.
Porridge (2017), [TV programme] BBC.
Reggie Perrin (2009–10), [TV programme] BBC.
The Rebel (1961), [Film] Dir. Robert Day, UK: Associated British Picture Corporation.
The Ring of Spies (1964), [Film] Dir. Robert Tronson, UK: British Lion Films.
Saluting Dad's Army (2018), [TV programme] UKTV.
Saving Mr Banks (2013), [Film] Dir. John Lee Hancock, USA: Walt Disney Pictures.
Scrubs (2001–10), [TV programme] ABC.
Shakespeare and Hathaway: Private Investigators (2018–), [TV programme] BBC.
Shaun of the Dead (2004), [Film] Dir. Edgar Wright, UK: StudioCanal.
Sherlock (2010), [TV programme] BBC.
The Squirrels (1974–7), [TV programme] ITV.
Still Open All Hours (2013–), [TV programme] BBC.
Suburgatory (2011–14), [TV programme] ABC.
Terry and June (1979–87), [TV programme] BBC.
The Thin Blue Line (1995–6), [TV programme] BBC.
This Happy Breed (1944), [Film] Dir. David Lean, UK: Two Cities Films.
Together (2016), [TV programme] BBC.
The Tourist Trap (2018), [TV programme] BBC.
Tunnel Visions (2011), [Short] Dir. Djonny Chen, UK: The Way Forward Productions.
Twenty Twelve (2011–12), [TV programme] BBC.
Two Doors Down (2016), [TV programme] BBC.
W1A (2014–17), [TV programme] BBC.
While You Were Sleeping (1995), [Film] Dir. Jon Turteltaub, UK: Hollywood Pictures.
The Wild House (1997–9), [TV programme] BBC.
We're Doomed: The Dad's Army Story (2015), [TV programme] BBC.
Young Hyacinth (2016), [TV programme] BBC.

Bibliography

Novels, poetry and plays

Barnes, Julian. *Metroland* (London: Pan Books, 1990).
Barrie, J. M. *Peter Pan and Wendy* (London: Penguin Books, 1994).
Bennett, Arnold. *Anna of the Five Towns* (London: Methuen, 1919) [Kindle Edition].
Bennett, Arnold. *Hilda Lessways* (London: E. P. Dutton, 1911).
Bennett, Arnold. *A Man from the North* (New York: George H. Doran, 1911).
Betjeman, John. *Collected Poems* (London: John Murray, 1962).
Bullock, Shan. *Mr Ruby Jumps the Traces* (London: Chapman and Hall, 1917).
Bullock, Shan. *Robert Thorne: The Story of a London Clerk* (London: T. Werner Laurie, 1907).
Canning, Victor. *Mr Finchley Discovers His England* (London: Pan Books, 1970).
Christie, Agatha. *The ABC Murders* (Harmondsworth, UK: Penguin, 1948).
Christie, Agatha. *The Big Four* (Glasgow: William Collins Sons & Co., 1978).
Christie, Agatha. *Death in the Clouds* (London: Pan Books, 1964).
Christie, Agatha. *Murder on the Orient Express* (Harmondsworth: Penguin, 1948).
Church, Richard. *Over the Bridge* (London: William Heinemann, 1956).
Collins, Norman. *London Belongs to Me* (London: Collins, 1947).
Conan Doyle, Arthur. *Beyond the City: The Idyll of a Suburb* (Fairfield, IA: 1st World Library, 2004).
Crosland, W. H. *The Suburbans* (London: John Long, 1905).
Delderfield, R. F. *The Dreaming Suburb* (London: Hodder and Stoughton, 1987).
Dickens, Charles. *Dombey and Son* (Ware, Herts.: Wordsworth Classics, 1995).
Dickens, Charles. *Great Expectations* (London: Penguin, 1994).
Dickens, Charles. *Sketches by Boz* (London: Penguin, 1995).
Eliot, T. S. *Collected Poems and Plays* (London: Faber and Faber, 1969).
Forest, Julian (pseud.). *The Wooden Angel* (London: Hodder and Stoughton, 1938).
Forster, E. M. *Howards End* (Harmondsworth: Penguin, 1961).
Gervais, Ricky, and Stephen Merchant. *The Office: The Scripts: Series 1* (London: BBC, 2004).
Gissing, George. *A Freak of Nature or Mr Brogden, City Clerk, an Uncollected Short Story* (Edinburgh: Tragara Press, 1990).
Gissing, George. *The Odd Women* (London: Virago Press, 1987).
Grey, C. T. *Fifty Sheds of Grey: Erotica for the Not-Too-Modern Male* (London: Boxtree, 2012).

Grossmith, George, and Weedon. *Diary of a Nobody* (Hertfordshire: Wordsworth Editions, 2006).

Honeyman, Gail. *Eleanor Oliphant Is Completely Fine* (London: HarperCollins, 2017).

Houlston's Industrial Library. *No. 7: The Clerk: A Sketch in Outline of His Duties and Discipline* (London: Houlston, 1878).

Howard, Keeble. *The Smiths of Surbiton: A Comedy without a Plot* (London: Fisher Unwin, 1925).

Huxley, Aldous. *Along the Road: Notes and Essays of a Tourist* (London: Chatto & Windus, 1927).

James, P. D. 'A Very Commonplace Murder'. In *The Mistletoe Murder and Other Stories* (London: Faber and Faber, 2016): 45–74.

Johnson, B. S. *Christie Malry's Own Double-Entry* (London: Picador, 2001).

Knight, Martin. *Barry Desmond Is a Wanker* (London: London Books, 2010).

Kureishi, Hanif. *Buddha of Suburbia* (London: Faber and Faber, 1990).

Lanchester, John. *Mr Phillips* (London: Faber and Faber, 2000).

Lawrence, D. H. *Lady Chatterley's Lover* (London: Peacock Books, 2001).

Lawrence, D. H. *Sons and Lovers* (London: Penguin, 2005).

Lewis, Jeremy. *Chatto Book of Office Life* (London: Chatto and Windus, 1992).

Masterman, C. F. G. *The Condition of England* (London: Methuen, 1909).

Matthews, Christopher. *Diary of a Somebody* (London: Arrow Books, 1980).

May, Sarah. *The Rise and Fall of the Queen of Suburbia: A Black-Hearted Soap Opera* (London: HarperCollins, 2006).

Melville, Herman. *Bartleby the Scrivener* (London: Penguin Classics, 2016).

Nobbs, David. *The Fall and Rise of Reginald Perrin* (London: Mandarin, 1990).

Nobbs, David. *The Return of Reginald Perrin* (Harmondsworth: Penguin, 1978).

Orwell, George. *Coming Up for Air* (London: Penguin, 1989).

Orwell, George. *Keep the Aspidistra Flying* (London: Penguin Classics, 2000).

Orwell, George. *Nineteen Eighty-Four* (London: Penguin, 2000).

Osbourne, John. *Look Back in Anger* (London: Faber and Faber, 1978).

Pain, Barry. *The Eliza Stories* (Boston, MA: Dana Estes, 1904).

Plater, Alan. *The Beiderbecke Trilogy* (Kent: Mandarin, 1993).

Poe, Edgar Allen. *Selected Tales* (Oxford: Oxford University Press, date unknown).

Postgate, Raymond. *Somebody at the Door* (London: British Library Publishing, 2017).

Pugh, Edwin. *The Broken Honeymoon* (London: John Milne, 1908).

Priestley, J. B. *Angel Pavement* (London: Mandarin Paperbacks, 1993).

Reid Banks, Lynne. *The L-Shaped Room* (London: Vintage, 2004).

Ridge, William Pett. *Outside the Radius* (London: Hodder and Stoughton, 1899).

Rowling, J. K. *Harry Potter and the Chamber of Secrets* (London: Bloomsbury, 1998).

Simmons, Jack (ed.). *The Railway Traveller's Handy Book of Hints, Suggestions and Advice: Before the Journey, On the Journey and After the Journey* (Bath: Adams and Dart, 1862).

Swinnerton, Frank. *The Young Idea: A Comedy of Environment* (London: Hutchinson, 1910).
Townsend, Sue. *The Secret Diary of Adrian Mole, Aged 13¾* (London: Arrow Books, 1998).
Waterhouse, Keith. *Mrs Pooter's Diary* (London: Black Swan, 1984).
Waterhouse, Keith. *Office Life* (London: Grafton Books, 1986).
Wells, H. G. '*42 to '44: A Contemporary Memoir upon Human Behaviour during the Crisis of the World Revolution* (London: Secker and Warburg, 1944).
Wells, H. G. *The History of Mr Polly* (London: Collins, 1969).
Wells, H. G. *Kipps: The Story of a Simple Soul* (London: Fontana Press, 1973).
Wells, H. G. *Love and Mr Lewisham* (London: Odhams Press, 1900).
Wells, H. G. *The New Machiavelli* (London: Penguin, 2018).
Wells, H. G. *Tono-Bungay* (London: Odhams Press, 1909).
Wells, H. G. *The War of the Worlds* (London: Pan Books, 1975).
Wells, H. G. *The Wheels of Chance* (London: J. M. Dent, 1896).
Williams, Nigel. *They Came from SW19* (London: Corsair, 2013).
Williams, Nigel. *The Wimbledon Poisoner* (London: Faber and Faber, 1990).
Wodehouse, P. G. 'A Sea of Troubles'. In *The Man with Two Left Feet* (Library of Alexandria, 27 December 2012) [Kindle Edition]: 128–39.
Wodehouse, P. G. *Psmith in the City* (Rockville, MD: Arc Manor, 2008).
Woolf, Virginia. *Night and Day* (London: George H. Doran, 1920).

Secondary sources

Alborn, Timothy. 'Quill-Driving: British Life Insurance Clerks and Occupational Mobility, 1800–1914'. *Business History Review* 82, no. 1 (Spring 2008): 31–58.
Anderson, Gregory. *Victorian Clerks* (Manchester: Manchester University Press, 1976).
Anderson, Gregory. *The White-Blouse Revolution: Female Office Workers since 1870* (Manchester: Manchester University Press, 1988).
Attewell, Paul. 'The Clerk Deskilled: A Study in False Nostalgia'. *Journal of Historical Sociology* 2, no. 4 (1989): 357–87.
Bailey, Peter. 'White Collars, Gray Lives? The Lower Middle Class Revisited'. *Journal of British Studies* 38 (July 1999): 273–90.
Baldry, Christopher. 'The Social Construction of Office Space'. *International Labour Review* 136 (1997): 365–78.
Banville, Scott. "'A Book-Keeper, Not an Accountant": Representing the Lower Middle Class from Victorian Novels and Music-hall Songs to Television Sitcoms'. *Journal of Popular Culture* 44, no. 1 (2011): 16–36.
Barker, Paul. *The Freedoms of Suburbia* (London: Frances Lincoln, 2009).
Batchelor, John. *H. G. Wells* (Cambridge: Cambridge University Press, 1985).

Berebitsky, Julie. *Sex and the Office: A History of Gender, Power and Desire* (New Haven, CT: Yale University Press, 2012).

Betjeman, John, and John Gay. *London's Historic Railway Stations* (London: John Murray, 1972).

Birch, Dinah. 'A Life in Writing: Ruskin and the Uses of Suburbia'. In *Writing and Victorianism*, edited by J. B. Bullen (London: Longman, 1997): 234–49.

Bishop, Nicola. 'Mundane and Menacing: "Nobodies" in the Detective Fiction of Agatha Christie'. *Clues: A Journal of Detection* 34, no. 1 (Spring 2016): 82–95.

Bishop, Nicola. 'Presenting the Past: New Directions in Television History'. In *Histories on Screen: The Past and Present in Anglo-American Cinema and Television*, edited by Sam Edwards, Michael Dolski and Faye Sayer (London: Bloomsbury, 2018): 277–92.

Bishop, Nicola. 'Ruralism, Masculinity and National Identity: The Rambling Clerk in Fiction, 1900–1940'. *Journal of British Studies* 54, no. 3 (2015): 654–78.

Booker, John. *Temples of Mammon: The Architecture of Banking* (Edinburgh: Edinburgh University Press, 1990).

Boyd, Kelly. *Manliness and Boys' Story Paper in Britain: A Cultural History, 1855–1940* (Basingstoke: Palgrave Macmillan, 2003).

Bradbury, Malcolm. 'The Opening World, 1900–1915'. In *Edwardian and Georgian Fiction*, edited by Harold Bloom (Philadelphia: Chelsea House, 2005): 279–308.

Brooks, Susan. 'Suburban Space in The Buddha of Suburbia'. In *British Fiction of the 1990s*, edited by Nick Bentley (London: Routledge, 2005): 209–25.

Bueka, Robert. *SuburbiaNation: Reading Suburban Landscape in Twentieth-century American Fiction and Film* (New York: Palgrave Macmillan, 2004).

Carey, John. *The Intellectuals and the Masses* (London: Faber and Faber, 1992).

Clapson, Mark. *Invincible Green Suburbs, Brave New Worlds: Social Change and Urban Dispersal in Post-war England* (Manchester: Manchester University Press, 1998).

Clapson, Mark. 'The New Suburban History, New Urbanism and the Spaces In-between'. *Urban History* 43, no. 2 (2016): 336–41.

Clapson, Mark. 'The Suburban Aspiration in England since 1919'. *Contemporary British History* 14, no. 1 (2000): 151–74.

Clapson, Mark. Suburban Century: Social Change and Urban Growth in England and the USA (London: Berg, 2003).

Crossick, Geoffrey. 'The Emergence of the Lower Middle Class'. In *The Lower Middle Class in Britain: 1870–1914*, edited by Geoffrey Crossick (London: Croom Helm, 1977): 11–60.

Crossick, Geoffrey (ed.). *The Lower Middle Class in Britain: 1870–1914* (London: Croom Helm, 1977).

Crossick, Geoffrey. 'The Petite Bourgeoisie in Nineteenth-Century Britain: The Urban and Liberal Case'. In *Shopkeepers and Master Artisans in Nineteenth-Century Europe*, edited by Geoffrey Crossick and Heinz-Gerhard Haupt (London: Methuen, 1984): 62–94.

Crozier, Michel. *The World of the Office Worker* (Chicago: University of Chicago Press, 1965).

Cunningham, Gail. 'Houses in Between: Navigating Suburbia in Late Victorian Writing'. *Victorian Literature and Culture* 32, no. 2 (2004): 421-34.

Cunningham, Gail. 'London Commuting: Suburb and City, the Quotidian Frontier'. In *London Eyes: Reflections in Text and Image*, edited by Gail Cunningham and Stephen Barber (Oxford: Berghahn, 2007): 7-25.

Cunningham, Gail. 'The Riddle of Suburbia: Sub fictions of the fin de siècle'. In *Expanding Suburbia: Reviewing Suburban Narratives*, edited by Roger Webster (New York: Berghahn Books, 2000): 51-70.

Davies, Helen, and Sarah Ilott (eds). *Comedy and the Politics of Representation: Mocking the Weak* (London: Palgrave Macmillan, 2018).

Dennett, Laurie. *A Sense of Security: 150 years of Prudential* (Cambridge: Granta, 1998).

Dennis, Richard. *Cities in Modernity: Representations and Productions of Metropolitan Space* (Cambridge: Cambridge University Press, 2008).

Duffy, Francis. 'Office Buildings and Organisational Change'. In *Buildings and Society*, edited by Antony D. King (London: Routledge and Keagan Paul, 1980): 140-57.

Dutton, Julian, *Keeping Quiet: Visual Comedy in the Age of Sound* (Gosport: Chaplin Press, 2015).

Dyos, H. J. *Victorian Suburb: A Study of the Growth of Camberwell* (Leicester: Leicester University Press, 1966).

Felski, Rita. 'Nothing to Declare: Identity, Shame, and the Lower Middle Class'. *PMLA* 115, no. 1 (January, 2001): 33-45.

Fishman, Robert. *Bourgeois Utopias: The Rise and Fall of Suburbia* (New York: Basic Books, 1987).

Flint, Kate. 'Fictional Suburbia'. In *Popular Fiction: Essays in Literature and History*, edited by Peter Humm, Paul Stigent and Peter Widdowson (New York: Berghahn Books, 2000): 111-26.

Freeman, Michael. *Railways and the Victorian Imagination* (London: Yale University Press, 1999).

Giles, Judy. *The Parlour and the Suburb: Domestic Identities, Class, Femininity* (Oxford: Berg, 2004).

Gunn, Simon. 'Class, Identity and the Urban: The Middle Class in England, c. 1790-1950'. *Urban History* 31, no. 1 (2004): 29-46.

Gunn, Simon. 'Translating Bourdieu: Cultural Capital and the English Middle Class in Historical Perspective'. *British Journal of Sociology* 56, no. 1 (2005): 49-64.

Haggett, Ali. *A History of Male Psychological Disorders, 1945-1980* (London: Palgrave Macmillan, 2015).

Haigh, Gideon. *The Office: A Hardworking History* (Melbourne: Melbourne University Publishing, 2012).

Hammerton, A. James. 'The Perils of Mrs Pooter: Satire, Modernity and Motherhood in the Lower Middle Class in England, 1870-1920'. *Women's History Review* 8, no. 2 (1999): 261-76.

Hammerton, A. James. 'Pooterism or Partnership? Marriage and Masculine Identity in the Lower Middle Class, 1870–1920'. *Journal of British Studies* 38 (July 1999): 291–321.

Hapgood, Lynne. *Margins of Desire: The Suburbs in Fiction and Culture 1880–1925* (Manchester: Manchester University Press, 2005).

Harris, Richard, and Peter Larkham (eds). *Changing Suburbs: Foundation, Form and Function* (London: Spon, 1999).

Heller, Michael. *London Clerical Workers 1880–1914: Development of the Labour Market* (London: Pickering & Chatto, 2011).

Higgins, Richard. 'Feeling Like a Clerk in H. G. Wells'. *Victorian Studies* 50, no. 3 (Spring, 2008): 457–75.

Highmore, Ben. *The Great Indoors: At Home in the Modern British House* (London: Profile, 2014).

Hilliard, Christopher. 'Modernism and the Common Writer'. *Historical Journal* 48, no. 3 (2005): 769–87.

Hinton, James. '"The 'Class Complex'": Mass-Observation and Cultural Distinction in Pre-War Britain'. *Past and Present* 199 (May 2008): 207–36.

Howell, David. 'The Property-Owning Democracy: Prospects and Policies'. *Policy Studies* 4, no. 3 (1984): 14–21.

Humble, Nicola. *The Feminine Middlebrow Novel, 1920s to 1950s: Class, Domesticity and Bohemianism* (Oxford: Oxford University Press, 2001).

Jackson, A. *Semi-Detached London: Suburban Development, Life and Transport, 1900–39* (London: Allen and Unwin, 1973).

James, Simon J. *Maps of Utopia: H. G. Wells, Modernity and the End of Culture* (Oxford: Oxford University Press, 2012).

Jeacle, Ingrid. 'The Bank Clerk in Victorian Society: The Case of Hoare and Company'. *Journal of Management History* 16, no. 3 (2010): 312–26.

Jeacle, Ingrid. '"Beyond the Boring Grey": The Construction of the Colourful Accountant'. *Critical Perspectives on Accounting* 19, no. 8 (2008): 1296–320.

Jeacle, Ingrid, and Lee Parker. 'The "Problem" of the Office: Scientific Management, Governmentality and the Strategy of Efficiency'. *Business History* 55, no. 7 (2013): 1074–99.

Jeffrey, Tom. 'A Place in the Nation: The Lower Middle Class in England'. In *Splintered Classes: Politics and the Lower Middle Class in Interwar Europe*, edited by Rudy Koshar (London: Holmes and Meier, 1990): 70–96.

Jeffery, Tom. 'Politics and Class in Lewisham'. In *Metropolis, London: Histories and Representations since 1800*, edited by David Feldman and Gareth Stedman Jones (London: Routledge, 1989): 189–218.

John, Angela (ed.). *Unequal Opportunities: Women's Employment in England 1800–1914* (Oxford: Blackwell, 1986).

Jordan, Paul. *The Author in the Office: Narrative Writing in Twentieth-Century Argentina and Uruguay* (Woodbridge: Boydell and Brewer, 2006).

Kalviknes Bore, Inger-Lise. *Screen Comedy and Online Audiences* (London: Routledge, 2017).

Kern, Stephen. *The Culture of Time and Space 1880–1918* (Cambridge, MA: Harvard University Press, 1983).

Kessel, Martina. 'Introduction: Landscapes of Humour: The History and Politics of the Comical in the Twentieth Century'. In *The Politics of Humour: Laughter, Inclusion and Exclusion in the Twentieth Century,* edited by Martina Kessel and Patrick Merziger (London: Toronto University Press, 2012).

Kirk, Russell. *Eliot and His Age: T. S. Eliot's Moral Imagination in the Twentieth Century* (Wilmington, DE: ISI Books, 2014).

Kirkham, Linda, and Ann Loft. 'Gender and the Construction of the Professional Accountant'. *Accounting, Organizations and Society* 18, no. 6 (1993), 507–58.

Klingender, F. D. *The Condition of Clerical Labour in Britain* (London: Lawrence, 1935).

Kruse, Kevin M., and Thomas J. Sugrue (eds). *The New Suburban History* (Chicago: University of Chicago Press, 2016).

Kuchta, Todd. *Semi-detached Empire: Suburbia and the Colonization of Britain, 1880 to the Present Day* (Charlottesville: University of Virginia Press, 2010).

Kynaston, David. *The City of London: Illusions of Gold 1914–1945* (London: Chatto and Windus, 1999).

Lange, Alexandra. 'White Collar Corbusier: From the Casier to the cités d'affairs'. *Grey Room* 9 (Fall 2002): 58–79.

Le Roux, Brigitte, et al. 'Class and Cultural Division in the UK'. *Sociology* 42, no. 6 (2008): 1049–71.

Lockwood, David. *The Blackcoated Worker: A Study in Class Consciousness* (Oxford: Oxford University Press, 1969).

Lodge, David. *The Art of Fiction: Illustrated from Classic and Modern Texts* (London: Penguin, 2002).

Lowe, Graham. 'Class, Job and Gender in the Canadian Office'. *Labour/Le Travailleur* 10 (Autumn 1982): 11–37.

Lowe, Graham. *Women in the Administrative Revolution* (Oxford: Basil Blackwell, 1987).

Lucas, John. *Arnold Bennett: A Study of His Fiction* (London: Methuen, 1974).

Lukács, Georg. *History and Class Consciousness: Studies in Marxist Dialectics* (London: Merlin Press, 1968).

Mayer, Arno J. 'The Lower-Middle Class as Historical Problems'. *Journal of Modern History* 47, no. 3 (1975): 409–36.

McKibbin, Ross. *Classes and Cultures: England 1918–1951* (Oxford: Oxford University Press, 2000).

McKinley, A., and R. G. Wilson. '"Small Acts of Cunning": Bureaucracy, Inspection and the Career, c.1890–1914'. *Critical Perspectives on Accounting* 17 (2006): 657–78.

Medhurst, Andy. *A National Joke: Popular Comedy and English Cultural Identities* (London: Routledge, 2007).

Medhurst, Andy. 'Negotiating the Gnome Zone: Versions of Suburbia in British Popular Culture'. In *Visions of Suburbia*, edited by Roger Silverstone (London: Routledge, 1997): 240–68.

Mihm, Stephen. 'Clerks, Classes, and Conflicts: A Response to Michael Zakim's "The Business Clerk as Social Revolutionary"'. *Journal of the Early Republic* 26 (Winter 2006): 605–15.

Mills, Brett. *The Sitcom* (Edinburgh: Edinburgh University Press, 2009).

Mills, Brett. *Television Sitcom* (London: British Film Institute, 2005).

Moran, Joe. *Queueing for Beginners: The Story of Daily Life from Breakfast to Bedtime* (London: Profile Books, 2007).

Moran, Joe. *Reading the Everyday* (London: Routledge, 2005).

Moseley, Merritt. *Understanding Julian Barnes* (Columbia: University of South Carolina Press, 1997).

Mülder-Bach, Inka. 'Cinematic Ethnology: Siegfried Kracauer's the White Collar Masses'. *New Left Review* 226 (1997): 41–56.

Mundy, John, and Glyn White. *Laughing Matters: Understanding Film, Television and Radio Comedy* (Manchester: Manchester University Press, 2012).

O'Dell, Tom. 'My Soul for a Seat: Commuting and the Routines of Mobility'. In *Time, Consumption and Everyday Life: Practice, Materiality, Culture*, edited by Elizabeth Shove, Frank Trentmann and Richard Wilk (Oxford: Berg, 2009): 85–98.

Oliver, Paul, Ian Davis and Ian Bentley. *Dunroamin: The Suburban Semi and Its Enemies* (London: Pimlico, 1981).

Panayiotou, Alexia. '"Macho" Managers and Organizational Heroes: Competing Masculinities in Popular Films'. *Organization* 17, no. 6 (2010): 659–83.

Parker, Lee. 'From Scientific to Activity Based Office Management: A Mirage of Change', *Journal of Accounting and Organizational Change* 12, no. 2 (2016): 177–202.

Parker, Lee, and Ingrid Jeacle. 'The Construction of the Efficient Office: Scientific Management, Accountability and the Neo-Liberal State'. *Contemporary Accounting Research* (2019): 1883–926.

Pope, Ged. *Reading London's Suburbs: From Charles Dickens to Zadie Smith* (London: Palgrave Macmillan, 2015).

Popp, Andrew, and Michael French. '"Practically the Uniform of the Tribe": Dress Codes among Commercial Travellers'. *Enterprise and Society* 11, no. 3 (2010): 437–67.

Price, Leah, and Pamela Thurschwell (eds). *Literary Secretaries/Secretarial Culture* (Aldershot: Ashgate, 2005).

Price, Richard. 'Society, Status and Jingoism: The Social Roots of Lower-Middle-Class Patriotism, 1870–1900'. In *The Lower Middle Class in Britain: 1870–1914*, edited by Geoffrey Crossick (London: Croom Helm, 1977): 89–112.

Priestley, J. B. *English Humour* (London: Longman, Green, 1930).

Rhodes, Carl, and Robert Westwood. *Critical Representations of Work and Organisation in Popular Culture* (Oxon: Routledge, 2008).

Richards, Jeffrey. *Films and British National Identity: From Dickens to Dad's Army* (Manchester: Manchester University Press, 1997).

Richards, Jeffrey, and John Mackenzie. *The Railway Station: A Social History* (Oxford: Oxford University Press, 1986).

Rose, Jonathan. *The Intellectual Life of the Working Classes* (London: Yale University Press, 2001).

Routh, Guy. *Occupation and Pay in Great Britain 1906–79* (London: Macmillan, 1980).

Rubinstein, David. *Victorian Homes* (Newton Abbot: David & Charles, 1974).

Savage, Mike. 'Changing Social Class Identities in Post-War Britain: Perspectives from Mass Observation'. *Sociological Research Online* 12, no. 3 (2006): n.p.

Savage, Mike. *Social Class in the 21st Century* (London: Penguin, 2015).

Savage, Mike, Gaynor Bagnall and Brian Longhurst. 'Ordinary, Ambivalent and Defensive: Class Identities in the Northwest of England'. *Sociology* 35, no. 4 (2001): 875–92.

Scott, Peter. *The Making of the Modern British Home: The Suburban Semi and British Life Between the Wars* (Oxford: Oxford University Press, 2013).

Scott, Peter. 'Marketing Mass Home Ownership and the Creation of the Modern Working-Class Consumer in Inter-War Britain'. *Business History* 50, no. 1 (2008): 4–25.

Silverstone, Roger. *Visions of Suburbia* (London: Routledge, 1997).

Siebert, Sabina. "'A Deeply Troubled Organization': Satire in the BBC's W1A Comedy Series'. *Scandinavian Journal of Management* 35 (2019): 56–63.

Spurr, Geoffrey. 'The London YMCA: A Haven of Masculine Self-Improvement and Socialization for the Late-Victorian and Edwardian Clerk'. *Canadian Journal of History* 37, no. 2 (August 2002): 275–301.

Strain, Tessa, Paul Kelly, Nanette Mutrie and Clare Fitzsimons, 'Differences by Age and Sex in the Sedentary Time in Adults in Scotland'. *Journal of Sports Sciences* 36, no. 7 (2018): 732–41.

Sundstrom, Mary Graehl. *Work Places: The Psychology of the Physical Environment in Offices and Factories* (Cambridge: Cambridge University Press, 1986).

Tebbutt, Melanie. 'Rambling and Manly Identity in Derbyshire's Dark Peak, 1880s-1920s'. *Historical Journal* 49, no. 4 (2006): 1125–53.

Thompson, Ben. *Sunshine on Putty: The Golden Age of British Comedy from Vic Reeves to The Office* (London: HarperPerennial, 2004).

Thompson, E. P. *The Making of the English Working Class* (London: V. Gollancz, 1963).

Thompson, F. M. L. *Hampstead: Building a Borough, 1650–1964* (London: Routledge, 1974).

Thompson, F. M. L. *The Rise of Respectable Society: A Social History of Victorian Britain 1830–1900* (London: Fontana Press, 1988).

Thompson, F. M. L. *The Rise of Suburbia* (Leicester: Leicester University Press, 1892).

Thompson, Graham. '"Dead Letters! … Dead Men?": The Rhetoric of the Office in Melville's "Bartleby the Scrivener"'. *Journal of American Studies* 34, no. 3 (2000): 395–411.

Thorns, David. *Suburbia* (St. Albans: Paladin, 1972).
Tosh, John. *Manliness and Masculinities in Nineteenth-Century Britain* (Harlow: Pearson Longman, 2005).
Wagg, Stephen. "'At Ease, Corporal": Social Class and the Situational Comedy in British Television, from the 1950s to the 1990s'. In *Because I Tell a Joke or Two: Comedy, Politics and Social Difference*, edited by Stephen Wagg (1998): 1–31.
Walker, Stephen. 'Identifying the Women behind the Railed-in Desk: The Proto-Feminisation of Bookkeeping in Britain'. *Accounting, Auditing and Accountability Journal* 4, no. 4 (2003): 606–39.
Walters, Ben. *The Office: A Critical Reading of the Series* (London: BFI, 2005).
Webb, Simon. *Commuters: The History of a British Way of Life* (Barnsley: Pen and Sword, 2016).
Webster, Roger. *Expanding Suburbia: Reviewing Suburban Narratives* (New York: Berghahn Books, 2000).
White, Robert. 'Wanted: A Rowton House for Clerks', *Nineteenth Century* 42 (October 1897): 594–601.
Wild, Jonathan. "'A Merciful, Heaven-sent Release": The Clerk and the First World War in British Literary Culture'. *Cultural and Social History* 4, no. 1 (2007): 73–94.
Wild, Jonathan. *The Rise of the Office Clerk in Literary Culture, 1880–1939* (Basingstoke: Palgrave Macmillan, 2006).
Young, Arlene. *Culture, Class and Gender in the Victorian Novel: Gentlemen, Gents and Working Women* (Basingstoke: Macmillan, 1999).
Young, Arlene. 'Virtue Domesticated: Dickens and the Lower Middle Class'. *Victorian Studies* 39, no. 4 (1996): 483–511.
Zakim, Michael. 'Business Clerk as Social Revolutionary; or, a Labor History of the Nonproducing Classes'. *Journal of the Early Republic* 26 (Winter 2006): 563–603.
Zimmeck, Meta. 'Jobs for the Girls: The Expansion of Clerical Work for Women, 1850–1914'. In *Unequal Opportunities: Women's Employment in England 1800–1918*, edited by Angela Johns (Oxford: John Wiley, 1986): 152–77.

Newspaper and magazine articles

'A. Thomas & Co'. *Daily Mail*, 11 September 1967. Available online via *Daily Mail Historical Archive, 1896–2004*: http://tinyurl.galegroup.com/tinyurl/8j8cy3 (accessed 9 December 2019).
'Education and Wages'. *Spectator*, 2 October 1886. Available online: http://archive.spectator.co.uk/article/2nd-october-1886/11/education-and-wages (accessed 3 November 2018).
'Hyacinth's Home Has Buckets of Style!' *Coventry Live*, 12 January 2005. Available online: https://www.coventrytelegraph.net/news/coventry-news/hyacinths-home-buckets-style-3138216 (accessed 17 March 2017).

'Modern Machines Take Charge of the Office'. *The Queenslander*, 16 February 1938. Available online: http://nla.gov.au/nla.news-article18902901 (accessed 15 December 2013).

'Multiple Display Advertising Items'. *Daily Mail*, 20 August 1953. Available online via *Daily Mail Historical Archive, 1896–2004*: http://tinyurl.galegroup.com/tinyurl/8j8Q87 (accessed 9 December 2018).

'No Robert Thorne'. *The Spectator*, 7 September 1907. Available online: http://archive.spectator.co.uk/article/7th-september-1907/25/no-robert-thorne-mr-shan-bullocks-excellent-autobi (accessed 1 April 2018).

'The Smiths of Surbiton'. *Saturday Review of Politics, Literature, Science and Art*, 17 February 1906: 210. Available online: https://search-proquest-com.ezproxy.mmu.ac.uk/docview/9161703?accountid=12507 (accessed 9 May 2017).

'The Smiths of Surbiton by Keble Howard (Book Review)'. *The Spectator*, 10 February 1906. Available online: https://search-proquest-com.ezproxy.mmu.ac.uk/docview/1295577594?accountid=12507 (accessed 9 May 2017).

'Sonnets of a Commuter'. *Shields Daily Gazette*, 3 August 1903, Issue 14676: 3.

'Too Strenuous Exercise'. *Daily Mail*, 8 August 1922. Available online via *Daily Mail Historical Archive*: http://tinyurl.galegroup.com/tinyurl/8j7yg6 (accessed 3 December 2018).

'Two Hour Daily Commute 'on Rise among UK Workers'. *BBC News*, 18 November 2016. Available online: http://www.bbc.co.uk/news/uk-38026625 (accessed 21 November 2018).

Anderson, R. J. 'Top Hat and Mortarboard', *Spectator*, 25 February 1955. Available online: http://archive.spectator.co.uk/article/25th-february-1955/10/top-hat-and-mortarboard (accessed 2 May 2018).

Atkinson, Louise. 'Losing Weight in the Office'. *Daily Mail*, 25 February 1992. Available online via *Daily Mail Historical Archive, 1896–2004*: http://tinyurl.galegroup.com/tinyurl/8j8vi4 (accessed 9 January 2019).

Barr, Sabrina. 'UK Weather: The Unspoken Rules of Commuter Etiquette during a Heatwave', *Independent*, 25 June 2018. Available online: https://www.independent.co.uk/life-style/commuter-etiquette-heatwaves-unspoken-rules-heat-summer-deodorant-water-eye-contact-a8415821.html (accessed 25 June 2018).

Ellis, Lee. 'Then We Came to the Next Office Novel', *New Yorker*, 2 February 2010. Available online: https://www.newyorker.com/books/page-turner/then-we-came-to-the-next-office-novel (accessed 23 January 2017).

Flanders, Judith. 'Why Don't Novels Do Work?'. *Guardian*, 30 March 2009. Available online: https://www.theguardian.com/books/booksblog/2009/mar/30/work-novels-fiction-flanders (accessed 1 February 2018).

Foster, Dawn. 'Commuting Is Now a Fact of Life. We Just Need to Make It Less Awful'. *Guardian*, 28 April 2016. Available online: https://www.theguardian.com/public-leaders-network/2016/apr/28/commuting-british-life-transport-links-housing (accessed 1 December 2018).

Frick, Thomas. 'The Art of Fiction, No. 85'. *The Paris Review*, Winter 1984. Available online: https://www.theparisreview.org/interviews/2929/j-g-ballard-the-art-of-fiction-no-85-j-g-ballard (accessed 15 November 2018).

Gallagher, James. 'Office Workers "Too Sedentary"'. *BBC News*, 27 March 2015. Available online: http://www.bbc.co.uk/news/health-32069698 (accessed 3 March 2017).

Green, Emma. 'The Origins of Office Speak'. *The Atlantic*, 24 April 2014. Available online: https://www.theatlantic.com/business/archive/2014/04/business-speak/361135/ (accessed 13 May 2018).

Grierson, Jamie. '"Tube Chat" Campaign Provokes Horror among London Commuters'. *Guardian*, 29 September 2016. Available online: https://www.theguardian.com/uk-news/2016/sep/29/tube-chat-campaign-provokes-horror-among-london-commuters (accessed 21 June 2018).

Hogan, Michael. 'Colin's Sandwich Boxset Review – Mel Smith's Wannabe Horror Writer is a Timeless Sitcom Hero'. *Guardian*, 11 September 2014. Available online: https://www.theguardian.com/tv-and-radio/2014/sep/11/colins-sandwich-box-set-review-mel-smith (accessed 13 June 2018).

Jenkins, Patrick, and Harriet Agnew. 'London: Sexism and the City'. *Financial Times*, 16 January 2015. Available online: https://www.ft.com/content/7c182ab8-9c33-11e4-b9f8-00144feabdc0 (accessed 3 November 2018).

Lanchester, John. 'When Fiction Breaks Down'. *Telegraph*, 29 January 2010. Available online: https://www.telegraph.co.uk/culture/books/7093699/When-fiction-breaks-down.html (accessed 23 January 2017).

Lawson, Mark, 'Dad's Army at 50: The Secret History of 'Comedy's Finest Half Hour'. *Guardian*, 24 July 2018. Available online: https://www.theguardian.com/tv-and-radio/2018/jul/24/dads-army-50-bbc-tv-comedy-home-guard-secret-history (accessed 3 September 2018).

Lesser, Wendy. 'Who's Afraid of Arnold Bennett?'. *New York Times*, 27 September 1997. Available online: https://www.nytimes.com/books/97/09/28/bookend/bookend.html (accessed 1 July 2015).

McKay, Alistair. 'The W1A Way'. *Evening Standard*, 26 March 2014. Available online: https://www.standard.co.uk/lifestyle/london-life/the-w1a-way-why-the-bbcs-new-office-comedy-feels-awfully-familiar-9216556.html (accessed 22 January 2018).

Power, Chris. 'Art Work: The Strange Appeal of Office-Bound Fiction'. *Guardian*, 26 March 2007. Available online: https://www.theguardian.com/books/booksblog/2007/mar/26/artworkthestrangeappealof (accessed 1 February 2018).

Rhind-Tutt, Louise. 'The Manchester Building That's Been a Refuge since the 1890s'. *I Love Manchester*, 13 September 2017. Available online: https://ilovemanchester.com/city-centre-building-thats-manchester-refuge-since-1890s/ (accessed 5 January 2019).

Scott, Andrew. 'AI and White-Collar Jobs'. *London Business School Review*, 21 May 2018. Available online: https://www.london.edu/faculty-and-research/lbsr/ai-and-white-collar-jobs (accessed 8 January 2019).

Stolworthy, Jacob. 'BBC's Most Popular Show Overseas Is … *Keeping Up Appearances*'. *Independent*, 18 February 2016. Available online: http://www.independent.co.uk/arts-entertainment/tv/news/bbcs-most-popular-show-overseas-is-keeping-up-appearances-a6880806.html (accessed 13 June 2017).

Stott, Sally. 'How to Become a Successful Writer and Get Paid'. *BBC Writers' Room*, 29 January 2014. Available online: http://www.bbc.co.uk/blogs/writersroom/entries/4e0cbb6f-c20d-3cda-95ec-0b884df9b961 (accessed 13 December 2018).

Wilde, Jon. 'I Hope *Diary of a Nobody* Is in Safe Hands'. *Guardian*, 23 April 2007. Available online: https://www.theguardian.com/culture/tvandradioblog/2007/apr/23/ihopediaryofanobodyisin (accessed 24 May 2017).

Zinser, Stephanie. 'Chairs That Stop You Getting a Bad Back'. *Daily Mail*, 15 June 1999. Available online via *Daily Mail Historical Archive, 1896–2004*: http://tinyurl.galegroup.com/tinyurl/8j8kZ7 (accessed 9 January 2019).

Web sources

Crick, Bernard. 'Blair, Eric Arthur (pseud. George Orwell)'. *Oxford Dictionary of National Biography*, 23 September 2004. Available online: https://doi-org.ezproxy.mmu.ac.uk/10.1093/ref:odnb/31915 (accessed 3 June 2011).

Davis, Kevan. 'Diary of a Nobody'. Available online: https://www.diaryofanobody.net/ (accessed 13 June 2017).

Department for Transport. 'Transport Statistics Great Britain 2017', 2017. Available online: https://assets.publishing.service.gov.uk/government/uploads/system/uploads/attachment_data/file/661933/tsgb-2017-report-summaries.pdf (accessed 8 January 2019).

Dunstan, Marsha. 'The Great British Commute'. *BBC Genome Blog*, 30 January 2018. Available online: http://www.bbc.co.uk/blogs/genome/entries/d64a2859-b651-4767-a9f6-8e808880caac (accessed 4 October 2018).

Landow, George P. 'London Bridge', 2001. Available online: http://www.victorianweb.org/photos/postcards/08.html (accessed 3 February 2018).

Lyddon, Dave. 'Britain at Work: 1945–1995'. Available online: http://www.unionhistory.info/britainatwork/narrativedisplay.php?type=healthandsafety (accessed 24 November 2018).

Morton, Peter. 'Diary of a Nobody'. Available online: https://sites.google.com/site/petermortonswebsite/home (accessed 4 January 2019).

Sanders, Mark. 'Urbis'. Available online: www.marksanders.co.uk (accessed 3 February 2018).

Index

The ABC Murders (*see also* Christie, Agatha) 17
Absolute Power 24, 41, 65, 71, 75
accounting 92
    accounting history 32, 64, 92–3
Act of Betrayal 151
Along the Road (*see also* Huxley, Aldous) 112
Angel Pavement (*see also* Priestley, J. B.) 45, 96–7
Anna of the Five Towns (*see also* Bennett, Arnold) 48
Are You Being Served? 68, 168
As Time Goes By 12, 85, 86
authorship 61, 62, 137, 174, 176
    clerk authors 172
    suburban authorship 174–81

banking 1, 7, 19, 31, 68, 69, 75, 80, 82, 88
Barnes, Julian 6, 110, 125, 126, 141, 166, 176, 179, 180
    Metroland 6, 29, 105, 125, 141, 166, 179, 180
Barry Desmond is a Wanker (*see also* Knight, Martin) 24, 115, 85, 142
Bartleby the Scrivener 36
Bennett, Arnold 1, 11, 12, 23, 26, 36, 44, 46, 48, 57, 58, 61, 62, 63, 76, 109, 116, 117, 130, 131, 150, 156, 157, 162, 163, 164, 172, 174, 175, 177, 180, 182
    Anna of the Five Towns 48
    Hilda Lessways 116
    A Man from the North 23, 26, 44, 46, 57, 61, 76, 90, 126, 130, 155, 156, 179, 180
Betjeman, John 11, 26, 43, 109
The Big Bang Theory 149
The Big Four (*see also* Christie, Agatha) 164
A Bit of Fry and Laurie 46
Blackadder Goes Forth 44
Bodyguard 66

Brazil 64
Brent, David (*see also The Office* and Gervais, Ricky) 7, 13, 14, 15, 20, 24, 41, 43, 66, 71, 72, 74, 77, 78, 85, 89, 91, 92, 99, 100, 144, 167, 172, 173
Bridget Jones's Diary 86
Brief Encounter 121
British Broadcasting Corporation (BBC) 6, 11, 17, 18, 39, 50, 121, 144, 173
The Brittas Empire 148
The Broken Honeymoon (*see also* Pugh, Edwin) 172
Bucket, Hyacinth (*see also Keeping Up Appearances*) 13, 15, 16, 26, 70, 71, 79, 99, 140, 142–6, 148–9, 151, 158–9, 166–71, 183, 189
Buddha of Suburbia (*see also* Kureishi, Hanif) 6, 120, 141, 142, 143, 149
bungalow 100, 139, 140, 142, 151, 158, 167, 168, 169
Bullock, Shan 11, 17, 13, 18, 24, 26, 30, 47, 61, 107, 138, 144, 145, 146, 147, 149, 150, 155, 156, 157, 160, 168, 169, 176, 183, 185
    Mr Ruby Jumps the Traces 17, 36, 88, 106, 119, 120, 163–5
    Robert Thorne 36, 44, 48, 51, 53, 57, 60, 61, 69, 72–6, 80, 95–6, 106, 123, 156, 162, 163, 171, 178, 186
bureaucracy 22, 25, 31, 34, 35, 36, 46, 56, 57, 58, 60, 63, 98, 104

Campus 73, 74
Canning, Victor (*see also* Forest, Julian) 17, 57, 58, 62, 95
    Mr Finchley Discovers His England 17
    The Wooden Angel 57–8
Car Share 121–4, 126
Charles Pooter 7, 11, 13, 18, 24, 26, 30, 47, 61, 107, 138, 144, 145, 146, 147, 149, 150, 155, 156, 157, 159, 160, 168, 169, 176, 183, 185

The Chatto Book of Office Life 35
Christie, Agatha 17, 113, 164
   The ABC Murders 17
   The Big Four 164
   Murder on the Orient Express 113
Christopher Robin 90, 166
Church, Richard 72, 75, 157, 164, 179
   Over the Bridge 72, 156, 179
Cleese, John 7, 12
clerk 1–5, 7, 15–20, 22–37, 44–9, 51, 53, 56–64, 66–9, 72–9, 81–3, 85–97, 100, 101, 105–10, 113, 119, 128, 130, 138, 139, 143, 148, 155–7, 163, 166, 172, 174, 176–7, 179, 181, 185–8
clerical work 16, 24, 30, 31, 34, 42, 45, 51, 57, 58, 69, 76, 77, 81, 86, 175
   clerical worker 1, 3, 17, 26, 29, 40, 47, 48, 51, 52, 56, 57, 59, 61, 81, 86, 98, 100, 101, 125, 172, 174, 187
   clerical workforce 16, 29, 32, 34, 42, 45, 59, 60, 71, 81, 82, 83, 85, 86, 104, 108, 185, 187
clock watching 24, 33, 55, 94–7, 105, 106
Colin's Sandwich 14, 46, 62, 63, 94
Collins, Norman 1, 23, 24, 59, 60, 96, 177
   London Belongs to Me 23, 59, 96
comedy 8, 9–15, 16, 18, 24, 25, 26, 27, 42, 46, 52, 56, 73, 87, 91, 113, 114, 122, 134, 144, 146–8, 150, 151, 152, 154, 158, 167, 168, 182, 183, 186–8
Coming Up for Air (*see also* Orwell, George) 5, 138, 165, 177
commute 9, 22, 24, 25, 26, 46, 89, 103–27, 139, 153, 163, 187, 188
commuter 24, 25, 29, 89, 96, 101, 103–27, 137, 138, 139, 187
consumerism 167, 171, 173, 175, 182
corporate culture 39, 46, 63, 64, 65, 69, 70, 79, 85, 93, 121
Croft, David 12, 18, 19
Crosland, T. W. H. 2, 16, 68, 130, 131, 163, 164
   The Suburbans 2, 130, 131
Crossick, Gregory 2, 4, 5, 21, 76
Cuckoo 150
cul-de-sac 133, 141, 153
cycling 50, 78, 118, 157

Dad's Army 13, 17, 18, 20, 69, 91, 110, 144, 145, 148, 149

Daily Mail 1, 50
Damned 41, 42
dehumanisation 43, 55, 57–61, 104, 107
Delderfield, R. F. 17, 111, 112, 131, 158, 161
   The Dreaming Suburb 11, 158, 161
deskilling 3, 57, 81
Diary of a Nobody (novel) (*see also* Grossmiths, George and Weedon) 11, 12, 18, 26, 61, 76, 107, 144, 146, 147, 168–70
Diary of a Nobody (television adaptation) 11
Dickens, Charles 1, 9, 10, 12, 33, 34, 36, 37, 40, 43, 56, 93, 94, 154
   Dombey and Son 36
   Great Expectations 36, 154
   Sketches by Boz 10, 94
dinnerladies 18, 46
DIY 134, 139, 144, 153, 155, 157, 168
Dombey and Son (*see also* Dickens, Charles) 36
The Dreaming Suburb (*see also* Delderfield, R. F.) 11, 158, 161
dress 20, 45, 67–8, 73, 84–6, 109, 143
Drop the Dead Donkey 148

education 6, 20, 31, 33, 62, 81, 89, 113, 168, 171–3, 175, 176, 182
efficiency 30, 32, 34, 35, 56, 58, 59, 61, 64–6, 73, 79, 81, 83, 86
Elinor Oliphant is Completely Fine (*see also* Honeyman, Gail) 36, 38
Eliot, T. S. 45, 57, 109, 176
   'The Waste Land' 57, 109
   'The Love Song of J. Alfred Prufrock' 45, 176
The Eliza Stories (*see also* Pain, Barry) 12
emulation 20, 26, 141, 145, 163, 165, 171, 175, 190
Escape to the Country 160
Ever Decreasing Circles 10, 12, 13, 15, 22, 25, 38, 85, 86, 97, 135, 136, 147–50, 157, 172, 182
Everybody Loves Raymond 168

The Fall and Rise of Reginald Perrin (novel, see also *Fall and Rise of Reginald Perrin* (television series) and Nobbs,

David) 22, 24, 38, 74, 79, 84, 92, 106, 111, 119, 147, 173
The Fall and Rise of Reginald Perrin (television series, see also *Fall and Rise of Reginald Perrin* (novel) and Nobbs, David) 13, 22, 24, 38, 69, 74, 86, 88, 98, 100, 114, 137, 146, 149
Fawlty, Basil (*see also Fawlty Towers*) 7, 13, 14
Fawlty Towers (*see also* Fawlty, Basil) 13, 145
A Fine Romance 12
Forest, Julian (*see also* Canning, Victor) 57
Forster, E. M. 23, 45, 68, 129, 154
  Howards End 23, 45, 154, 160
Fraud (*see also* white-collar crime) 31, 73, 82
A Freak of Nature, or, Mr Brogden, City Clerk (*see also* Gissing, George) 48, 88, 119
Fresh Fields 166, 172, 182
Friday Night Dinner 135, 150, 160, 167
Friends 65, 149
The Full Monty 100

gardening 113, 139, 157–60, 168, 179
Gavin and Stacey 135, 137, 139–40, 142, 150, 169
George and Mildred 22, 25, 172
Gervais, Ricky (*see also The Office* and Brent, David) 12, 26, 41, 71, 91, 95
Girl from Rio 47, 72, 73, 82
Gissing, George 1, 48, 83, 88, 93, 119, 175, 181
  A Freak of Nature, or, Mr Brogden, City Clerk 48, 88, 119
  The Odd Woman 83, 93
Gogglebox 148
The Goldbergs 150–2
golf 70, 79
The Good Life 22, 25, 26, 43, 61, 70, 79, 91, 99, 100, 117, 228, 122, 134, 135, 137, 140, 147, 154, 158, 161, 169, 172, 182
Great Expectations (*see also* Dickens, Charles) 36, 154
Grossmith, George and Weedon 1, 11, 26, 68, 91, 138, 156, 157, 160, 183, 186
  Diary of a Nobody 11, 12, 18, 26, 61, 76, 107, 144, 146, 147, 168–70

Hancock, Tony 14, 52, 88, 95, 117
Harry Potter and the Chamber of Secrets (see also *Rowling, J. K*) 70
health and safety 39, 52
Henry 9 'til 5 74, 114
Hilda Lessways (*see also* Bennett, Arnold) 116
The History of Mr Polly (*see also* Wells, H. G.) 17, 157
hobbies 130, 139, 149, 157, 158, 172, 182
Holborn Bars 35
Home Guard 17, 110
Honeyman, Gail 36, 38, 62
  Elinor Oliphant is Completely Fine 36, 38
Hook 166
hot-desking 130, 139, 149, 157, 158, 172, 182
Hot Fuzz 146
Howard, Keble 160–2
  The Smiths of Surbiton 160–2
Howards End (*see also* Forster, E. M.) 23, 45, 154, 160
Huxley, Aldous 45, 112, 113
  Along the Road 112

ill health 47–53, 105
The Inbetweeners 13, 142, 149, 150
The Incredibles 65
The Island with Bear Grylls 49
insurance 2, 12, 35, 62, 78, 98
interior design 157, 160
Is It Legal? 78, 79, 87
The IT Crowd 24, 73, 148

James, P. D. 37, 39, 92, 113, 186
  'A Very Commonplace Murder' 37, 39, 92, 113, 186
Jerome, Jerome K. 11
jerry-built 129, 132, 134
Johnson, B. S. 23, 47, 92, 113, 186
  Christie Malry's Own Double Entry 23, 47, 92, 113, 186
Jonathan Creek 95
Juliet Jekyll and Harriet Hyde 134

Keep the Aspidistra Flying (*see also* Orwell, George) 44, 61, 117, 143, 144, 174, 176, 178, 179, 180

Keeping Up Appearances (*see also* Bucket, Hyacinth) 12, 15, 22, 25, 26, 71, 79, 99, 134–5, 145–6, 148, 149, 154, 159, 166, 167–70, 189
Kiss Me Kate 80
Knight, Martin 85, 115, 142, 143, 149, 150
   Barry Desmond is a Wanker 24, 115, 85, 142
Kureishi, Hanif 6, 120, 141, 142
   Buddha of Suburbia 6, 120, 141, 142, 143, 149

Lady Chatterley's Lover (*see also* Lawrence, D. H.) 87
Lanchester, John 35, 39, 40, 51, 74, 85, 98, 110, 116, 118
   Mr Phillips 39, 51, 74, 75, 85, 87, 98–100, 110, 116, 118
Larbey, Bob 12, 22, 38, 62, 152
The Last of the Summer Wine 91
Lawrence, D. H. 49, 175
   Lady Chatterley's Lover 87
   Sons and Lovers 49
Leffingwell, W. H. 56
The Legacy of Reginald Perrin (television series) 98–9
Location, Location, Location 133
London 1, 2, 17, 19, 21, 23, 25, 29, 34, 37, 43, 50, 51, 57, 68, 75, 76, 82, 84, 92, 104, 105, 107, 108, 109, 110, 114, 115, 116, 118, 119, 121, 125, 126, 128, 129, 131, 133, 136, 137, 140, 147, 149, 150, 151, 155, 156, 157, 160, 163, 164, 169, 174, 175, 177, 178
London Belongs to Me (*see also* Collins, Norman) 23, 59, 96
London Bridge 1, 57, 108, 109, 119
London Underground (*see also* Tube) 115
Love Actually 41, 77, 86, 123
Love and Mr Lewisham (*see also* Wells, H. G.) 68, 156, 174, 175, 178–80
'The Love Song of J. Alfred Prufrock' (*see also* Eliot, T. S.) 45, 176
lower middle class 1–19, 21–7, 30, 33, 34, 40, 44, 46, 49, 50, 53, 67, 67, 80, 88, 97, 100, 101, 103, 108, 112, 113, 126, 128, 129, 130, 135, 137–9, 144, 149, 150, 152–6, 159, 165, 168, 171, 175, 176, 178, 180, 182, 183, 185, 187–9

clerk 19, 23, 29, 67, 93, 138, 155
comedy 8, 9–15, 18, 25, 113, 144, 146–8, 150, 154, 169, 182, 186–8
culture 4, 5, 7, 23, 26, 114, 145, 168, 172, 178, 188, 189
home 130, 166, 179
identity 8, 27, 132, 178, 187
masculinity 16, 17, 49, 88, 145, 186
politics 20–2
stereotypes 9, 13, 14, 16, 18, 20–2, 29, 43–4, 88, 90, 93, 97, 113, 145, 168, 187
suburbs 68, 112, 142, 155, 166, 168, 175, 177
values 7, 18, 20, 22, 26, 27, 130, 137, 142, 173
Lowry, L. S. 109
The L-Shaped Room (*see also* Reid Banks, Lynne) 37–8

Magritte, René 108
A Man from the North (*see also* Bennett, Arnold) 23, 26, 44, 46, 57, 61, 76, 90, 126, 130, 155, 156, 179, 180
Manchester 30, 34, 104, 106
marriage 47, 69, 70, 77, 82, 135, 136, 144, 145, 147, 149, 158–67
Mary Poppins 19, 69, 82, 88
masculinity 16, 17, 19, 20, 31, 49, 51, 68, 78, 86, 87, 88, 119, 144, 185–6
Masterman, C. F. G. 44, 49, 107, 125, 138, 146
   The Condition of England 49, 107
Matthews, Christopher 11
   Diary of a Somebody 11
May, Sarah 113, 141
   Rise and Fall of the Queen of Suburbia 113, 141
mechanization 3, 24, 29, 32, 33, 45, 55, 56–63, 77, 78, 81, 97, 101, 107, 109, 153, 182
Melville, Herman 36
   Bartleby the Scrivener 36
Men Behaving Badly 24, 52, 76, 87, 88, 90, 91, 99, 137, 143, 147, 148, 166, 167, 172
Merchant, Stephen (*see also* Gervais, Ricky) 26, 41
Metroland 29, 105, 179

Metroland (*see also* Barnes, Julian) 6, 29, 105, 125, 141, 166, 179, 180
middlebrow 11, 21, 26, 135, 155, 161, 162, 167, 175, 176, 183
mid-life crisis 16, 43, 87–93, 119, 121, 163
middle class 2, 4, 8, 10, 14, 17, 18, 20–1, 24, 40, 67, 68, 70, 81, 86, 93, 104, 108, 112, 128, 129, 132, 133, 138, 139, 145, 150, 151, 155, 160, 161, 165–8, 170, 171, 173, 187–9
middle manager 9, 16, 36, 44, 45, 63, 87, 88, 89, 100
The Mindy Project 80
Motherland 16, 146, 150
Mr Finchley Discovers His England 17
Mr Phillips (*see also* Lanchester, John) 39, 51, 74, 75, 85, 87, 98–100, 110, 116, 118
Mr Ruby Jumps the Traces (*see also* Bullock, Shan) 17, 36, 88, 106, 119, 120, 163–5
Mrs Brown's Boys 150, 188
Mrs Pooter's Diary (*see also* Waterhouse, Keith) 11
Murder on the Orient Express (*see also* Christie, Agatha) 113
music hall 11, 13, 18, 68, 146
Mutiny 49
My Family 135, 147, 166
My Parents Are Aliens 134

Night and Day (*see also* Woolf, Virginia) 108, 125
Nineteen Eighty-Four (*see also* Orwell, George) 64
Nobbs, David 12, 22, 24, 38, 39, 70, 74, 95, 106, 111, 114, 119, 163
  The Fall and Rise of Reginald Perrin (novel, see also *Fall and Rise of Reginald Perrin* (television series)) 22, 24, 38, 74, 79, 84, 92, 106, 111, 119, 147, 173
  The Return of Reginald Perrin 173
nostalgia 149, 150, 167
Not Going Out 135, 149, 151, 157
Notting Hill 47

The Odd Woman (*see also* Gissing, George) 83, 93

The Office 7, 12, 15, 20, 24, 26, 40, 41, 43, 44, 52, 53, 61, 66, 71, 75, 78, 85, 86, 89–92, 95, 100, 144, 147, 172–3, 175
office building 1, 2, 29, 30, 33–7, 41–3, 53, 57, 64, 67, 75, 106
Office Gossip 73
office guidebook 67–9
office interior 30, 33, 42, 44, 53, 64, 66
Office Life (*see also* Waterhouse, Keith) 41, 79, 84
One Foot in the Grave 25, 134, 135, 143, 148
On Your Feet Britain 50
open-plan office 30, 40–1, 63–6, 73
Open University 172, 182
Oriel Chambers 34
Orwell, George 4, 43, 44, 61, 62, 64, 100, 117, 138, 142, 143, 144, 165, 173–4, 177–8, 182–3
  Coming Up for Air 5, 138, 165, 177
  Keep the Aspidistra Flying 44, 61, 117, 143, 144, 174, 176, 178, 179, 180
  Nineteen Eighty-Four 64
Osbourne, John 141
  Look Back in Anger 141
Outnumbered 13, 135, 146, 149
Outside the Radius (*see also* Pett Ridge, W) 110, 130, 165
Over the Bridge (*see also* Church, Richard) 72, 156, 179

Paddington 47, 166
Paddington 2 90
Pain, Barry 12
  The Eliza Stories 12
Pan, Peter 90, 91, 166
The Parole Officer 52
People Like Us 18, 24, 41, 60
Perrin, Reginald 13, 22, 24, 38, 39, 69, 74, 79, 84, 86, 87, 88, 90, 92, 98, 99, 106, 119, 128, 147, 163, 173
Perry, Jimmy 12, 18, 19
Peter Pan 165, 166
petite bourgeoisie 1, 5, 6, 7, 10, 14, 19, 21, 26, 131, 143, 185, 187, 188
Pett Ridge, W. 110, 130, 165
piecework 56, 58, 59
Plater, Alan 154
  The Beiderbecke Trilogy 154

2point4 Children 134, 135, 148
Postgate, Raymond 113
   Somebody at the Door 113
Priestley, J. B. 13, 45, 96, 97, 98
   Angel Pavement 45, 96–7
proletarianization thesis 3–4, 81
Prudential Life Insurance Company 35, 78, 79, 81, 82
Psmith in the City (*see also* Wodehouse, P. G.) 66, 72, 76, 80, 107
Pugh, Edwin 36, 39, 45, 62, 172
   The Broken Honeymoon 172
Punch 11, 18, 68, 77, 85

radio 11, 12, 18, 123, 178
railways 24, 25, 29, 46, 47, 62, 90, 94, 103, 104–6, 109, 112–15, 117, 120, 121, 123, 124, 126, 179, 181
The Rebel 53, 88, 95, 110, 117
redundancy 24, 33, 45, 51, 56, 60, 93, 95, 97, 98, 99, 100, 116, 172, 189
Refuge Life Assurance Company 34, 35, 82, 106
Reggie Perrin 24, 39, 40, 43, 66, 70, 71, 87, 114, 121, 124
Reid Banks, Lynne 37–8
   The L-Shaped Room 37–8
retirement 24, 32, 45, 56, 60, 76, 93, 94–7, 99, 100
retirement clock 94–7
Return of Reginald Perrin 173
The Rise and Fall of the Queen of Suburbia (*see also* May, Sarah) 113, 141
Rising Damp 136
Robert Thorne (*see also* Bullock, Shan) 36, 44, 48, 51, 53, 57, 60, 61, 69, 72–6, 80, 95–6, 106, 123, 156, 162, 163, 171, 178, 186
routinization 3, 24, 55, 56, 62, 97, 101, 116
Rowling, J. K. 70
   Harry Potter and the Chamber of Secrets 70
rush hour 103, 104–18, 122, 123, 125
Ruskin, John 105, 128, 129

Saluting Dad's Army 18
Saving Mr Banks 19
scientific management 55, 56, 64
Scrubs 80

secretary 16, 50, 71, 74, 75, 78, 82–7, 90, 98, 99
self-sufficiency 43, 61, 117, 154, 179, 182
semi-detached 9, 25, 29, 130, 133, 134, 140, 148, 150, 152, 153, 162, 167, 168, 181
The 7.39 87, 89, 90, 112, 115, 118, 119, 123, 126, 163, 180
sexuality 16, 74, 75, 83–7, 114, 124, 142–5
Shakespeare and Hathaway: Private Investigators 94
Shaun of the Dead 146
Sherlock 26, 67, 82
sitcom 6, 10, 11–18, 25, 26, 38, 43–6, 52, 60, 62, 65, 68–71, 73, 76, 78–80, 82, 85, 86, 88, 91, 95, 97, 99, 110, 117, 135–7, 140, 143, 145–51, 155, 157, 158, 160, 166–70, 172, 183, 186, 188–9
Sketches by Boz (*see also* Dickens, Charles) 10, 94
The Smiths of Surbiton (*see also* Howard, Keble) 160–2
social mobility 6, 93, 127, 132, 168, 173, 186
Sons and Lovers (*see also* Lawrence, D. H.) 49, 175
sport 49, 77–9, 182
The Squirrels 45, 71, 75, 82, 83, 84, 86, 95, 186
Still Open All Hours 150
suburb 17, 26, 92, 11, 127, 128, 131, 134–6, 141, 147–9, 151, 152, 167, 179, 188
suburban 1, 2, 5, 6, 9, 11, 12, 16, 20, 21, 22, 25–7, 29, 38, 47, 63, 68, 70, 91, 99, 100, 101, 103–5, 107, 110, 112, 113, 117, 119, 120, 122, 125, 127–52, 153–183, 185–9
The Suburbans (*see also* Crosland, T. W. H.) 2, 130, 131
suburbia 5, 12, 16, 20–23, 25, 26, 104–5, 113, 119, 120, 127–53, 155, 157, 159, 161–6, 168, 169, 173–9, 181–3, 186–8
Suburgatory 151, 152
surveillance 32, 55, 59, 63–75, 103, 122, 158
Swinnerton, Frank 23, 36, 45, 94, 155
   The Young Idea 23, 94, 155

Taylor, Frederick 23, 55–9, 61, 63, 64, 67, 79, 81, 95
teenage 89, 141–2
telephone 35, 38, 41, 111, 169–70
Terry and June 25, 79, 136, 140, 146, 188
Thatcher, Margaret 4, 6, 83
The Thin Blue Line 13, 18, 60
This Happy Breed 141
Together 150
The Tourist Trap 41
traffic 103, 108, 118, 122, 125, 126
Tube (*see also* London Underground) 104, 108, 114, 121–3
Tudor Walters Report (1918) 128
Twenty Twelve 24
2 Broke Girls 149
Two Doors Down 149, 188
2point4 Children 134, 135, 148
typewriter 58, 59, 60, 81, 83, 86
typist 3, 53, 86, 138, 177

'A Very Commonplace Murder' (*see also* James, P. D.) 37, 39, 92, 113, 186
Villa Toryism 20

W1A 24, 41, 42, 47, 65, 67, 75, 87, 118, 119, 121
The War of the Worlds (*see also* Wells, H. G.) 117, 155
'The Waste Land' (*see also* Eliot, T. S.) 57, 109
Waterhouse, Alfred 35
Waterhouse, Keith 11, 41, 79, 84
  Mrs Pooter's Diary 11
  Office Life 41, 79, 84
Wells, H. G. 17, 68, 95, 106, 117, 120, 129, 135, 136, 155–7, 171, 172, 174–8, 180, 182
  The History of Mr Polly 17, 157
  Love and Mr Lewisham 68, 156, 174, 175, 178–80

The War of the Worlds 117, 155
The Wheels of Chance 157
We're Doomed: The Dad's Army Story 18
The Wheels of Chance (*see also* Wells, H. G.) 157
While You Were Sleeping 124
'white-blouse revolution' 16, 56, 83
white-collar crime 31, 73
white-collar work 4, 16, 29, 31, 44, 51, 52, 57, 78, 81, 83, 88, 90, 97, 100, 157, 181
white-collar worker 1, 3, 4, 7, 9, 10, 11, 16, 29, 31, 34, 42–4, 48, 50–3, 55, 56, 59, 60, 61, 68, 71, 81, 86, 92, 93, 97, 98–101, 103, 104, 108, 111, 129, 138, 146, 153, 167, 185–6
The Wild House 134
Williams, Nigel 12, 39, 92, 113, 142, 151, 159, 160
  The Wimbledon Poisoner 39, 92, 113, 151, 159, 160
The Wimbledon Poisoner (*see also* Williams, Nigel) 39, 92, 113, 151, 159, 160
Wodehouse, P. G. 48, 61, 66, 72, 76, 107
  Psmith in the City 66, 72, 76, 80, 107
Wood, Victoria 46, 144
  'Ballad of Barry and Freda' 144
The Wooden Angel (*see also* Canning, Victor) 57–8
Woolf, Virginia 45, 108, 125
  Night and Day 108, 125
working class 4, 5, 6, 8, 15, 16, 21, 22, 31, 37, 51, 62, 87, 101, 127, 129, 139, 142, 147–9, 153–4, 159, 165, 167, 170

YMCA 49
Young Hyacinth 171
The Young Idea (*see also* Swinnerton, Frank) 23, 94, 155

www.ingramcontent.com/pod-product-compliance
Lightning Source LLC
Chambersburg PA
CBHW072143290426
44111CB00012B/1958